Praise for *100 Places in Italy Every Woman Should Go*

"Makes me want to pack my bag and follow Van Allen's alluring suggestions...she reveals an intimacy with Italy and a honed sense of adventure. *Andiamo!*"

—Frances Mayes, author of *Under the Tuscan Sun*

"I've just returned from six weeks in Italy and how I wish I'd had Van Allen's book. It positively sparkles with delight in all matters female, which, it turns out, is an optimal way to reveal particularly delicious matters Italian. Italy has a new portrait: sexy and savvy. Makes a gal smile in English and Italian, to eat up this compendium of Italy's most delectable women's outings."

—Anne Calcagno, author of *Pray for Yourself*
and editor of *Travelers' Tales Italy*

"I knew that Italy was the land of *la dolce vita* and *far niente*, but this is the first book to present an organized way to find your way through her earthly and soulful wonders. I want all my girlfriends to have a copy of *100 Places*."

—Camille Cusumano, editor of *Italy, A Love Story*

"A wonderful gift for any woman traveling to Italy. With Van Allen's advice you won't be overwhelmed and you'll discover how nurturing it is to travel in a country that has honored us since we all descended from Venus."

—Marybeth Bond, author of *Gutsy Women*
and *Best Girlfriends Getaways Worldwide*

"Part guidebook, part history, and part manual to the good life in the land of La Dolce Vita, Susan Van Allen's magnum opus on all things Italian is essential reading for women (and men) who either want to get the most out of their next trip or want to be spirited back to their last."

—David Farley, author of *An Irreverent Curiosity:*
In Search of the Church's Strangest Relic in Italy's Oddest Town

"Susan Van Allen's writing makes the magic of Italy jump off the page. She has a knack for capturing the charms, quirks, and authenticity of this magnificent land."

—Kathy McCabe, editor and publisher,
Dream of Italy Travel Newsletter

"That old Freudian chestnut—'What do women really want?!'— has been answered once again in yet another appealing Travelers' Tales opus. Susan Van Allen has romped through an Italy replete with seductive goddesses and female saints, architectural wonders, beauty spas, entrancing beaches, shopping sprees and craft/cultural courses, and picked the very best, mixing dreamy delights with drops of dainty decadence."

—David Yeadon, author of *Seasons in Basilicata*

"No matter how many times you've been to Italy and think you know it, reading Susan Van Allen's book almost guarantees a return trip. Now I must visit Siena, not for the Palio, but because it was here that St. Catherine bucked family expectations and proclaimed her commitment to Christ, thereby becoming a medieval woman to be reckoned with. Susan whipped up a delightful book you'll only put down long enough to check the flights to that fascinating country."

—Carol Coviello-Malzone, author of *Flavors of Rome:*
How, What & Where to Eat in the Eternal City

100 *Places in Italy Every Woman Should Go*

SUSAN VAN ALLEN

TRAVELERS' TALES
AN IMPRINT OF SOLAS HOUSE, INC.
PALO ALTO

Travelers' Tales and Solas House are trademarks of Solas House, Inc., 853 Alma
Street, Palo Alto, California 94301. www.travelerstales.com

Art Direction: Stefan Gutermuth
Cover Photograph: Cinque Terre, Vernazza, Picturegarden
Author Photograph: Erin Champion
Interior Design and Page Layout: Howie Severson
Production Director: Christy Quinto

Library of Congress Cataloging-in-Publication Data
Van Allen, Susan.
 One hundred places in Italy every woman should go / Susan Van
Allen. -- 1st ed.
    p. cm.
Includes bibliographical references and index.
ISBN 978-1-932361-65-0 (pbk.)
  1. Italy--Guidebooks. 2. Women--Travel--Italy--Guidebooks. 3.
Women travelers--Italy--Guidebooks. I. Title. II. Title: 100 places in
Italy every woman should go.
 DG416.V36 2009
 914.504'93--dc22
                        2009016345

First Edition
Printed in the United States
10 9 8 7 6 5 4 3 2 1

To my mother
Who opened the door to Italy
And always told me:
"Do what you love!"

Whenever I go anywhere but Italy for a vacation,
I always feels as if I have made a mistake.

—ERICA JONG

Table of Contents

SECTION II
VILLE, PALAZZI, AND AN APARTMENT   81

SECTION III
GARDENS   125

Preface

I FELL IN LOVE WITH ITALY at a dining room table in Newark, New Jersey. It was Nana and Papa's dining room, my maternal grandparents—immigrants from Southern Italy. The walls were painted in a pale-rose stenciled pattern, the table spread with an ivory-colored lace cloth. On the mahogany sideboard sat a soccer-ball-sized jar of wild cherries marinating in syrup, next to a Capodimonte lamp, with porcelain figures of fancy ladies in flouncy dresses fanning themselves under the shade. A soprano on the hi-fi sang "*Un Bel Di Vedremo*"—"One Beautiful Day We'll See Each Other."

Nana, with her apron tied up under her marshmallow-baggie arms, lit the candles. My mother and aunts carried in platters heavy with mozzarella, roasted peppers, shiny black olives, steaming bowls of macaroni. I sat propped up on a telephone book, clinking my tumbler of half-red wine/half-water along with the grown-ups toasting, "*Salute!*" By the time the feasts were finished, the candles had burnt to their bottoms, dripping onto the lace cloth. Papa poured Strega, a golden liqueur, into curvy glasses, and sliced a dome-shaped, slathered-with-whipped-cream rum cake.

This was my first Italy: a big, delicious, loving heart.

Every August Papa would get on a ship to visit his sisters who still lived near Naples. He'd send back postcards of statues and churches. He'd return after Labor Day with beads from Venice, rosaries blessed by the Pope, rocks from Mount Vesuvius.

Italy became magical and mysterious, beckoning me—a billowy cartoon finger wafting out of a pot of bubbling tomato sauce.

When I got there for the first time in 1976, I arrived in Roma Termini with a pack on my back and a bursting anticipation. The trip was a sweltering August blur of standing awestruck in the Sistine Chapel, tasting my first gelato, getting my bottom pinched. Naturally there was romance: on the train I'd met a *bel ragazzo* named Luciano who'd sat across from me in the compartment. We fell madly in love for forty-eight hours and rendezvoused in the Forum: moonlight, a Chianti bottle with a straw-covered bottom, two nineteen-year-olds singing Beatles songs to each other.

Feeling transformed into a woman of the world, I headed to my Roman cousins where I was embraced with smothering-lovering and seated at their dining room table, coming full circle to my childhood Italy.

The spell was cast. Italy grabbed hold of my heart forever. Over these many years it's drawn me back, again and again.

Tonight as I'm sitting here in an apartment on Rome's Piazza Paradiso, way past bedtime, even for Italy, I'm realizing there's been absolutely no logic to my times here. The trips started off with visits to the major sights in the big cities, but then out went the plans, and instinct flung me to such spots as a classroom near Rome's Colosseum where I struggled to tackle the subjunctive, a quiet farm road in Puglia surrounded by old olive trees, dancing at the Excelsior in Florence with my husband one New Year's Eve.

I became the "girlfriend with the lists"—scribbling down places I'd loved visiting and passing them along to my traveling pals. If I was back in the States counting the days till my next trip, I lived in Italy vicariously—knowing that Babs was in Rome seeing all those provocative Bernini sculptures with my notes in hand, Sheila at a glove shop in Florence, Louise drinking wine at my favorite *bacaro* in Venice.

When the opportunity to write this book came along, so did elation, gratitude, and then a freezing panic. How could I choose 100 out of the infinite pleasures I'd experienced in Bell'Italia? So let's just get the most obvious fact out of the way: there are more places than any one book could hold. I've even left out some of the most obvious—such as the Sistine Chapel, Pisa, and Michelangelo's *David*—things well covered in other guidebooks.

In these pages, I'm sharing with you some places from my list of favorites, along with those my savvy Italian and American friends have raved to me about. I've put a spotlight on goddesses, the Madonna, female saints, beauties who've inspired masterpieces, women who've taken power. After all, isn't the fact that women have been worshipped here for thousands of years one of the reasons we love Italy so much? Though in modern times females haven't yet triumphed as far as business and political realms go, as Luigi Barzini in *The Italians* says: "Men run the country, but women run men." Here where *la famiglia* is the power source, women are at the core of it.

What about your male traveling partners? They're likely to enjoy a lot of these places, too, whether it's a museum, beach, or spots for adventure and learning. O.K., the guys probably won't be into buying lace in Rapallo, but they'll certainly enjoy Venus of the Beautiful Buttocks in Naples!

Italy seduces both sexes, with irresistibly feminine appeals. Shaped like a boot we'd love to strut around in, she transforms herself as she transforms travelers. She's the nurturing mama, the drop-dead-gorgeous vixen, the compassionate spirit. She's even the unreliable girlfriend who exasperates you with travel snafus, but you forgive her because she's so darn charming. She's constantly coaxing, "Come on, lighten up and enjoy my beauties and flavors."

Treat this book like a cookbook. What do you want a taste of? Botticelli's *Birth of Venus*? The best chocolate in Rome? A ceramic painting class in Deruta? A wine therapy spa treatment in the Veneto? Allow your mood to be your guide, savoring the experience Italian style, letting it unfold with an unhurried Old World pace.

To make a full meal of it, I've included suggestions for *Golden Days*—matching a place to a nearby restaurant, just like I do when I send out lists to girlfriends. These are only suggestions, because each of us has our own deeply personal experience of encountering Italy.

But as unique as each encounter is, I'm amazed at always hearing, even from travelers without a drop of Italian blood in them, the same words: "It felt like home." Home, in the sweeping sense of a place that brings peace and comfort, a place that stirs the soul.

For me, it's that childhood dining room table feeling. It sneaks up on me now, looking out the window of this apartment in late-night Rome. There's a light shining on a little Madonna altar across the way, her robe the same rose as those dining room walls. Out of the shadows, from a nearby restaurant, comes a dark-haired *signorina*, walking as if she absolutely knows she's a descendant of Venus, with her Adonis—a *bel ragazzo* in a leather jacket—linked to her side. They stop for a smooch under the

Madonna, pressing up against each other as if this was their last night on earth.

Italy, once again, playing an endless beautiful song.

My wish for you is to enjoy her many places of pleasure, wherever your desires lead you to go.

—Susan Van Allen
Rome

I

The Divine:
Goddesses, Saints,
and the Blessed
Virgin Mary

I taly begins with **Venus—Goddess of Love, Beauty, Fertility, and Sexual Healing.** She's that gorgeous divine gal you'll see posed naked all over the country.

The Ancient Romans believed they were her chosen descendants. It was Venus who seduced a Greek mortal and thus became the great grandmother of Romulus and Remus, those twins suckled by a she-wolf on Rome's Palatine Hill who founded the Eternal City.

Her presence is eternal. If you have doubts, watch Italian women striding down the *via*, knowing that spark of Venus lives inside them.

Moving from Pagan to Christian times, churches honoring the **Blessed Virgin Mary (aka the BVM)** were built smack over Venus's temples. Mary is everywhere: dangling off taxicab mirrors, popping out of alleyway altars, wowing you in masterpieces.

Madonna Mia! Two divine females embody the essential spirit of Italy.

* Italy is Venus: Country of beauty, freedom, mercurial passions, surprising possibilities.
* Italy is Mary: Country of motherly love, compassion, serenity.

With those two adored beauties and many more goddesses and saints surrounding you, go and have a divine time exploring...

Mythology 101

Nude Venus is the easiest goddess to recognize. The others that made up Ancient Rome's Big Six (the major goddesses who were worshipped equally alongside six major gods) are:

Juno (Jupiter's Queen and Goddess of Marriage) dressed like a soldier for her job of protecting the finances of the Rome.

Minerva (Virgin Goddess of Rome, Wisdom, and War) with her helmet and spear.

Ceres (Goddess of Agriculture, Motherhood, and Patron of Sicily) holding a cornucopia of wheat.

Diana (Virgin Goddess of the Hunt and the Moon) carrying bows and arrows, with a moon crowning her.

Vesta (Goddess of Hearth and Home) veiled, surrounded by her perpetual flame.

Mary's Rites of Passage 101

Italian artists wore down paintbrushes and chisels to express the divine human nature of the BVM. Some scenes are familiar, others may be less so:

Presentation in The Temple: She accepts her fate. Three-year-old Mary, brought to the temple by her parents, dances up the steps.

Annunciation: She receives the announcement that the Divine is within her. Angel Gabriel swoops in to tell the virgin she's pregnant with the Son of God.

Visitation: She shares the miraculous news. Pregnant Mary visits her cousin Elizabeth, who was way beyond childbearing years but pregnant with John the Baptist.

Assumption: She triumphs. Mary dies and rises body and soul to be crowned queen of heaven.

1 The Campidoglio, Roman Forum, and Palatine Hill

YOU'LL NEVER FORGET YOUR FIRST TIME. You'll be walking along or speeding in a cab from the airport and then will appear... the Colosseum...the Arco di Tito...the whole glorious spread of jaw-dropping triumph and ruin.

It's a place to let your imagination run wild. Picture women rattling tambourines in torch-lit processions, chariots carrying tanned muscular men in togas to the baths.

Goddesses' temples, Empresses' tombs, and churches dedicated to the Virgin Mary are all to be discovered in the thousand-plus years of history that surrounds you. It's impossible to absorb it all in one shot. Hiring a good guide is best since hardly any of the sculptures and ruins are marked. Or just stroll around and surrender to your fantasies.

Here are some places where women take center stage:

The Campidoglio

The Michelangelo-designed piazza is a perfect place to begin, where Minerva (just behind Marcus Aurelius) sits on a throne holding her mighty spear. To either side of her are the Capitoline Museums, packed with sculptures of characters who once roamed the area surrounding you.

In the Palazzo Nuovo (museum to the left of Minerva) head to the first-floor hallway to see *The Capitoline Venus*. She's featured in a sunlit niche, posed as Venus *Pudica* (modest Venus), with one hand over her breast, the other covering her Cupid's cloister. Yes, she's modest, but also teasing, as if to say: "Look what I'm hiding..."

Venus was the deity who flitted from passion to passion. She was married to Vulcan, God of Fire, but even the best couple's counselor couldn't have kept this beauty tied to that angry, crippled god. Venus had hot affairs with Mars (God of War), the devastatingly handsome Adonis, and disguised herself as a mortal for trysts with men she found attractive. Every year she bathed herself in the sea from which she was born to renew her virginity.

In the same hallway, you'll see a statue of a **Roman Woman Dressed As Venus** (hardly dressed), proving how closely Romans associated themselves with the Goddess. The Roman woman breaks out of the Modest Venus pose, standing proud and naked with one hand on her hip. For a laugh further down the hall, check out the **Drunken Old Woman**, who's crouched, laughing, and guzzling a jug of wine.

The Roman Forum

Here in the ongoing archaeological excavation, is the **Temple of the Vestal Virgins**, now rows of pillars with remains of female statues.

The Cult of Vesta, Goddess of Hearth and Home, was the oldest of the Ancient Roman world, which carries through in today's Italy, where *la famiglia* remains as the country's core. Back then girls from noble families, between the ages of six and ten were chosen to guard Vesta's perpetual flame, vowing to "not lie with men" for their entire thirty-year term.

The upside for the Vestals, in a time when women didn't have that much freedom, was that they could come and go as they pleased and got perks all over town, like special seats at games and festivals. The downside was gruesome: if they let Vesta's flame go out they'd be flogged and if they had sex with anyone they'd be buried alive.

The Palatine Hill

Walking up from the Forum, you come to this pretty and serene place, where Romulus (great grandson of Venus) chose to begin the city. It went on to become the Beverly Hills of Ancient Rome, where noble palaces were built. In the sixteenth century the Farnese family created gardens here, so you can wander through rows of boxwood shrubs, cypress trees, laurel and rose bushes, and enjoy lovely views of the sights below.

As for the palaces, the **Home of Augustus** is now open to the public, but be prepared to wait in a long line to see the emperor's frescos unless you get there when the site opens. His wife Livia's house is closed for restoration, but the Palatine is still a great place to fantasize about the grand days of Livia and Augustus, who ruled Rome for forty-five years, bringing the city into its Golden Age.

Back in 39 B.C., just after Julius Caesar's assassination, Livia was a beautiful nineteen-year-old, married to the much older Tiberius Claudius Nero, and pregnant with their second child. Along came Octavius, a rising star on the military scene, married with a pregnant wife. Octavius fell in love with Livia, divorced  his wife the day she gave birth, and married the pregnant Livia. Livia's husband gave her away at the ceremony, even throwing in a dowry. It turned out to be a good political move for all involved and in those days the citizenry didn't even blink over it.

Octavius became Emperor Caesar Augustus and ruled Rome with his perfect mate Livia, who took charge of all the biz at home when he set off to conquer distant lands. Livia was an exemplary Roman wife. She was famously chaste, "worked wool" (made her husband's togas), and never showed off with fancy jewelry or dress. The couple lived simply here throughout their fifty-one years of marriage, with Livia putting up with philandering Augustus, who was known for his S&M exploits. Together they revived Rome, restoring monuments in the Forum and building new ones throughout the city.

Livia's become famous in fiction, particularly through Robert Graves' *I Claudius*, where she's portrayed as a conniving woman who poisoned potential heirs to make sure her family line would inherit the throne. Whatever version of the story you believe, Livia's descendants did end up ruling Rome. She died at the ripe old age of eighty-six and was honored as Diva Augusta. Her image was revered in the streets that surround you, carried in celebrations by elephant drawn carriages.

To get a more vivid experience of Livia's lifestyle, head to the **Palazzo Massimo alle Terme**, near the Termini station. The entire garden room of her suburban villa has been moved to the top floor of this museum, so you can stand in the midst of amazing frescos that feature a harmonious, abundant landscape of trees, flowers, and birds.

www.pierreci.it
www.romaturismo.it
www.museicapitolini.org
WWW.

TIPS: *Don't go to the Forum between 10 A.M. and 2 P.M., the heaviest tourist times. The museums, on the other hand, are rarely crowded, and in addition to the Palazzo Nuovo, the Palatine Museum, with its mosaics and sculptures, is a good choice.*

Palazzo Massimo alle Terme: Via di Villa Peretti 1 (near Termini), Tuesday-Sunday 9-7:30.

Capitoline Museums: Tuesday through Sunday (Closed Monday) 9-8.

Roman Forum and Palatine Hill: Daily 9 until one hour before sunset.

❧

Golden Day: Start out at the **Capitoline Caffè** (to the right of the Campidoglio's steps) to rev up with coffee or even have lunch, enjoying beautiful views from its terraces. Time your visit so you'll be on the **Palatine Hill** at sunset, or circling back to the caffè at the **Campidoglio** to unwind with a glass of wine and go in for that view again.

TOURS

For the best guided small group tours, contact **Context Travel** at www.contexttravel.com.

RECOMMENDED READING

A Traveller in Rome by H. V. Morton
A Traveller in Italy by H. V. Morton

The Pietà, Saint Peter's Basilica–Rome

YOU'LL FEEL THE PULL of the greatest sculpture ever made as soon as you enter the doors of Saint Peter's. It's over there, to your right. Where the cameras are flashing. Where tourists are posing. Where among the crowd there is at least one nun. Get close: the *Pietà*. *Pietà* means pity. And compassion.

Has compassion ever looked more beautiful? How did Michelangelo make marble flow? How did he capture such grace and serenity in Mary's face?

Michelangelo modeled the face of Mary after his mother: his mother who died when he was six.

He got all kinds of criticism for it. "Mary looks too young," people said. "If she has a thirty-three-year-old son, she's gotta be at least forty-five."

And Michelangelo said: "A woman so pure of body and soul is eternally young."

He was twenty-two, in 1498, when French Cardinal Jean de Bilheres, thinking ahead, commissioned Michelangelo to sculpt it for his tomb. The Cardinal gave him 450 papal ducats. Not that Michelangelo cared much about money. He slept in his clothes in his studio; got his nose broken in drunken street brawls.

After he signed the contract, Michelangelo took off to Carrara in Tuscany to pick out the best piece of marble for the *Pietà*. He believed the statue is already in the stone since the beginning of time. The sculptor's job is to free the form from the stone.

Michelangelo was supposed to have the *Pietà* done in 1500, for the Holy Year. But when the pilgrims came through, he was still working on it. They stood back and watched Michelangelo free the form from the stone. *Can you imagine?* They thought it was amazing—divine grace made flesh. They went back home spreading the word.

When it was finally unveiled, Michelangelo heard visitors saying he didn't sculpt it, that another artist, Gobbio di Milano did. He got so enraged he snuck in late at night and carved his name onto Mary's sash. It was the only work he ever signed. He always regretted it.

This is one of the many masterpieces in Italy that may hold a memory for you of the first time you saw it. Maybe it was on a postcard or a slide in art history class.

For me, each time I see it in Rome, I'm pulled back to 1964, when the *Pietà* came to New York for the World's Fair. I lined up with the crowd, my mother behind me. The Vatican Pavillion!

We stepped onto a moving walkway. I heard a chorus singing "Alleluia, Alleluia." I felt my mother's hands on my shoulder. The room was draped in blue velvet with a sparkling light over the *Pietà*.

We floated by. It was the first A-R-T that I ever saw. I was seven, the age of reason. I wondered: How could something sad be beautiful? I heard gasps. I took a long look and reasoned: Beautiful.

www.saintpetersbasilica.org

Saint Peter's Basilica: Daily 7-6 (October through March), 7-7 (April through September). Best to go later in the day, after the tour groups have gone. Avoid Wednesdays when there are Papal Audiences in the mornings.

❧

Golden Day: See the *Pietà*. Have lunch at **La Veranda dell'Hotel Columbus** (Via della Conciliazone 33, 06 6865435), a gorgeous frescoed loggia from the sixteenth century.

3 Santa Maria Churches–Rome

IF YOU SAY YOU'VE BEEN TO **Santa Maria and the Martyrs** church, no one will know what you're talking about, except maybe a priest. Everybody else knows it as the **Pantheon**, a fantastic monument built to honor all the Goddesses and Gods. It was consecrated in the seventh century as a church dedicated to Mary and the Martyrs.

The "Eye of God"—the humongous, uncovered circular opening at the top of the Pantheon's dome, frames the dramatic Roman sky, making the ever-changing city a part of this architectural wonder. It's fabulous near sunset. One winter I got there just before closing when a rosy cotton-candy-tinged-with-gold cloud floated across it, inspiring even one of the guards to throw his head back and sigh. And it's great in the rain. Especially in the rain, when water pours through and drains out the holes in its floor.

You also should take a moment to look at the plaque to the right of artist Raphael's tomb. On it is the name of the girl he was engaged to, Maria Bibbiena, his patron's niece. Raphael died at thirty-seven without ever marrying Maria. According to his biographer Vasari, he died from too much sex. Not with Maria, but with a baker's daughter who was his steady mistress.

Besides Santa Maria and the Martyrs, there are approximately eighty churches in the Eternal City dedicated to Mary.

The winner for best photo op is **Santa Maria in Cosmedin** with the *Bocca della Verità* (Mouth of Truth) at its entrance, along with long lines of tourists unless you get there early or late in the day. The medieval legend of this big-faced stone disk says if a liar sticks his hand in its mouth, it'll get bitten off. Gregory Peck did a great job of faking his hand being eaten in *Roman Holiday*, and Audrey Hepburn's freaked-out yet charming reaction is a gem of a scene I replay on You Tube when I am Rome-sick.

Two favorite Santa Maria churches in Rome are:

* **Santa Maria in Trastevere**
  You cross the Tiber, head through a zigzag of narrow streets, arrive at the piazza and BAM: topping this church is a vibrant mosaic frieze of Mary nursing Jesus, surrounded by ten lamp-holding virgins.

  This was the first church in Rome dedicated to Mary, built on a spot where it's said oil spurted from the ground and flowed the entire day Jesus was born.

  Over the inside altar, Mary's life story is told in Pietro Cavallini's thirteenth-century mosaics, culminating with her being crowned Queen of Heaven. It's best to get there on a sunny day, when the light bounces and sparkles off the gold background.

  One of the most popular spots in the huge church is Saint Anthony's statue, surrounded by candles and covered with hand-scribbled notes, written to beg for miracles or help finding whatever's lost.

  A plus to this Santa Maria church is that it doesn't close down midday. And at night the piazza surrounding it gets magical. The lit-up mosaic makes it seem like Mary's blessing the whole Fellini-esque scene of tourists and locals passing through or hanging around the fountain. I can never resist indulging in a caffè or Campari at the **di Marzio** to take it all in.

❋ **Santa Maria della Pace**

"Every moment is an opportunity for something wonderful to happen," was the baroque artists' philosophy. It's how I feel when this church appears like a pearl tucked at the end of a cobblestoned street in one of Rome's most theatrical settings.

Maybe I love della Pace so much because its opening hours (Monday, Wednesday, and Saturday 9-12) make it so elusive—like an ultra-handsome guy who's hardly ever available. When your timing is right, you open the door to the small sanctuary and get a glorious blast of Raphael's frescos of four sibyls—prophetesses in flowing robes, beautifully blending grace and power.

Sibyls were brilliant older women of Greece, Italy, and Persia who studied the moon and the stars, predicting eclipses and creating the basis for astrology. Catholics adopted them, believing Cumae (the sibyl on the left) predicted the birth of Christ. In this painting, completed by Raphael's students after he died, sibyls listen to the words of swooping angels.

To the left of that fresco is a chapel designed by Michelangelo and throughout the church are paintings of events of Mary's life, from her birth to Assumption. Lots of female saints are honored here as well, including Bridget and Catherine who border Mary in the painting opposite Raphael's. Sculptures of Cecilia, Agnes, and Chiara adorn the arches.

Even if Santa Maria della Pace isn't open, you'll find another treasure if you head left from the church's entrance: the **Bramante Cloister**. This was the first work Bramante did in Rome, right before he went to work on Saint Peter's Square, and shows on a smaller scale his genius for harmony. If you take the stairs from the cloister, you can peek through the bookshop window into the church for a view of Raphael's masterpiece, which takes the edge off disappointment if the sanctuary is closed.

Pantheon: Monday–Saturday 8:30-7:30, Sunday 9-6.

Santa Maria in Cosmedin: Piazza Bocca della Verità, daily 9-1, 3-5.

Santa Maria in Trastevere: Daily 9:30-6:30.

Santa Maria della Pace: Vicolo del Arco della Pace 5, Monday/Wednesday/Saturday 9-12.

☙

Golden Day: Visit **Santa Maria della Pace**, stop for an espresso or apertivo at **Caffè della Pace** (via della Pace 3), and eat at **da Francesco** (Piazza del Fico), a casual place with a great antipasti bar and delicious Roman pasta specialites.

4 Churches Dedicated to Female Saints—Rome

WOMEN OF STEADFAST CONVICTION, who struggled, suffered, and triumphed in Rome, were elevated to sainthood and are remembered in churches all over the city.

Each has their special domain. There's Saint Cecilia, Patron of Musicians, the young martyr who sang heavenly hymns even when her throat was slashed. She's honored in a Trastevere church that's built over her former home. There's Saint Monica, Patron of Mothers, who spent most of her life worrying about her nee'r-do-well son, Augustine. She lived to see him change his ways and is entombed in the church named after him, Sant' Agostino.

Two of the prettiest churches dedicated to Roman saints in the historic center are:

❈ **Saint Agnes in Agone: Patron Saint of Virgins and Girl Scouts (Piazza Navona)**
Don't let the word "Agone" make you think of "Agony" and keep you away from this glorious Borromini-designed structure that graces the Piazza Navona with its splendid curves and towers. "Agone" comes from the Latin "Campus Agonis," meaning "the site of competitions," which is what this piazza was in the Middle Ages, when it was filled with water for boat races.

Soft baroque music pipes through the ornate, dripping-with-gold church sanctuary. To the right of the altar is a statue of Saint Agnes, set against a pale blue background, with her arms outstretched and flames lapping at her feet. It was sculpted by a pupil of Bernini, and features Agnes in a breathtaking, transcendent moment.

Back in 304, men all over Rome were hot for beautiful thirteen-year-old Agnes, but she turned them away with her sweet smile, saying she was engaged to Jesus. "Let's strip her naked and have her walk to a whorehouse, that'll show her!" was the governor's idea to solve the problem. But miraculously, right where this church was built, Agnes' golden hair grew down to her knees to cover her up, Lady Godiva style. Totally flummoxed by the cheerful virgin, the governor had her head cut off. A side chapel that holds Agnes' shrunken head will be re-opened after renovation.

Streams of light flow through the cupola, illuminating a rich painting of Paradise and medallions below it where women personify such virtues as Temperance and Prosperity.

The church is the perfect place to escape the Piazza Navona hubbub and one of the few left in Rome where you can light real candles.

  ❀ **Church of Santa Brigida a Campo de' Fiori: Patron of Scholars and Sweden (Piazza Farnese)**
If you get to this jewel-box between four and five in the afternoon, you'll hear nuns singing vespers in sweet harmonies.

They're Brigittines, the best-dressed sisters in Rome, with long gray habits and tight headpieces accented by a white band and shining red studs. They belong to an order founded by Saint Bridget of Sweden in the fourteenth century.

Bridget's famous mystical visions started coming to her when she was just a girl. She married when she was fourteen and had eight children. When her husband died, Bridget was forty-two, and she decided to follow her childhood visions by founding an order of nuns. The monastery she built became a Swedish literary center (thus her scholarly patron side), because she allowed her holy assistants to have as many books as they wanted.

Bridget came to Rome in 1349 for two reasons. One, she wanted the Pope to approve her order, and two, she'd had a vision that he'd die soon so she thought she should tell him. She met the Pope, he approved the Brigittines and died four months later. Bridget stayed in Rome, living near what is now her church, and died there at the age of seventy-one.

Bridget's convent, around the corner from her church, is now the **Casa di Santa Brigida guesthouse**, run by her nuns. The downstairs rooms where the saint lived are furnished with dark antiques and elegant draperies, and the rooftop terrace has amazing views. The guest rooms are simple but comfy and you've got to reserve way in advance, as this is one of the best bargain digs in the historic center.

The roof of Saint Bridget's church is graced with baroque statues of Bridget and her daughter, Saint Catherine. Inside it's prettily done up in rust-colored marble and gold moldings, with frescos telling Bridget's life story. It's located right on the Michelangelo-designed Piazza Farnese, which features fountains made from tubs taken from the Baths of Caracalla, the harmonious façade of the Palazzo Farnese, and handsome priests passing by on their way to Vatican City.

ॐ

Golden Day: Visit the **Sant' Agostino** church to see Caravaggio's stunning *Madonna di Loreto* and Saint Monica's tomb. Get to **Saint Bridget's** between 4 and 5 to hear vespers. Have a caffè or aperitivo at the **Caffè Farnese**, and a traditional Roman dinner at **Ai Balestrari** (Via dei Balestrari 41, closed Monday).

RECOMMENDED READING

Saints Preserve Us! by Sean Kelly and Rosemary Rogers

The Pilgrim's Italy: A Travel Guide to the Saints by James and Colleen Heater

5 Bernini's Beautiful Broads and the Galleria Borghese—Rome

YOU'D THINK THE ARTIST WHO SCULPTED the Fountain of the Four Rivers in Piazza Navona, the Triton in the Piazza Barberini, and Saint Peter's flamboyant altar would have been a wild man. But actually Gian Lorenzo Bernini took on his masterpiece work like a monk, sculpting seven hours a day, up until his death at eighty-one. He poured all his passion into his creations—sculptures of figures caught in theatrical moments that absolutely define baroque Rome.

Bernini did have one enticing affair, with Constanza Bonarelli, the wife of one of his assistants. Things heated up when Constanza started to fool around with Bernini's younger brother. Bernini flew into a violent rage, threatening to throw acid on Constanza's face and beating up that younger brother until the Pope stepped in to put a stop to the whole deal. Bernini's *Constanza* bust is in the Bargello in Florence. With her lips slightly parted and blouse unbuttoned, it seems as though she was sculpted just before they were going to have a good time in bed.

Bernini calmed down after Constanza, married at forty-one, and fathered eleven kids. His daily routine was morning mass at the Gesu, work-work-work, and then back to church where he prayed with the Jesuits.

Unlike Michelangelo's sculptures (such as the *Pieta* and *David*) that have a powerful meditative style, Bernini's creations seem to be formed in wax. Their robes flow, they laugh, scream, sigh, and pulse with vitality.

On the **Ponte Sant'Angelo** you'll be surrounded by the dramatic angels he designed. And in these sculptures, you'll see how Bernini captures women in climactic moments...literally:

* *Ecstasy of Saint Teresa,* **1647-1652** (Santa Maria della Vittoria, Via XX Settembre 17)

    It looks like the Carmelite Spanish nun Bernini placed in a stage set altar is having quite an "ecstasy" as an angel pierces her with a golden shaft.

    Saint Teresa had loads of mystical visions, and wrote that this piercing left her "on fire with the love of God" and "The pain was so great that it made me moan; and yet so surpassing was the sweetness of this excessive pain that I could not wish to be rid of it." Clearly, Bernini's genius took Teresa's account and ran with it.

* *Beata Ludovica Albertoni,* **1671-1674** (San Francesco a Ripa, Piazza San Francesco d'Assisi 88)

    Here the mystic Ludovica is sprawled out in bed with her head thrown back as she clutches her breast. Some say she's in her death throes, but since she has her shoes on, others believe Bernini caught her in a private, earth-shattering, "seeing the Divine" pose. It's best to visit the church in the morning when sunlight streams over Ludovica from the cupola above.

The Galleria Borghese

* *Daphne and Apollo,* **1622-1625** (**Room III**)

    The virgin water nymph manages a fantastic escape from Apollo by transforming into a laurel tree before your eyes.

Her hair and fingertips become leaves, her feet and ankles the tree trunk.

❋ *Pluto and Proserpina*, 1621-1622 (Room IV)

A teardrop runs down Proserpina's face as she smushes her hand into Pluto's chin, fighting him off with a heaven-help-me look. Pluto scoops her up and gets a firm grab on her thigh. The three-headed barking dog adds to the drama.

This is Bernini's version of the Greek myth that told how Pluto, God of the Underworld, got struck by the beautiful Goddess of Vegetation he saw picking flowers in a field, and swooped up to kidnap her.

www.galleriaborghese.it

Other fabulous women in the Borghese are:

❋ *Venus Victrix*, 1805-1808 (Room I)

Here's Pauline Bonaparte (Napoleon's sister), posed regally on a chaise as the nude goddess. Pauline came to Rome as a ravishing twenty-three-year-old widow, won the heart of Prince Borghese, married him, and became mistress of the Villa. Though it caused quite a scandal when Pauline stripped to model for the sculptor Canova, and her husband kept this  statue hidden away while he was alive, Pauline's only comment on the affair was, "The room was well heated." Famously vain woman that she was, Pauline was also known to have used her servants as footstools and liked to have, in her words, "a large Negro" carry her to her bath.

✷ *Sacred and Profane Love,* 1805-1808 **(Room XX)**
Painted by Titian when he was just twenty-five for a Venetian
nobleman's marriage, the Venuses here are named differently than what you'd expect. The Profane Venus is in proper
Renaissance dress, drawing a pot of gold to her side, signify-
ing "fleeting earthly happiness." The Sacred Venus is naked,
holding an eternal flame, meaning "eternal happiness in
heaven." She wears only her magic girdle, which gave her the
power to attract her many lovers.

TIP: *Reservations for the Borghese are a must, you can make them easily by phone
or online (see URL on previous page). This turns out to be a good thing, because
you get to browse without crowds.*

❦

Golden Day: Stop by **Roscioli** (Via dei Chiavari 34, near
Campo dei Fiori, www.rosciolifinefood.com) to pick up picnic
supplies and then head over to spend the day at the **Galleria
Borghese.** Your picnic supplies will not be allowed inside, but
you can stash them in lockers and take a break for lunch in the
park that was once the Borghese family's backyard.

6

Venuses, Madonnas, and Judith at the Uffizi–Florence

FLORENCE IS THE HOT SPOT WHERE the Renaissance burst forth, with artists creating masterpieces that revered the female form. In the Uffizi, you'll see women adored in such paintings as:

* ***The Birth of Venus*, 1484, by Sandro Botticelli (Rooms 10-14)**
Describing a woman as a Botticelli automatically brings up this famous image of a naked, curvy Venus stepping off a seashell to the shore. But Botticelli actu-ally translates to "little barrel." It was the artist's nickname, because in truth he was a roly-poly guy.

  A better description of a beautiful woman would be to call her a Simonetta Vespucci, the name of the model for this painting. Simonetta was Botticelli's muse, the most adored woman in Florence, and his neighbor's wife.

  She came to Florence from Genoa as the fifteen-year-old bride of Marco Vespucci, whose cousin was the famous Italian explorer Amerigo. Her fans called her *La Bella Simonetta* and liked to say she was born in the Ligurian coastal town of Portovenere, where the Romans believed Venus arose from the sea.

Though these days she'd be ordered to do Pilates to tighten her abs, in 1469 Simonetta's pear shape was ideal. Only poor starving gals were skinny back then, and Renaissance guys adored chicks with childbearing hips. In Florence, artists clamored to have Simonetta pose for them, writers sent her love poems, and she was showered with gifts from admirers.

Botticelli, an artist on the rise, introduced Simonetta to the men who ran Florence, the brothers Lorenzo and Giuliano de Medici. Lorenzo was involved with being Magnificent and his banking and philosophy biz, but smitten with Simonetta, ordered a painting of her for his bed chamber, which some say became Botticelli's *Venus*.

Giuliano, a sporty type, called for a jousting tournament to be held in honor of this glamour-puss who had quickly become the Marilyn Monroe of Florence. Botticelli painted Giuliano's joust banner with the words "The Unparalleled One" under Simonetta's image. Giuliano won and Simonetta was declared "Queen of Beauty." Since she was married, there's no record of nooky between Simonetta and Giuliano, though the locals imagined their steamy affair as fervently as the Brangelina romance of our times.

www.florenceart.it www.uffizi.com

A year after the joust, twenty-two-year-old Simonetta died of consumption. Her funeral was an Italian day of mourning. Thousands came to Florence to join in her casket procession, weeping and tossing flowers.

Botticelli had started painting *The Birth of Venus* before Simonetta died. It took him nine years to finish it, perhaps because the thought of his nude muse being gone from him was too tragic to bear.

As you look around the room, you'll see how Botticelli used Simonetta's inspiration again and again—from *Primavera* to *The Annunciation*. He never married, in fact said the idea of marriage was a nightmare. And there were reports of him "liking boys," followed by charges of sodomy, that were dropped.

When he died, thirty-four years after *La Bella Simonetta*, Botticelli asked to be buried at her feet. In the Church of Ognissanti, which was Simonetta's family parish, you can see his wish was granted.

✻ ***Venus of Urbino*, 1538, by Titian (Room 28)**
Here's the most erotic painting in the museum. Titian probably used a Venetian prostitute for his model, as there were around 10,000 in Venice during the time he did this painting and they traditionally took on the extra work.

Venus stretches out on a couch *au naturale* in elegant surroundings, with a confident look and roses in one hand that symbolize Venus. The most attention goes to her other hand, with her curled fingers between her legs.

The painting was commissioned by the Duke of Urbino, probably as a hint for his young bride. They married when the girl was only ten years old, but things couldn't be consummated—which meant the Duke couldn't have heirs—until she became a woman at fourteen. The medical belief in those days was that conception could only occur if both man and woman had orgasms, so Titian's Venus is teaching the Duke's bride how to do her wifely duty.

❀ **Madonna with Child and Two Angels, 1505-1506, by Filippo Lippi (Room 8)**
In this totally enchanting painting, the Friar Lippi probably used the novice Lucrezia Buti as his model. The two had a scandalous love affair which lead to her getting pregnant. The baby here is probably their child, who grew up to be the painter Filippino Lippi.

❀ **Annunciation, 1472-1475, by Leonardo da Vinci (Room 15)**
It's amazing to think of Leonardo painting this when he was only twenty-one. Here Mary gracefully accepts her calling, looking up from her book, while the angel holds out a lily, the symbol of Florence.

❀ **Holy Family, aka Doni Tondo, 1506-1508, by Michelangelo (Room 25)**
The master who sculpted the *David* and *Pieta* always claimed he wasn't good at painting. But he shows his genius here with vibrant color and his sculptural sense of dimension. I see it as a great example of shared parenting, with Mary passing her son off to father Joseph, who seems to be able to handle it.

It was commissioned by the Doni family when their second child was born, as their first child had died in infancy. At first the Donis didn't appreciate Michelangelo's background nudes, but then accepted it as symbolic of the passing of pagan times.

❀ **Madonna of the Goldfinch, 1505, by Raphael (Room 26)**
Mary, who symbolizes "The Seat of Wisdom," gets interrupted from reading, by her son and his cousin, John the Baptist, at her feet. (It's my sister's favorite—as the mother

of two she relates.) The goldfinch John the Baptist hands to Jesus is a symbol of his future violent death.

It was a wedding gift to Raphael's friend, was destroyed in an earthquake, breaking into seventeen pieces, and has undergone many meticulous restorations.

❉ *Judith Beheading Holofernes,* **1614-1620, by Artemisia Gentileschi (Room 43)**

Finally a painting by a woman! It's displayed on the lower floors along with some awesome Caravaggios, and was done by the great Renaissance artist Artemisia Gentileschi.

Gentileschi began painting in her father's workshop, showing her talent early on. She was raped by a painter her father teamed her up with, one Agostino Tassi. To ensure she was telling the truth during the trial, she was tortured. Horribly tortured, with a gynecological examination and wrapping and tightening of leather thongs around her fingers to the point of excruciating pain. It was believed if she could tell the same horrendous rape story under torture as the one she'd told as an accusation, it had to be true. Paintings such as this one, which tells the story of the Jewish heroine Judith cutting off the head of an enemy's general, have been interpreted as Gentileschi's revenge against that gruesome treatment.

Gentileschi's life story is ultimately inspiring. She went on to have a successful career and six children and was highly respected by her contemporaries, even though it was very unusual for a woman to be among them. Since she was passed over for the high altar commissions the men around her were getting, she moved around to find work—from Florence to Rome to Venice, and finally settled in Naples.

Feminists have always taken an interest in her life, and playwright Wendy Wasserstein used her in *The Heidi Chronicles*, in scenes of the main character lecturing about female painters.

TIP: *Be sure to make a reservation for the Uffizi Gallery to avoid long lines.*

❧

Golden Day: Visit the **Uffizi**, then have dinner at **La Sostanza** (Via Porcellana 25r, 055 212 691), a fantastic place that serves wonderful *bistecca* and chicken. Be sure to leave room for the meringue cake dessert.

7 Annunciations—Florence

FLORENTINES ARE SO WILD ABOUT MARY they've always celebrated their New Year on her Annunciation, March 25.

These days there's partying to celebrate the event in the Piazza of the **Church of the Most Holy Annunciation (Santissima Annunziata)**, where a thirteenth-century miracle is believed to have taken place. An artist (some say Pietro Cavallini) was painting a fresco of the Annunciation, and felt so overwhelmed when he got to the face, he stepped away and fell into a deep sleep. When he woke up, the painting was finished. (There's a universal dream of every artist if I've ever heard one.) The Annunciation fresco is to the left of the church entrance in an ornate tabernacle and Florentine brides traditionally visit it to drop off their bouquets.

Besides the Chiesa Santissima Annunziata, Florence is chock-a-block with Annunciations. Renaissance painters loved interpreting the action-packed scene and the variations you'll see all over the city go from austere to absolutely flirty. I'm partial to Pontormo's Mannerist one in **Santa Felicitá**, where Mary's a willowy figure with a rose robe swirling about her, like a runway model.

The most famous Annunciation painting can be found in **Museo San Marco.** The Dominican Friars of this fifteenth-century monastery were very lucky to have a talented painter in their gang, Guido di Pietro. He was such a great guy, they named him Fra Angelico, which means Brother Angel. This Fra Angelico is not to be confused with the monk from northern Piedmont, for whom the hazelnut liqueur is named.

This Fra Angelico (now called Beato Angelico) spent eight years with his assistants frescoing San Marco's hallways and  monks' cells, with images to support them in their meditation and prayer. He was so spiritually on fire, he prayed every time he picked up a brush, never changed what he'd done (thinking it would insult the Divine who gave him inspiration), and wept every time he painted a crucifixion. The frescos here, painted over gold backgrounds downstairs and in muted jewel tones upstairs, clearly reflect his deep faith and humility.

On your way up the stairs to the cells, you'll turn on a landing and get hit with the sight of his most well-known Annunciation, which has been called the most beloved painting of the Renaissance. It's been reproduced so many times you'll get that weird brain readjustment that happens when suddenly you're in front of the real thing. Stay on that landing, with the stairs ahead of you to get the viewpoint Fra Angelico intended.

Peaceful power! Mary is timid, leaning forward with her hands crossed over her heart in acceptance. In its soft, luminous style, the moment of her transformation is striking. Taking in the whole image, you'll realize Fra Angelico's message. He included the beams of the house, to ground the event in reality. At the same time the figures are totally out of proportion—as tall as the pillars and doors that surround them, so the expansive nature of the moment is palpable.

In Cell Number 3, believed to be Fra Angelico's, is a more simple Annunciation. There Saint Dominic, the monks' patron, stands in a corner. It's as if the painter, through the saint, was teaching the monks to contemplate this image of humility.

In 1982, Pope John Paul officially beatified Fra Angelico, praising the divine beauty he painted, and putting him on the path to become the Patron Saint of Artists.

Also in the Museo are beautiful paintings of Madonnas and female saints by other Fras. Two very memorable ones of the Virgin and Child by Fra Bartolomeo have been placed in one of the cells that belonged to Savonarola, the fanatic friar who inspired masterpieces to be burned in the famous 1497 Bonfire of the Vanities. Go figure.

Museo San Marco: Piazza San Marco, weekdays 8:15-1:50, weekends 8:15-4:15. Closed 1st, 3rd, and 5th Sunday, and 2nd and 4th Monday of month.

୬୯

Golden Day: Visit **San Marco** in the morning, when the light is best for viewing the frescos. There's also a pretty cloister in the complex that's a good place for a breather after the art overload. Then have lunch at **Trattoria Mario** (Via Rosina 2r, closed Sunday, no reservations), a great folksy place near the Mercato Centrale.

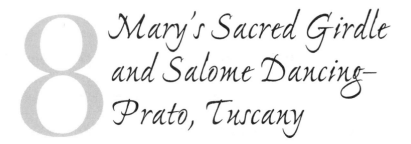

8 Mary's Sacred Girdle and Salome Dancing— Prato, Tuscany

SALOME, THE BIBLE'S VIRGIN FLOOZY, fantastically frescoed by Fra Filippo Lippi, is the logo for the town of Prato and it's well worth it to take the half-hour train ride from Florence to see it. This town first got on the tourist map back in medieval days when Mary's sacred girdle ended up here. In a classic example of Italians combining such concepts, both the Virgin Mother's Girdle and the Virgin Floozy can be found in Prato's Romanesque Duomo.

Mary's girdle, kept locked in a sacred chapel, is nothing like the "this girdle is killing me" kind of my mother's day. It's a green belt that Mary untied when she ascended into heaven and threw to doubting Saint Thomas to prove that yes, it was she whooshing away.

The girdle was passed down to Thomas' disciples, and then to a Jerusalem priest who was married (a.o.k. back in those days) and had a gorgeous daughter. The priest disapproved of a merchant named Michael who fell in love with his daughter, but the girl's sympathetic mother helped the couple elope and threw in Mary's girdle as a dowry. Michael and his bride sailed from Jerusalem to Prato, where Michael slept with the girdle under his mattress to protect it, until on his deathbed he handed it over to a Prato priest. The Chapel of the Sacred Girdle is decorated with frescos that tell that whole story.

Five times a year, with much pomp and incense, Mary's girdle is taken from the chapel and shown to thousands. Because the event attracts more than the Duomo can hold, Donatello sculpted a pulpit attached to the outside of the church, adorned with flying *putti*. There's a copy of the original pulpit up there now, but you can see Donatello's original in the attached museum.

The Duomo's main attraction, on the center altar, is Fra Filippo Lippi's cycle of The Life of John the Baptist, especially *The Feast of Herod*, featuring Salome.

As the Bible story goes, Salome danced so fabulously for her stepfather, King Herod, that he "was pleased" and told her he'd do anything for her. Young Salome didn't have an answer for Herod, so she asked her mother, Herodias, for advice. "Bring me John the Baptist's head on a platter," was her mother's demand.

Herod didn't want to have John's head cut off, but since he'd made that promise to Salome in front of everyone at his birthday party, he couldn't back down. He'd put John in prison because the holy man had called him and Herodias adulterers. Yes, it was true they'd had a wild affair when they were married to others, got divorced, and then became husband and wife. Herod didn't want to kill him because John, that holy man, had so many followers, but his wife Herodias held quite the grudge.

I blame Herodias for Salome going down in history as a bloodthirsty whore, when actually she was just a naïve Shirley Temple-like ten-year-old, who didn't have an answer to "your wish is my command." Over the years Oscar Wilde and Hollywood screenwriters have taken Salome's story and spiced it up, so now her name brings visions of "The Dance of the Seven Veils," and it's assumed Herod's "being pleased" meant she stripped for him.

In Lippi's image that follows Salome dancing, she's shown holding out the head of John the Baptist to her nonplussed mother Herodias, while others look on shocked. Only Salome and Herod look straight out at the viewer, as if Lippi was guiding us to have compassion for these two.

It took Lippi thirteen years to finish these frescos, because he had major *amore* distractions from his work. While fresco-ing and friar-ing, he became smitten with Lucrezia Buti, a beautiful novice, and asked the nun's permission to use her for a model. Sparks flew in Lippi's studio, and during one of the Feasts of the Sacred Girdle when the whole town was partying, the two ran off together. Lucrezia got pregnant and gave birth to Filippino, who would also grow up to be a great painter. Because Lippi was so talented, and his patrons wanted to end the scandal, the Pope stepped in and gave Lippi and Lucrezia dispensation from their vows so they could marry. Lucrezia was Lippi's model for most of his masterpieces, which inspired Botticelli and Michelangelo.

A visit to this Duomo is not only a chance to enjoy Lippi's frescos; Prato is also a leisurely place to wander around with the locals, taste their famous *biscotti di Mattonella*, and get a break from the tourist crowds of Florence.

Duomo: Monday-Saturday 10-5, Sunday 1-5. NOTE: If you're there September 8, you'll hit the town's biggest Sacred Girdle party of the year, with parades and festivities all over Prato. Other Sacred Girdle showings are Christmas, Easter, May 1, and August 15.

ॐ

Golden Day: Train from Florence to the **Prato Porta al Serraglio Station** (half hour), walk a few blocks to the **Duomo** to see Lippi's masterpiece. Have lunch at **La Vecchia Cucina di Soldano** (Via Pomeria 23, 0574 34665, closed Sunday), a cozy budget place that is packed with locals.

9 Museum of the Madonna del Parto–Monterchi, Tuscany

THIS MAY BE THE ONLY MUSEUM on earth where pregnant women get in free. There's only one painting displayed here, the striking *Madonna del Parto*, that shows Mary in her ninth month of pregnancy.

It's a fifteenth-century masterpiece by Piero della Francesca, who dedicated it to his mother who was born in Monterchi. Mary stands in a pale blue robe, her hand over her full middle, flanked by boy angels who draw back curtains of a regal tent. It's dramatic

and serene—capturing Mary in a meditative moment, completely involved with the life growing inside her.

Francesca was a mathematician and in all his paintings there's an arresting symmetry of precise lines and lighting, combined with a gentle spirit of compassion. He created the *Madonna del Parto* for a Monterchi church that was built on a Cult of Fertility site. Back in pagan days pregnant women traditionally went to this site to bathe in a hilltop spring and pray for protection and abundant breastmilk. The church built over it, called the Momentana, was actually a cemetery chapel, so ceremonies for both birth and death took place there for centuries.

The Momentana became severely damaged over the years, and Francesca's fresco barely survived. Even though the only way to save the *Madonna del Parto* was to move it, the local women were so attached to it being in the cemetery chapel that they put up a fight, and ultimately lost.

It's been expertly restored and is displayed under glass in a sterile modern room in this museum that was once an elementary school. You've got to use your imagination to picture it in its original place, when all those Monterchi women would be kneeling in prayer before it. Now there's a bench in the room with the painting (handy for pregnant women), so you can settle in and absorb. In other rooms of the museum there's a theater where you can watch a movie about Piero della Francesca, displays about the *Madonna del Parto's* restoration, and a gift shop with books and prints.

Outside the museum, the tiny medieval village of Monterchi is a dreamy place to circle up cobblestoned streets and enjoy hilltop views of the valley. When I stopped by, I felt part of a classic Sunday afternoon, with two elderly town couples sitting next to me at a caffè, drinking beer and playing cards.

Nearby is Arezzo, where you'll find Piero della Francesca's most famous fresco, *The Legend of the True Cross*, in the Basilica di San Francesco. As for female images, a wonderful Annunciation and scene featuring the Queen of Sheba meeting Solomon are a part of that masterpiece.

Museum of the Madonna del Parto: Open April-October 9-1, 2-7; November-March, 9-1, 2-5. Closed Mondays. Pregnant women and children under fourteen get in free.

❧

Golden Day: Visit **Monterchi** (a half-hour drive from Arezzo), see *The Madonna del Parto* and have lunch at **Al Travato** (Piazza Umberto 1), an old-style enoteca. For luxury accommodations, and a great base to explore Tuscany and Umbria, stay at the **Palazzo Terranova**, an eight-room seventeenth-century palazzo that also has a fantastic spa and pool (www.palazzoterranova. com).

RECOMMENDED READING

Travelers' Tales Italy edited by Anne Calcagno, introduction by Jan Morris

30 Days in Italy edited by James O'Reilly, Larry Habegger, and Sean O'Reilly

10 City of Saint Catherine– Siena, Tuscany

THE EVENING SKY IN SIENA is a divine wonder to behold. Get a seat in the Piazza del Campo as the sun sets and you're in for a show. Colors change from blue-pink-golden to a rich navy. Then out pop the stars. Whoever is doing the lighting here is brilliant.

Any time of day, Siena is one of the most pleasant cities to stroll around. You'll be awed by the Gothic **Duomo** outside and in. There's Duccio's *Maestà* (Majesty) in the **Museo dell'Opera Metropolitana**, where the BVM sits enthroned, holding a rose-robed baby Jesus, surrounded by twenty angels and nineteen saints. When this masterpiece was unveiled in 1311, the whole town came out with candles to *ooh* and *aah* over it as church bells rang.

All over Siena, Saint Catherine, the most important woman of the Middle Ages, is honored with statues, paintings, and altars. The beloved *Mystic of Politics* was born here in 1347, in the area called Contrada dell' Oca, or Neighborhood of the Goose.

Pilgrims flock to the church she went to while growing up, which is now the **San Domenico Basilica**. There you'll find the richly decorated Santa Caterina Chapel, with frescos by Sodoma, who was a student of Leonardo da Vinci. In the center of it all is Catherine's head. Compared to a lot of other relics I've seen, it looks more like a mask, in amazing shape. Her thumb is nearby under a bell jar.

A short walk away is the **Santuario e Casa di Santa Caterina**, where the saint was born and grew up. It doesn't look as it probably did in her day, as it's been transformed to a shrine with Renaissance paintings that tell stories from her life. But still, as you walk through what was her kitchen and go upstairs to her bedroom you get a feel for the strong spirit of this brilliant woman. Get a load of the stone pillow she used—just one example of how she denounced creature comforts to feel closer to God.

Catherine was the twenty-fourth of twenty-five children, whose twin sister died in childbirth. She shocked her parents when she was seven and announced, "I've had a vision! I'm devoting my life to Christ!" Her mother tried to pull her away from her incessant praying and marry her off when she was twelve, but Catherine chopped off her hair and put up a fight. Her parents finally relented, and allowed her to join the Dominican nuns as a "tertiary," a lay person associated with the clergy.

Catherine devoted herself to nursing the sick, but even the devout around her were concerned about her religious zeal, as she'd only eat communion wafers. These days, psychologists who've examined the lives of female saints focus on Catherine. They say she had survivor's guilt because of the death of her twin, and it manifested as holy anorexia nervosa.

Despite her diet, Catherine became a powerful, influential woman. She had a vision that set her on a path to change the world through letter-writing. This was amazing, because she was illiterate. She dictated letters to her followers, and sent them off to the Pope in Avignon, encouraging him to come back to Rome. Those fourteenth-century times were a mess with divisions in the papacy and Italy. Dante and Petrarch had written to Pope Gregory XI to try to get him to come back to Italy, but it was Catherine's outright begging, addressing the Pope as "Sweet Babbo" (Sweet Daddy), and demanding "Up father, like a man!" that got him to think about budging.

For the ultimate push, Catherine went on horseback to Avignon and had a one-on-one meeting that got the Pope to pull up stakes. He died shortly after, and Catherine joined the new Pope in Rome, continuing to fight to unite the church through her writing. She died in Rome at thirty-three, of a paralytic stroke.

Catherine was canonized in 1461 as the Patron of Nurses and Fire Prevention. In 1939 she was named Co-Patron Saint of Italy (along with Saint Francis), in 1970 a Doctor of the Church, and in 1999, the Patron of Europe.

The Romans treasured her and have her body enshrined in the **Santa Maria Sopra Minerva** church, which coincidentally has a frescoed ceiling that to me resembles the Siena sky.

Her head is in Siena, because, according to legend, it was stolen by Sienese. When Roman guards caught the thieves on their way out of the Eternal City and asked them to open their sack, it appeared to be full of rose petals. But when they got it back to Siena, the head reappeared. Catherine's foot is now enshrined in Venice, at Santi Giovanni e Paolo. Everybody wanted a piece of this amazing woman. But you'll feel her presence living on most powerfully in Siena.

⁂

Golden Day: Enjoy **Siena** and **Saint Catherine** sights. Get to the **Campo** for sunset. If you don't want to splurge at the obvious caffès, head to **Key Largo**, where you can walk up a narrow stairway (more like a hole in the ceiling) with your glass of wine and wind up on a narrow wooden balcony to take in the whole scene. Eat at **Cane e Gatto** (Via Pagliaresi 6, 0577 287 545, dinner only, reservations necessary) where *Dream of Italy* editor Kathy McCabe says she had "one of the best meals of my life." Stay at **Palazzo Ravizza** (www.palazzoravizza.it), a restored Renaissance palace.

RECOMMENDED READING

Saint Cathrine of Siena as Seen in Her Letters edited by Vida Scudder

Holy Anorexia by Rudolph M. Bell

11 Town of Saint Margaret—Cortona, Tuscany

THIS PLACE HAS EVERYTHING on the checklist to fulfill the Tuscan hill town dream. Walls built by the Etruscans, which is where the name *Tuscany* comes from. A masterpiece *Annunciation* by Fra Angelico, in the **Museo Diocesano**. And a patron saint with a twisted story.

A steep, *very* steep, uphill walk from the Cortona historic center will take you to the place Saint Margaret once lived, where she's buried and honored: the **Chiesa di Santa Margherita**. It's a place that is worth the climb.

This is Saint Margaret's story:

Once upon a time in the thirteenth century, there lived a beautiful, high-spirited farmer's daughter named Margaret. Her mother died when she was young and Margaret's father remarried some shrew who had an automatic hate-on for Margaret. Meanwhile beautiful Margaret kept her spirits up by enjoying the attention from all the young lads in her little town. But no matter how hard she tried to enjoy her lot, she had the gnawing "there's gotta be something better than this" feeling. Lo and behold, along came a knight from Montepulciano who asked Margaret to come live with him...and work as his maid. Not insulted in the least, Margaret, then seventeen, jumped at the chance to get away from her evil stepmother. She moved into the knight's castle and surprise, surprise, he couldn't keep his

47

hands off her. Before you know it, she got pregnant and gave birth to a son.

"Now will you marry me?" Margaret asked her knight. "Uh... umm...uh...no," was his reply.

Margaret decided not to push it, looked on the bright side, and was grateful for her good fortune. She went out everyday to help the poor, even though the townsfolk would come by and call her a tramp. "Ha-ha, someday I'll be a saint," was her reply.

Then one day her knight went off for a trip and didn't come home as planned. But his dog did, and ala Lassie, led Margaret into the woods. There she came upon a horrifying site: her knight murdered and rotting. Margaret had a suspicion that she was the cause of it. She knew other men wanted her, and they probably whacked her knight, thinking they could take his place. "It's all my fault!" Margaret said. "If I weren't so beautiful none of this would have happened!"

She decided to repent big-time. She gave all the riches she'd gotten from the knight back to his family. She went home to her father and stepmother, all ready to confess that her whole life had been wrong up to this day. Her stepmother threw her out: "Wanton woman!"

In despair, she ran to Cortona, through a gate that's now called the **Porta Margherita**. Huffing and puffing, she arrived at the Franciscan Friars. "Please let me in, I want to repent!" They weren't going to make it so easy for her. To prove her faith, she put on a hair shirt. She fasted. She took out a knife and was all set to cut her beautiful nose off.

That's when the Franciscan monk, Fra Giunta, stepped in and became her confessor. Many tongues began wagging: "They're lovers!" But Giunta convinced his brothers that Margaret had suffered long enough, and after three years of penance they let her join their order.

Soon a miracle occurred. As Margaret was praying below a crucifix, Jesus himself leaned forward and whispered, "Poverella..." That began a whole bunch of conversation and ecstasies for Margaret.

Inspired, she went back to what she'd been doing in the first place when everyone called her a tramp: helping the poor. This time it was the poor of Cortona, and she really put muscle into it. She started an order of nuns she called "le Poverelle," founded a hospital for the poor and sick, and a charity organization—The Confraternity of Our Lady of Mercy—to support the hospital.

As she got older, Margaret wanted peace and quiet. So she moved up the hill to the Church of Saint Basil, and had it repaired. She died there in 1297. Immediately the people of Cortona forgot about Saint Basil, named the place Chiesa di Santa Margherita, and started rebuilding it. What you see up there now is mainly from the nineteenth century.

Margaret's body is in an open tomb above the high altar. She was canonized in 1728, as the Patroness of Fallen Women.

The view from up there—the rolling hills of the Val di Chiana—is awesome.

☙

Golden Day: Visit the **Museo Diocesano** to see Fra Angelico's *Annunciation*, walk to the **Chiesa di Santa Margherita**. Eat and stay near Cortona at **Il Falconiere** (www.ilfalconiere.com), a converted eighteenth-century country villa that's been elegantly turned into a Relais & Châteaux hotel.

Santa Maria Churches—Venice

VENICE IS A SEXY PLACE. The curves of its Grand Canal and palazzos, mysterious passageways, and flowing tides make it magically seductive.

It's always been closely tied to Mary and was officially established as an Italian republic on the same day as her Annunciation (March 25). It also has a history of being a bustling port town, and along with sailors and wealthy single merchants went prostitutes and high-class courtesans, like the famous poet Veronica Franco.

The mix of these two female aspects of Venice is literally carved in stone on the Rialto Bridge. On one side there's a bas-relief of the Annunciation. On the other side, to the left, is a woman with her legs spread, sitting over flames. The story of this gal is that she was a prostitute who was around when the idea for building the Rialto Bridge was first proposed. "Impossible," she said. "If you build it, I'll burn my crotch!" And so the bridge was built and the bawdy woman remembered.

Back on the BVM side of Venice, you'll see in its museums and churches how architects, painters, and sculptors pay homage to Mary in Venetian Renaissance style, bringing out the passionate emotions of her story.

Here are two of my favorite Santa Maria churches:

❋ Santa Maria della Salute (Dorsoduro)

At the opening of the Grand Canal, *The Salute*, or what my husband calls "the giant white boob," welcomes visitors to Venice.

Salute means health and salvation, which is what the Venetians needed desperately in 1631. For two years, the plague had ravaged the city, causing 45,000 deaths, a loss of one third of their population. The doge ordered prayers to Mary, the plague stopped, and it was decided to build a church to thank her.

Baldassare Longhena, at thirty-two years old, won a contest to design the church and came up with a Mary-centric plan. The dome represents her crown, the round shape her womb, the octagonal interior, her eight-sided star. The center of the marble floor features thirty-two roses, symbolizing the beads of her Rosary.

It's refreshing to step into the airy expanse of this church, with loads of light flooding through its giant dome. A marble sculpture at the main altar tells the plague story. In the center of it is the Madonna and child, bordered on one side by a pretty *signorina* who represents Venezia. On the other side is the plague—an old hag running from an angel who holds out a torch.

Pay the extra couple euros to get into the sacristy and see such masterpieces as Tintoretto's folksy hit on the the *Marriage at Cana*, where he got his friends to pose and women are in charge of pouring wine out of giant jugs. Titian's ceiling paintings here are also stunning, especially *The Sacrifice of Abraham*, where an angel swoops in to save Abraham's son Isaac, depicted as an adorable three-year-old with Titian-colored hair. Use the mirrors set on the side benches to get the best view.

In a corner are four simple Madonna portraits by Sassoferrato, a Baroque painter who was influenced by Raphael. Though critics call them too sentimental, they win me over.

❀ **Church of Santa Maria dei Miracoli, 1480s, Campo dei Miracoli (Cannaregio)**

This tiny glowing marble treasure chest looks like it should be kept under glass in a museum. If you catch it on a sunny day it shimmers. It was built with marble left over from San Marco, by Pietro Lombardo, who fitted pink, gray, and butter-yellow stones together to dazzling effect inside and out.

The motivation to build this church came from a portrait of the Madonna that back in the fifteenth century was kept in a Cannaregio neighborhood yard. Venetians used to stop and pray to it, and miraculously their prayers were answered. It became so popular that people started to leave money in front of the portrait—enough to fund the building of a church, which became Santa Maria dei Miracoli. In fact, so much money was given that a second story and a convent were added.

The miraculous Madonna portrait now sits at the altar, up a flight of marble steps. The church's gilded ceiling is painted with fifty portraits of saints and prophets, there are pillars carved with mermaids, *putti*, and floral motifs. It all blends seamlessly to create a romantic Renaissance masterpiece. It's no wonder this is the first choice for brides around the world who want to get married in Venice.

❧

Golden Day: Visit **dei Miracoli**, enjoy a caffè in the adjoining campo to gawk some more at the church exterior. Have lunch at **Fiaschetteria Toscana** (Salizada San Giovanni Grisostomo 5719), one of cookbook author Marcella Hazan's favorite Venice restaurants.

RECOMMENDED READING

The Honest Courtesan: Veronica Franco, Citizen and Writer in Sixteenth-Century Venice by Margaret F. Rosenthal

13 Madonnas by Titian, Bellini, and Tintoretto—Venice

THE MOST SPECTACULAR PAINTING of the Assumption you'll ever see is in **The Frari**. It's an action-packed transcendent scene. You'll gasp. The first time I saw it, there was an organ rehearsal going on. May you be so lucky.

It appears in the center of this massive church's altar. Mary dances while flying up to golden heaven, her red robe swirling, arms open to the light, she's lifted on a cloud by twenty-two happy *putti*. Bearded God swoops down, like Batman; an angel by his side crown a-ready. The earthbound apostles fall all over each other in awe over the miraculous moment, as if a wondrous storm is sweeping through.

The painting caused quite a sensation, like the opening of *Star Wars*, when folks back in 1518 first saw what Titian painted specifically for this chapel. I imagine he was miffed when the Franciscan friars (whose church it was) gave him flak and waffled about paying him, because they thought his dancing Mary was way too provocative compared to the calm scenes of her levitating on a throne, which was the proper, traditional way to portray her. But soon everybody else declared it revolutionary, Titian became a superstar, and to this day the painting is praised as the best Assumption out there.

Also beautiful is Titian's *Madonna di Ca' Pesaro*. Here he broke the rules again, placing Mary at the side of the painting and putting the Doge who paid for it in the center. Jesus playfully squirms away, tugging at Mary's veil. She was modeled after Titian's wife, who died in childbirth not long after the painting was finished.

Titian's teacher, Giovanni Bellini, painted the delicate, bathed in golden light *Madonna* triptych in the sacristy. You can take a seat here to admire this stunning, serene image of Mary surrounded by serenading angels. And yes, the Bellini that you'll be drinking in Venice, that fabulous prosecco and peach juice mixture, was named in honor of this artist.

Scuola San Rocco, Campo San Rocco, San Polo

Next door is another wonderful painting by Titian. It's an Annunciation, where a red-robed angel dances in to break the news to Mary. You'll find it upstairs in this Scuola, a place the artist Tintoretto covered with over fifty of his paintings, making it his lifelong project.

For a short time, Tintoretto was a student of Titian's, but the older artist kicked him out of his studio, some say because Titian was threatened by Tintoretto's talent. It looks to me more like their styles were so different, probably Titian couldn't stand to have this artist, nicknamed "Il Furioso" around.

Tintoretto's paintings have a folksy exuberance, with massive characters jammed together telling stories of dramatic biblical moments. The first painting of his you'll notice on the left as you enter the Scuola is the most bizarre Annunciation I've ever seen. Typically Mary is in a sacred bedroom, with a lovely garden in the background. But here she's in a broken down home, dropping a cloth from her spinning wheel, bewildered and anxious, as a muscular Angel Gabriel bursts in through the brick wall with tumbling *putti* overhead. In the background, Mary's husband Joseph works in the yard, oblivious to the event. It's quintessential Tintoretto, mixing the Divine with the everyday.

The Great Hall upstairs features wall-to-ceiling Old and New Testament scenes. You can pick up mirrors on side carts to get a better look at all that drama above you.

Though the overall effect of Tintoretto's Scuola borders on too Vegas-like for my taste, it's well worth it to stop by here for those two completely different Annunciations.

❦

Golden Day: Visit the **Frari** and **Scuola San Rocco**, have lunch at **La Bitte** (Campo San Barnaba, 041 5230531), a popular place for locals.

14 The Scrovegni Chapel—Padua

IT'S TOUGH TO PULL AWAY FROM VENICE, but a half-hour train ride will bring you to this splendid fourteenth-century chapel, dedicated to Mary and frescoed by Giotto, who inspired all the Renaissance greats. It was built over ruins of a Roman arena, which is why its real name is the **Church of the Madonna dell'Arena**. But it's better known as the **Scrovegni Chapel**, because it was originally a part of their family villa.

The inspiration to call in Giotto to fresco this place came from Enrico Scrovegni, who was desperate to not burn in hell. His father, Reginaldo, was a scumbag money lender—the embodiment of the worst credit card company you can imagine, who charged ridiculously high interest rates and awful late fees. Reginaldo was so despised that the church denied him a burial. Dante put him in the Seventh Circle of Hell, where he was doomed to sit on hot sand with his head bent while Florentines shouted in his ears for eternity.

Enrico, a wealthy merchant and banker, wasn't so different from his father, so to atone for Reginaldo's sins, save his soul and his family's, he went overboard and called in the best painter of the day to work on the church adjoining his home.

You'll walk in to be wowed by the intense blue of Giotto's curved star-studded ceiling that tops thirty-eight frescos, all backed by that heavenly blue, which narrate the life of Mary and then Christ.

Giotto broke the mold of the stiff Middle Ages, bringing emotion to these figures, which in 1306 was as radical as adding special effects to a movie. There's an innocent beauty to every panel. Characters plead, embrace, conspire and lament as angels sweep in like comets.

Here, sort of like how Ron Howard took the *Da Vinci Code* and made it into a movie, Giotto took *The Golden Legend*, a bestselling book of his day, and made a medieval graphic novel with Mary in the lead. *The Golden Legend*, written by a friar, told imaginative stories of Christianity's major players. Folks back then loved relating to holy people in a contemporary way for the first time.

Since you probably haven't read the book, the images need some explanation. Giotto's scenes play out in three tiers, beginning at the top left corner to "establish the conflict," as Hollywood script analysts would say. Joachim, Mary's father, gets thrown out of the temple because after twenty years of marriage, he and his wife Ann are still childless. What follows is Joachim retreating to his fields in despair, sacrificing a goat to lift the barren curse. Meanwhile home-alone Ann receives the news from an angel that she's finally pregnant. The couple rejoices, Mary is born and taken at three years old to the temple.

In the eighth fresco you'll see men lined up with sticks in their hands, for the *The Presentation of the Rods*, which would have given Freud a phallic field day. The story goes that when Mary was fourteen and marriage-ready, the high priest called in every bachelor in town to lay their rod on the altar and whoever had one that flowered could marry Mary. The guy standing to the side with a beard is Joseph, who figured he was too old to marry a fourteen-year-old, so he doesn't even enter the rod contest. In the next shot, the high priest has convinced him to add his rod and all the men are huddled and waiting. What follows is *The Betrothal of Mary and Joseph*, with Joseph proudly holding a rod with a blossoming lily, the symbol of Mary. Joseph's miffed contenders stand to the side, one of them breaking a rod over his knee as if to say, "Drat! I wanted to marry Mary!"

On the wall opposite Mary's Annunciation is the *Last Judgment*, said to be painted by Giotto's assistants because it doesn't have the elegance of the master. Amidst the fires of hell is Reginaldo Scrovegni holding up a model of the chapel to the Madonna in a, "Please forgive me! Look at this pretty chapel I made for you!" gesture.

It's good to visit the chapel knowing these stories because you'll only have fifteen minutes inside to view the frescos. The place has been restored and a sterilized, climate-controlled environment created to preserve the frescos. Your visit begins in an antechamber where you view a fifteen-minute film about the chapel before you're escorted in for your limited time with the masterpiece.

www.capelladegliscrovegni.it
www.selectitaly.com

Scrovegni Chapel: Daily 9-7. Reservations are a must, so book ahead through one of the websites listed on this page. (Though I did visit one November weekday without reserving, got a ticket for an hour later, and had pleasant waiting time strolling through the nearby Padua market.)

❧

Golden Day: Visit to **Scrovegni Chapel**, lunch at **Isola di Caprera** (Via Marsilio di Padova 11/15 049 8760244, closed Sunday) for great seafood, and caffè at the classic (since 1831) **Caffè Pedrocchi** (Via VIII Febbraio 15).

15 Venus of the Beautiful Buttocks and Other Museo Archeologico Nazionale Treasures—Naples

"DO YOU THINK ALL THE MEN here know how good looking they are?" Sheila asked as we took in the view from our table at the Piazza Bellini in Naples. This is a place where you could O.D. on infinite variations of bedroom eyes. Top it off with *delizioso* pizza, *sfogliatelle*, and the spontaneous theater that bombards you as you wander through Naples' lively markets and you'll be won over by the vibrant soul of this city.

The idea of stepping out of such fun into a place called the **Museo Archeologico Nazionale** may sound like a buzz kill, but get over it. Even here, the Neapolitan ambience—a mix of classic beauty, deep sensuality, and naughty humor is inescapable. On my last visit, the flirty guy at the ticket booth kept me waiting as he took bites of a huge chocolate torta, then held it out to me, insisting I have a taste. It was a perfect start for a couple of rich hours.

Here are just a few highlights of this amazing place:

* *Callipygian Venus* (*Venus of the Beautiful Buttocks*)
Sculptures of *Hercules* and the *Farnese Bull* dominate the ground-floor room where you'll find this enticing Venus. She's posed lifting up her robe and turning to peek at her rear end. The statue is a Roman copy of the Greek *Callipygian Aphrodite* (Venus to the Romans), that was found in Syracuse, Sicily.

There's a good story behind this behind.

Two Sicilian farm girl sisters were fighting over which one had the better rear. To settle the feud, they ran to the road, lifted their skirts, and asked a guy passing by to be the judge. He chose the older sister's rear, fell in love, and ran back home to tell his brother all about it. The brother decided to head out there and judge for himself—which he did, and chose the younger sister's behind. These guys were from a wealthy family, and their father tried to marry them off to rich girls, but they refused to give up on the sisters with the beautiful butts. And so those lucky farm girls ended up marrying money.

In gratitude they built a temple in Syracuse and dedicated it to Aphrodite Callipygos, because in Greek *calli* means beautiful and *pygos* means buttocks. A Sicilian cult grew around the temple, with many coming to worship at the statue, hoping that they would receive good fortune from those buttocks, just as those farm girls had.

The Callipygian Venus statue here in this museum was considered so pornographic in the nineteenth century only privileged men on the Grand Tour who paid were allowed to have a look at it. Notice how those beautiful buttocks got smudged by all the kisses they received from her admirers.

Upstairs you're going to love the mosaics and frescos from the villas of Pompeii, Herculaneum, and Stabia. Especially four small beautiful frescos from Stabia, where Medea, Flora, Leda, and Diana delicately float in pale blue and green backgrounds. There are also frescos from the Temple of Isis (the Egyptian mother goddess), whom

the Romans worshipped, where a deep Pompeii red backs
enchanting ornamental designs and figures.

And you definitely can't miss:

● **The Secret Cabinet (Il Gabinetto Segreto)**
Women weren't officially allowed to enter this room until
the year 2000. Men's logic was that the weaker sex shouldn't
see displays of what they labeled pornography, dug up from
Pompeii and Herculaneum in the eighteenth century.

What did they think females would do if we saw such
things as Pan screwing a she-goat or Zeus frolicking with a
naked maiden? Was it all those penises in so many shapes and
sizes that the fellas feared would make things dangerous?

Now even kids are allowed in to see the frescos and vases
here that are painted with scenes that bring to mind the *Kama
Sutra*, with a strong emphasis on doggie-style positions. When
they were first discovered, it was believed these objects came
from Pompeii whorehouses, as the town of 40,000 people
was known to have 400 brothels. But eventually the racy
scenes and objects were also found in the remains of noble
villas, where the images must have added inspiration to the
grand banquet-orgies of those days. Some are ancient jokes.
Such as a fresco of Pan, that lusty God of Shepherds, lifting
up the skirt of a maiden and discovering "she" has a penis!

As for the abundance of penises—made into wind chimes,
oil lamps, and gigantic ones hanging off dwarves—they were
fertility symbols used to bring luck, like our garden gnomes.
It all started with Priapus, the Greek god of fertility, whom
the Romans also worshipped. They put statues of him in
front of their homes and a stroke of his penis as you walked
by insured your good fortune.

Priapus was the son of Aphrodite (Goddess of Love and Beauty) and Dionysus (God of Wine and Sexual Ecstasy). Hera (Zeus' wife) cursed Priapus when he was in Aphrodite's womb, condemning him to ugliness and impotence. When Priapus was born looking like a freak with a huge erect penis, Aphrodite was horrified and threw him down to earth from Mount Olympus, where he was raised by shepherds.

Everywhere Priapus with the three-foot shlong went, animals started humping each other and plants sprouted up, which is why he became known as the God of Fertility. The irony was that he was impotent, which understandably frustrated the poor guy, so he ended up being ornery and couldn't even walk because of his permanent hard-on. Since he couldn't visit all the fields in person, farmers made statues of Priapus which were eventually pared down to his most prominent feature.

It's rare to be in a museum where jaw-dropping beauty, sex, and laughter blend together so well. But this is Naples, after all.

Museo Archeologico Nazionale: Piazza Museo 19, Wednesday-Monday, 9-7.

www.marketplace.it/museo.nazionale

❧

Golden Day: Spend a couple of hours in the **Museo** and take a break at the nearby **La Libreria delle Donne caffè** (Piazza Bellini 72). Dine at **Pizzeria Bellini** (Via Costantinopoli 79/80, 081 459 774, closed Sunday) where the house specialty, spaghetti cooked in parchment with seafood, is fantastic.

16 *Cloister of Santa Chiara—Naples*

TUCKED AWAY FROM NOISY, darker **Spaccanapoli** is this calm bright oasis where the followers of Santa Chiara once prayed.

The cloister's main attractions are rows of seventy-two majolica-tiled columns, painted in pretty blue, green, and gold floral designs. Tiled benches below show scenes of peasants dancing the *tarantella*, hunting, and enjoying jolly times in the fields, along with myths featuring Neptune and his mermaids. Citrus trees and shrubs fill the gardens, adding sweet smells.

On the convent walls surrounding the cloister are faded jewel-toned frescos where angels float on arches next to women representing virtues such as Wisdom and Temperance. Murals picture action-packed battle scenes and Bible stories, including one of Judith looking innocent and content as she cuts off the head of General Holofernes.

It all seems a bit much for the nuns who called themselves The Poor Clares and were famous for living lives of poverty and self-denial. As they had no contact with the outside world, these images must have been as entertaining as high-def TV.

The cloister didn't look at all like this originally. It was built in the fourteenth century when the second wife of Robert d'Anjou (the church founder) decided she wanted to live vicariously through the lives of nuns in seclusion so had this convent added on.

Four hundred years later the innovative artist Domenico Antonio Vaccaro came in and renovated the cloister, inspired by all the Neapolitan frivolity of his day. The nuns enjoyed it all to themselves until 1924, when they traded places with their Franciscan friar neighbors. The Franciscans invited upper-class intellectuals and artists to see the cloister and finally in the 1970s the space was opened to the public.

Although this is still a quiet spot, who knows what Santa Chiara (to us Clare) would think of it. She was a twelfth-century girl living in Assisi who got very inspired when Saint Francis came and gave a sermon at her church. Though many noblemen wanted to marry her, one Palm Sunday night Chiara snuck out of her wealthy parent's home and headed to Saint Francis to ask to join his gang.

Francis took her in, shaved her head, and gave her sackcloth to wear. Though Chiara's parents tried to force her to come back home, she fiercely resisted. Instead she founded the Poor Clares order of nuns, and became a fanatic about vows of poverty. The sisters wore no shoes, existed only on alms, slept on the ground, spoke little, and could own nothing.

Chiara became the Patron Saint of Embroidery and Sore Eyes because she was a sickly type and while in bed managed to get a lot of sewing done, making altar cloths and vestments for churches all over Assisi. One Christmas Eve, ailing in her bed, she heard songs from the church below. Then, miraculously, an image of the Bethlehem manger appeared on her bedroom wall. That's why in 1958, the Pope declared that she should also be known as The Patron Saint of TV.

There are many impressive churches nearby, including the **Cappella Sansevero** with its famous statue of the veiled Christ. And don't miss **Pio Monte della Misericordia**, where you'll find Caravaggio's *Sette Opere della Misericordia* (*Seven Acts of Mercy*), with angels carrying the Virgin Mary into a Spaccanapoli street.

Cloisters of Santa Chiara: Via Benedetto Croce, Monday-Saturday 9:30-1, 2:30-5, Sunday 9:30-1.

❧

Golden Day: Visit **Cloisters** and **Spaccanapoli**. For a wonderful lunch, go to **La Cantina della Sapienza** (Via della Sapienza 40, 081 459 078, lunch only, closed Sunday), a humble place for Neapolitan classics. Then stop by **Mary's** for the best *sfogliatelle* in town at the **Galleria Umberto**, or get pizza at **Sorbillo** (Via dei Tribunali 32, closed Sunday).

17 Cave of the Cumaean Sibyl—Cumae, Campania

THE EARTH PERCOLATES IN THIS PLACE northwest of Naples called the "Phlegrean Fields" or "Burning Fields." Steam rises from volcanic craters and lakes. The Tyrrhenian Sea is the backdrop for ruins of temples and a trapezoidal-shaped forty-foot tunnel that leads to a chamber where poets say there lived the mysterious and powerful Cumaean Sibyl. Archaeologists say the tunnel was built as a defense structure, but what fun is that?

If you're a *Sopranos* fan you'll recognize this Cumae cave from a Season 2 episode. Annalisa Zucca, that bombshell of a mafia boss, brought Tony to this otherworldly spot to discuss family business. As they walked through the shadowy cave, the sexual tension between the two of them sizzled.

According to myth, thousands of years ago another bombshell of a young maiden was wandering around here and caught the eye of Apollo, God of the Sun. To win her over, Apollo threw her the "Your wish is my command" line. The maiden pointed to a pile of sand and said, "I wish to live as many years as those grains of sand." So Apollo gave her one thousand years of life, but she still wouldn't put out. To get back at her he found a loophole—she hadn't asked for youth. That's the reason why through most of her long life the Cumaean Sibyl was a bent over, warty old gal. In her latter years, she shriveled into a small ball and hung like a bat in a jar from a tree. Kids would stand below her, taunting and asking: "What do you want, Sibyl?" Only her croaking voice was left and her answer was always: "I want to die!"

Apollo, who kept a soft spot for her, gave her the gift of prophecy. She was a sneaky one, writing enigmatic prophecies on oak leaves and leaving them on her cave's ledge. Often they were scattered to the winds, driving those looking for her answers crazy.

The poet Virgil wrote about the Cumaean Sibyl in the *Aeneid*, in a dramatic sequence where she inhales the smoke from burning laurel leaves and then "with wild hair, breast heaving, and foaming mouth" bellows to Aeneas that there's more trouble ahead for him.

All poor Aeneas wanted was to see his dead father. The Sibyl put him through a rigamarole of having to find a golden bough and burning animals in sacrifice. She finally escorted him into Hades, through a convenient door nearby in the foul-smelling, bubbling Lake Averno. The two of them rode across the River Styx and eventually got to Elysium, The Land of Joy, where Aeneas and his father had a tear-filled reunion.

Going to Cumae, you'll be visiting one of Italy's oldest settlements, founded by the Greeks in the eighth century B.C., way before Naples existed. To the right of the cave entrance is the Via Sacra which winds up to Lago Fusaro and remains of a church that used to be a temple dedicated to Jupiter. The views of Cape Misenum from here may inspire mythic thoughts.

Acropoli di Cuma: Open from 9 until one hour before sunset.

Phlegrean Fields: Tours can be arranged at www.retourcampiflegrei.com.

❧

Golden Day: Go to the **Acropoli di Cuma** by car or take the Cumana train from Naples to the Fusaro stop and then a Miseno-Cuma SEPSA bus. Back in Naples, eat at **Da Dora** (Via Ferdinando Palasciano 30, 081 680519), where the house seafood pasta is divine and the waitress who bursts into song is so soulful you may find yourself teary-eyed.

18 Goddesses and Madonnas—Palermo

ACCORDING TO THE ANCIENT ROMANS, the Goddess Ceres brought abundance to Sicily, scattering seeds all over the island so fields of wheat, tomatoes, eggplant, zucchini, you name it, sprung up and thrived under the blazing sun.

In Palermo, Sicily's capital, Ceres stands majestically in one of the city's most beautiful outdoor places, the **Piazza Pretoria** fountain. Venus and a racy collection of nymphs and mermaids surround her. When this fountain was first brought here from a Florentine villa in 1575, the shocked Palmeritani nicknamed it "The Fountain of Shame" because of all the nakedness.

The story of Ceres (Patron of Sicily, Motherhood and Agriculture) is interlocked with her daughter Proserpina, who caused Ceres tremendous grief. Beautiful Proserpina was picking flowers in a field near Enna in central Sicily when suddenly Pluto (God of the Underworld) caught sight of her, found her irresistible, swooped up, kidnapped or raped her (choose your version), and brought her down to Hades to make her his queen.

Distraught, Ceres left the heavens to wander Sicily in search of Proserpina, lured by the echoes of her daughter's cries. When she found out what Pluto had done, Ceres begged her husband

(and brother!) Jupiter to get their daughter back. Jupiter had to oblige Ceres, because what with all her wandering and neglecting the fields, everything had stopped growing. Pluto let Proserpina go, but being a tricky god, he offered her a pomegranate to eat before she left. As soon as Proserpina bit into the fruit, a deal was sealed with that King of Hades: Proserpina would have to return to be Pluto's wife for four months out of the year.

That's one explanation for the change of seasons. Winter is a time when Proserpina does her stint in hell and Ceres mourns for her daughter. Spring comes when mother and daughter are reunited. To this day Sicilians hold festivals that mark Proserpina's leaving (in December) and returning (in March).

Beyond Palermo's Pretoria Fountain of goddesses and nymphs, there are wonderful sights that pay homage to the BVM. Close by and up some stairs from it is the tiny, sparkling **Santa Maria dell'Ammiraglio** church, originally dedicated to a Greek admiral and styled in a Byzantine-Islamic mix with fantastic mosaics of blue, deep red, and green set against a gold background.

Benedictine nuns, headed up by Mother Superior Eloisa Martorana, took it over in the sixteenth century, so it was renamed **La Martorana**. The nuns baroque-icized the church, which wasn't exactly the best thing, as they tore out some of those mosaics and replaced them with frescos. There's one pretty Annunciation, and we can forgive those nuns for their mistakes in redecorating, because they did keep the original mosaic columns and archways. The best thing they did was invent one of Palermo's tastiest treats: *frutta di Martorana*, marzipan molded into fruit shapes. These were so realistic when they were hung on a tree they were mistaken for the real thing and can still be found today in shops all over Palermo. You must have a taste.

More BVM treasures can be found in **La Kalsa**, my favorite Palermo neighborhood, where crumbling baroque buildings, Spanish-Moorish architecture, and artists' studios blend together in a quiet area of the city that retains an exotic sense of the Arab port it once was.

In the Palazzo Abatellis, now the **Galleria Regionale**, you may think the *Annunciation* you see is mistitled, because there's no angel there. It's a close up of a gorgeous blue-veiled, dark-eyed Madonna, resembling the Sicilian women you'll see on the streets outside. Renaissance artist Antonello da Messina caught the moment where Mary receives her calling, with one hand raised from her book, in reaction to the offstage angel.

Also in this neighborhood is the awe-inspiring **Santa Maria dello Spasimo**, a sixteenth-century Romanesque church, named "Spasimo" to commemorate Mary's suffering at the crucifixion. What's amazing about the church is that it's roofless because a Turkish invasion kept it from being completed. Two huge sumac trees grow in the middle of what was once (almost) the sanctuary, forming a leafy cupola, opening to the Palermo sky. There's a natural grace to this setting and as you stand there looking up, you're likely to hear rehearsals going on in the attached music school that was once a monks' cloister. For a truly magical experience, get there for one of their evening concerts.

La Martorana (Santa Maria dell'Ammiraglio): Piazza Bellini 2, daily 8-1, 3:30-6.

Galleria Regionale della Sicilia: Via Alloro 4, daily 9-1 and Tuesday and Thursday 2:30-7.

Santa Maria dello Spasimo: Via Santa Maria dello Spasimo 13, daily 8-12. For concert schedules, check out www. thebrassgroup.it.

❧

Golden Day: Explore Palermo's **Kalsa district**, eat at **Antica Focacceria San Francesco** (Via A. Paternostro 58, 091 320264, closed Monday). To get a more luxurious side of Palermo, the pretty bar at the **Grand Hotel et des Palmes** (Via Roma 398) is fun for a cocktail.

19 Nymphs, Goddesses, and Santa Lucias— Ortygia, Sicily

To step into a Wonderful Way Back machine, head over a bridge in Syracuse to the island of Ortygia, one of Sicily's most intriguing and beautiful places. According to Homer, the sea nymph Calypso lured Odysseus here, and now amidst its remains of ancient civilizations and baroque architecture are treasures that pay homage to females, from nymphs to saints.

In Ortygia's main square, Piazza Archimede, is the baroque **Fontana di Diana**, that tells the story of the Greek Myth of Arethusa, a nymph dedicated to Artemis (Diana to the Romans), the Virgin Goddess of the Hunt.

Like Artemis, Arethusa loved frolicking about in nature. One fateful day she decided to take a dip in a lovely river, which just happened to be the god Alepheus's river. Trouble ensued, as he fell hopelessly in love with Arethusa, and went after her in hot pursuit. Desperate to keep her virginity, Arethusa begged Artemis for help, so the goddess swept in, lead Arethusa underground from Greece to Sicily's Ortygia island, and turned Arethusa into a spring.

Today the **Fonte Arethusa** spring at the Ortygia waterfront is a pretty papyrus-filled spot with swans floating about it. As for the rest of the Greek legend, Arethusa never did completely shake off her stalker, Alepheus. He remained connected to her through his river where she swam in Greece. When sacrifices were made there for the Olympics, the Fonte Arethusa here in Sicily would turn red. Even today it's believed that if you drop a cup into the Greek Arethusa River it'll turn up at this Ortygia spring.

The island's **Duomo** is built around the remains of a Greek Temple that honored the Goddess Athena, patron of Wisdom, Craftsmanship and Heroic Endeavors, who became Minerva to the Romans. Sprung from the head of Zeus, Athena was a real career goddess who did such great things as guide Odysseus home, think up the Trojan horse, and give Greece the olive tree.

The Duomo's Baroque and Norman designs blend around the massive Doric columns of Athena's temple. Once a sculpture of her graced the rooftop, where she stood with her golden shield, serving as a beacon to sailors. Now you'll see it's been replaced with a statue of the Virgin Mary.

Inside the Duomo, there's a chapel dedicated to the most celebrated saint in town—**Saint Lucy**, Patron of Syracuse and Eyes.

Lucy was born in the third century to a noble Syracuse family and early on decided to live for God and remain a virgin. This didn't sit well with her parents who wanted to marry her off, but Lucy managed to turn things around. She took her sick mother to pray at the tomb of Saint Agatha in Catania, and when her mother was miraculously healed, she took Lucy's side and stopped hounding her about finding a man. So Lucy could go about her saintly work, which was bringing food to Christians who were hiding out in underground tunnels. In order to guide her way through those dark tunnels, she wore a wreath of candles on her head, which is where the Swedes got the idea to always represent her with that wreath.

Despite herself, beautiful Lucy had many Syracuse admirers. One of them couldn't stop telling her how much he loved her eyes, so she plucked them out and handed them over to him on a plate, hoping he'd leave her in peace. But the guy was so insulted about being rebuffed, he turned Lucy over to the authorities for being a Christian. The governor's idea for a punishment was to drag Lucy to a whorehouse, but even with a team of oxen pulling her, Lucy miraculously could not be budged. When burning her at the stake didn't work, she was finally beheaded at a place on the Syracuse mainland where a church, Santa Lucia al Sepolcro, now stands.

If you're in Syracuse for Lucy's Feast Day (December 13), there'll be torch-lit processions and you'll be eating *cuccia*, wheat soaked in milk and sugar. The wheat commemorates a sixteenth-century Syracuse event, where the locals prayed to Saint Lucy to end a famine, and miraculously a ship sailed into the Ortygia harbor loaded with grain.

Finally, you shouldn't miss stopping by the **Museo Regionale di Arte Mediovale** (Palazzo Bellomo) to see Caravaggio's dark and intense masterpiece, the *Burial of Saint Lucy*. It was painted just a few months before Caravaggio died, when he was exiled to Syracuse, having been accused of murder in Rome. It's a powerfully haunting work, showing Lucy with her throat slashed, surrounded by mourners and gravediggers.

Duomo: Piazza del Duomo, daily 8-noon, 4-7.
Museo Regionale di Arte Mediovale e Moderna: Via Capodieci 16, Ortygia, Monday-Saturday 9-6:30, Sunday 9-1:30.

᪣

Golden Day: Explore **Ortygia**, eat at the extraordinary **Ristorante L'Ancora** (Via G. Perno 7, 0931 462 369) for fantastic seafood and lemon cake dessert. For a splurge, stay at the **Grand Hotel Ortigia Siracusa** (www.grandhotelortigia.it), a Liberty-style building set grandly on the seaside. Or go for good budget digs at **Domus Mariae** (www.sistemia.it/domusmariae), which is run by nuns and has simple rooms with sea views.

20 Temple of Segesta—Sicily

FOR AN UNFORGETTABLE, ROMANTIC EXPERIENCE of the ancient world, head to **Segesta**, an hour's drive west of Palermo. There you'll find one of the most perfectly preserved temples in the world, from the fifth century B.C., set in the midst of a remote grassy field.

According to the Roman writer Cicero, the temple once held a statue of the Goddess Diana. When a governor ordered it removed, all the townswomen gathered to anoint the statue with perfume, cover it with flowers, and burn incense to give her a sacred send off.

Mystery surrounds this place. It's unknown why the Elymians, settlers who came before the conquering Greeks, never put a roof on it. Its thirty-six Doric columns clearly show Greek influence, and there's a theory that the Elymians built it to get on the good side of those powerful Greeks. At the time they were having a rivalry with their southern Selinunte neighbors, who'd aligned themselves with Syracuse. The Elymians, wanting the Greeks to think they were worth supporting, started building the temple because they knew a delegation from Athens would be coming through to check them out. Once the Athenians came and went, convinced the Segesta Elymians were rich and had good taste in architecture, they stopped work on the temple.

When the wind whips through the temple's columns, it sounds as if an organ is being played. And in spring, when it's surrounded by wildflowers, it's glorious. From the Segesta hilltop, there's a sweeping view of the valley towards the Gulf of Castellammare. Unlike places such as Agrigento, where modern developments break the ancient mood, in Segesta there are no such distractions.

A short walk away is an amphitheater from the third century B.C., where revivals of Greek plays, ballets, and avant-garde performances are staged in the summer.

Segesta Temple: Open November-March 9-4 and April-August 9-7. It can be reached by driving an hour west from Palermo, or you can take a half-hour train or bus ride from Trapani.

&

Golden Day: Visit the **Segesta Temple**, and driving toward Erice, check into the **Eremo Casa del Sorriso** (www. eremocasadelsorriso.it), a converted monastery that also serves wonderful meals.

II

Ville, Palazzi, and an Apartment

If these pretty walls could talk, you'd hear whispers of sweet nothings, laughing, crying, knock-down drag-out fights. The drama! In these grand homes, often adorned with masterpieces, heroines or courtesans or foreigners who moved here, lived and left a lasting legacy.

You may find yourself in the 500-room Palazzo Ducale, where Isabella d'Este, the brilliant gutsy Renaissance woman, became a patron of the arts and ruled Mantua. Or in a humble apartment in Florence, where Elizabeth Barrett Browning spent the happiest years of her life.

My first thoughts as I wander through these places always veer to: *Imagine the parties! A princess waltzing, a poet entertaining her writer friends, a courtesan playing a lute.*

Then my mind wanders…. *What about an ordinary day? A Savoy Queen waking up with that gigantic chandelier hanging over her bed. What would it have been like to have been Eleonora de' Medici, flinging open the curtains to her Boboli Gardens' view?*

History comes alive in these places. Go, admire, and indulge in your own imaginings as you walk in these women's footsteps.

RECOMMENDED READING

Sarah Dunant's Renaissance Trilogy:
In The Company of the Courtesan
The Birth of Venus
Sacred Hearts

21 Palazzo Barberini– Rome

IN *ROMAN HOLIDAY*, THE PRINCESS PLAYED by Audrey Hepburn escapes from this palace to end up on a romantic adventure with reporter Gregory Peck. It's sublime to play Audrey's moves backward and escape inside the Barberini to peacefully take in Renaissance masterpieces.

The palace was the digs of Maffeo Barberini, who transformed it when he became Pope Urban VIII in 1623. He went all out to make it *splendido*, calling in the best artists of the day, including Bernini and Borromini. You'll climb Borromini's spiral staircase as you enter. Inside you'll get a dizzying hit looking up at his Grand Salone ceiling, frescoed by Pietro Da Cortona. Go ahead and lie back on a couch to admire this *Triumph of Providence*, where golden bees (the Barberini family emblem) ascend to the heavens.

Most of the rooms you'll be walking through were originally the apartment of Princess Anna Colonna Barberini, who had married the pope's nephew. She was the palace hostess and the most powerful woman in Rome during the Barberini's seventeenth-century heyday. The family's fortunes got dispersed over the years, and the palace was sold to the State in 1949, becoming the National Gallery of Art.

In the galleries, you'll see beautiful women immortalized by masters, including:

❀ *Fornarina* (Raphael's Girlfriend)

The subject of Raphael's most famous portrait is his longtime lover, Margherita Luti, who he called Fornarina, which translates to "little oven." The dark-haired, bare-breasted, mischievous-looking beauty was a Trastevere baker's daughter. She wears a bracelet with Raphael's signature on it, as if they were going steady.

❀ *Beatrice Cenci* (Who Murdered Her Daddy)

With those legendary huge eyes and innocent over-the-shoulder look, it's hard to imagine this sixteen-year-old bludgeoned her father to death. That is until you hear the story of the man's atrocious cruelty to his whole family, who joined Beatrice in the murder. The painting, said to have been completed the night before Beatrice's execution, is attributed to Guido Reni, but many believe Elisabetta Sirani, a female artist, is the one who painted it.

❀ *Judith Beheading Holofernes* (Bible's Gutsiest Widow)

Master painter Caravaggio captures a gory biblical moment here. It's Judith, chopping off the head of General Holofernes, complete with spurting blood. Her maid stands by with a "Take that, you bastard!" look.

According to the Old Testament, Judith was a widow who got fed up with her Israeli countrymen in their fight against the Assyrians, so she took matters into her own hands, got all dolled up, and went to visit the enemy's General Holofernes. Clever woman that she was, Judith promised him helpful information and sexual favors, which she never made good on. The general lusted after Judith, and threw a banquet where he became "sodden with wine," expecting some nooky afterward. Imagine his surprise when Judith snuck into his tent, found Holofernes sprawled out drunk as a skunk, and lopped his head off.

Caravaggio's brilliant brush strokes illuminate Judith's conflicted expression. She's repulsed, curious, a bit repentant, but committed. For his model, he used one of Rome's most popular courtesans of the day, Fillide Melandroni. A few years after the painting was completed, Caravaggio got into a street brawl with Melandroni's "protector," Ranuccio Tomassoni. It's believed Caravaggio was trying to castrate Tomassoni, but instead gave his thigh a fatal artery-severing slash. Caravaggio was exiled from Rome for the murder, never to return.

Palazzo Barberini: Via delle Quattro Fontane 13, 8:30-7:30. Closed Monday.

꙳

Golden Day: Morning at the **Barberini** and lunch at **Colline Emiliane** (Via degli Avvignonesi, 22, 06 481 7538) for specialties of the Emilia-Romagna region.

RECOMMENDED READING

The Families Who Made Rome: A History and Guide by Anthony Majanlahti
Beatrice's Spell: The Enduring Legacy of Beatrice Cenci by Belinda Jack

22 Villa Farnesina–Rome

LE DELIZIE OR "THE DELIGHTS" was the original name of this villa, known back in Renaissance days as the best party house in Rome. It was built by Agostino Chigi, banker to the Popes, aka the Richest Man in the World. On the same site in 44 B.C. was a villa where Cleopatra had carried on with Julius Caesar.

Chigi was a generous patron of the arts, so in 1506 he called in the top architect (Baldassare Peruzzi) and best painters to create luscious gardens and a villa packed with frescos of mythological love scenes to inspire his guests. Spectacles with singers and dancers were staged here, followed by opulent banquets. For the grand finale, Chigi had his servants toss his used china and silverware into the Tiber. Little did his guests know he kept a net down there to catch it all.

The stars of Chigi's parties were Rome's adored courtesans. These beautiful ladies, called "honest prostitutes," in addition to providing their expected services, could recite classical poetry at the drop of a hat and serenade their admirers with lutes or violins. They were treated well by Rome's many wealthy bachelors, who ranged from merchant traders to priests. Like movie stars, when courtesans rode through the streets in their fancy carriages, people would run out to gawk at their elegant get-ups, jewels, and hairstyles.

Imperia, one of Rome's most famous courtesans, was a favorite of Chigi's; he planned on living with her in this villa when he first decided to build it.  The painter Raphael, who also spent quality time with Imperia, had her model for one of the first frescos you'll see here in the *Loggia of Galatea*. The image of the half-naked sea nymph (surprisingly muscular and fleshy) is a scene from a Greek myth that began with the Cyclops Polyphemus falling madly in love with Galatea. Unfortunately for Polyphemus, Galatea fell in love with a mortal shepherd, Acis. When Polyphemus saw the two of them cavorting, he flipped out and threw a boulder at the couple, killing Acis. The blood of Galatea's dead lover turned into a river that she rides away on in this painting, triumphantly escaping Polyphemus.

Raphael's model Imperia was not so triumphant. The courtesan had many men besides Chigi, and fell in love with one of them. When he tired of her, Imperia feared she was losing her beauty, and at the age of twenty-six swallowed poison and died. The exact date of her suicide was August 15 (coincidentally, the celebration of Mary's Assumption into heaven), and in Rome there was a huge storm, with folks in the city saying Jupiter had thundered down to take away their beloved beauty.

Imperia's image appears again upstairs in this villa, where the artist Sodoma frescoed Chigi's bedroom with scenes from the life of Alexander the Great. There *The Wedding of Alexander and Roxanne* reeks with sexual anticipation, as Roxanne's clothes are tugged at by *putti* and Alexander stands awaiting his bride.

Chigi and Imperia had broken up before her suicide, and he'd gone to Venice and gotten himself another courtesan, Francesca. The couple moved in here and, after having four children, the Pope insisted they marry. Their wedding was one of the biggest bashes ever held in the villa, with Pope Leo and twelve cardinals in attendance.

For all the great parties at Le Delizie, guests would enter through the *Loggia of Psyche*, the villa's most beautiful setting, that originally opened to the gardens and wasn't enclosed like it is today. Raphael designed it, but had no time to paint it, as he was busy with other jobs and his romance with Margherita Luti, a baker's daughter who lived in the neighborhood. His students completed it, bringing in the surrounding nature with ornamentation of lush greenery, flowers, and fruits that surround frescos which tell the love story of Amore and Psyche. Here's a myth that fit right in with the Renaissance philosophy of joining the Divine (Amore) with the Mortal Mind/Soul (Psyche). The Goddess Venus is of course involved, and after many trials, the main characters are united in a marriage celebration painted on the ceiling.

www.lincei.it

After Chigi's death, the Farnese family bought Le Delizie, renamed it Farnesina, and planned on connecting it to their palazzo near the Campo dei Fiori. The proposed bridge was never completed, but part of it forms that beautiful, dripping-with-vines archway you'll see over the Via Giulia.

Villa Farnesina: Villa della Lungara 230, Open Monday-Saturday, 9-1. This is one of the few museums in Rome that is open on a Monday.

❧

Golden Day: Visit the **Farnesina**, eat at **Romolo** (Via di Porta Settimiana 8, 06 5818284) to enjoy Roman specialties right where Raphael's girlfriend once lived.

23 The Costume Gallery at the Pitti Palace— Florence

DUCHESS ELEONORA DI TOLEDO DE' MEDICI got fed up living in the gloomy Palazzo Vecchio. So in 1549, with her own money, she bought a palace on the other side of the Arno that the Pitti family had up for sale. What with her eight kids and failing health (hubby Duke Cosimo I had given her syphilis), Eleonora wanted someplace away from the city racket where she could have a garden. The choice was connected to her past: she'd been born in sunny Spain and grew up around lush gardens in Naples, the daughter of the city's Viceroy.

She was so raring to relocate she even moved in while renovations were going on, with architect Vasari doubling the palace in size. Right off the bat, she hired a landscaper for the backyard.

Now the Pitti Palace Eleonora bought is home to six museums and the beautiful Boboli Gardens. It's all too much for one visit, so I say go to the Costume Gallery for a change of scene from painting and sculpture. It's an absolutely glam place, the only museum in Italy dedicated to fashion design and is relatively new to the Pitti, opened in 1983.

You'll find it in the Palazzina della Meridiana, that was added to the palace and completed in 1858. Luscious chandeliers, gold-framed mirrors, and brocade walls decorate room after room (eighteen in all), that takes you through 300 years of Italian fashion.

Displays rotate every two years and on my last visit, the show began with eighteenth-century Marie Antoinette styles—impossibly wide skirts of richly textured fabrics. There were fantastic silk Neapolitan wedding dresses, satin bustled ensembles worn by contessas in the nineteenth century, beaded Italian flapper wear from the 1920s.

But what I most adored were the post-World War II fashions, where Italian designers broke loose and the styles were outrageously chic. There's a scrumptious blue velvet cocktail dress from 1950, completely covered in primary-colored beads, by Alma Maria Lami, who was a protégé of Elsa Schiaparelli. There are sparkling gowns by Florentine designer Cesare Fabbri, choice vintage pieces from revered fashion artists like Valentino, Gianfranco Ferre, and Maurizio Galante. It's fun to imagine Italian women out and about flaunting these threads. Many come from the closet of an eccentric Bologna department store heiress, Cecilia Matteucci Lavarini, who's world famous for collecting couture and has sent some of her overflow to the museum.

The last room of the exhibit honors Eleonora. The dress she was buried in is displayed there. It's in tatters, spread out in a glass case, but you still can get an idea of the style of this fabulous woman, who kept a staff of ten weavers working full time to create her elegant get-ups.

Eleonora married Cosimo I de' Medici in 1539, when she was seventeen and he was just a year older. The Medici rep was at a low point, so it was a coup for them to have this beautiful woman descended from Castilian royalty added to their mix. Eleonora became a beloved first lady, winning the Florentines over with her generous patronage of artists and the peasantry. The marriage worked out: she put up with Cosimo's notorious mood swings, he put up with her penchant for gambling. He even named her regent when he'd take trips away from Florence, which was a most unusual position for a woman of those days.

Most importantly, Eleonora popped out heirs, bearing eleven children in their first fourteen years of marriage, five of them male. This was tough on her five-foot-tall body. By the time she was forty, she was emaciated, there were hairline fractures on her pelvis from the child-birthing, and her bones were deteriorating from the syphilis. She took a trip with her son Garzia to see her older son Giovanni in Pisa, even though he'd warned them there was a malaria outbreak. One by one, first Garzia, then Giovanni, then Eleonora succumbed to the disease. From the looks of the dress, her funeral must have been grand.

Right down the steps from the gallery is the wondrous expanse of the Boboli Gardens. In the warmer months, you can stroll paths bordered by lemon trees and blooming flowerbeds, just as Eleonora did.

Pitti Palace: Houses the Palatine Gallery, Gallery of Modern Art, Porcelein Museum, Boboli Gardens, and the Costume Gallery. Costume Gallery open daily 8:15-4:30 or 6:30, depending on the season. Closed 1st, 3rd, and 5th Mondays of the month, and 3rd Sunday of each month.

ॐ

Golden Day: Enjoy wandering around the **Costume Gallery** and **Boboli Gardens**, linger in the **Oltrarno** with lunch nearby at **Olio e Convivium** (Via Santo Spirito 4, 055 2658198),

www.polomuseale.firenze.it

which is not only a restaurant, but a high-end shop that stocks Tuscan wines, fresh baked breads, and other regional specialties. They also offer cooking classes.

RECOMMENDED READING

The House of Medici, Its Rise and Fall by Christopher Hibbert

24 Casa Guidi–Florence

WHEN WE THINK OF "How do I love thee, Let me count the ways," Elizabeth Barrett Browning's most famous line, it seems only natural that this romantic poet would wind up in Italy. It was *amore* that brought her to Florence, where she lived for fourteen years with her husband Robert Browning. Stop by their former Oltrarno apartment to get a hit of what life was like for these bohemians back in the nineteenth century.

When Barrett met Browning in London, she was thirty-eight and at an all-time low. Her poetry books were a smash, but she was a semi-invalid with lung problems that began with a spinal injury she got as a teenager and left her dependent on opium for the rest of her life. And she was in mourning for her beloved brother. He'd gone with her to a lovely lakeside spot to help restore her health, and ended up drowning in that lake.

In swooped poet-on-the-rise Robert Browning, who wrote her a fan letter that began, "I love your verses with all my heart..." It was a little too over the top for Elizabeth, but the two started writing to each other and after a few months Robert showed up at her father's house, where she was living as a recluse. Robert was six years younger than Elizabeth, a strapping, healthy guy, and it was hard for her to even imagine he could love her. Elizabeth's wealthy, tyrannical father was dead set against any of his twelve children coupling, but after their first meeting, a secret romance between Elizabeth and Robert began.

A year later, in 1846, they eloped, and Robert whisked Elizabeth off to Italy for their honeymoon, along with her nurse and cocker spaniel. Elizabeth described it as "living a dream." After toodling around, they found this gem of a six-room apartment in Florence. They bargained with the landlord, giving him back the grand furniture the place came with, and getting the rent down to twenty-five guineas a year, which included free entrance to the nearby Boboli Gardens.

The apartment is on the *piano nobile* (what we think of as the second floor) of this fifteenth-century palazzo, once owned by Count Guidi. You pass through a big dining room to get to the main attraction: the drawing room where Elizabeth wrote and hung out with artists and writers like the Hawthornes and Harriet Beecher Stowe.

Thanks to an oil painting Robert had done, the room looks almost exactly as it was when the Barrett-Brownings lived here. It has a cozy Victorian style, with intense olive green walls, soft lighting, velvet upholstered furniture, and a little table with a mother of pearl tea set. In the middle of it all is a tiny writing desk where you can imagine Elizabeth composing *Aurora Leigh*—a love story of a woman writer making her way in the world. The gilt-framed mirror over the fireplace is the one piece that's original to Casa Guidi. Elizabeth wrote to her sister about how thrilled she was Robert bought it, even though to her the five-pound price was an extravagance.

Elizabeth got her strength back in Florence. At forty-three she gave birth to a son, whom she nicknamed Pen. She got passionately involved with the Italian fight for independence, and wrote the poem "Casa Guidi Windows" in support of the Florentines she saw from her terrace, who protested fiercely against Austrian occupation.

Though most biographies claim "they lived happily after," Elizabeth and Robert were real people, so it wasn't a fifteen-year honeymoon. At some points it got a little Madonna-Guy Ritchie-esque. Elizabeth was the poet star of the duo, paying all the bills for the house and many wonderful vacations, with her writing profits and money she'd inherited from an uncle. She got her way when it came to dressing Pen, outfitting him in effeminate velvet get-ups and having his hair grow in long curls like his mommy's. Robert didn't stand behind Elizabeth's passions—feminism, the fight for Italian unification, and most of all her explorations into spirituality, which involved consulting mediums. Add to that her four miscarriages and opium addiction to give some shadings to the "happily ever after" story.

A photograph of Elizabeth just months before her death shows her dressed in billowing black silk, with that signature cascade of curls surrounding a face that looks pained and cadaverous. The story goes she died in Robert's arms in 1861 in Casa Guidi, at the age of fifty-five. Some suspect Robert may have upped the dose of morphine to put an end to her suffering.

Robert left Florence after Elizabeth died and never returned. In England, he finally reached his success as a poet.

In Elizabeth's memory (no mention of Robert), the Florentines placed a plaque over the doorway of the Casa Guidi apartment building, honoring her for poetry they said "made a golden ring between Italy and England."

Casa Guidi: Piazza San Felice 8 (Oltrarno), Monday-Wednesday-Friday, 3-6, April to November. NOTE: The attached rooms of the Barrett-Browning place that aren't being used for a museum have been turned into a **vacation apartment**, so you can sleep where the Brownings slept. It's three bedrooms, three bathrooms, and kitchen (www.landmarktrust.org.uk).

English Cemetery: Elizabeth Barrett Browning's grave, Piazzale Donatello.

❧

Golden Day: Visit **Casa Guidi**, enjoy the **Oltrarno**. Have dinner at **Osteria del Cinghiale Bianco** (Borgo San Jacopo 43r, 055 215706, closed Wednesday), set in a thirteenth-century tower, serving robust versions of tradtional Florentine dishes.

RECOMMENDED READING

Elizabeth Barrett Browning by John Henry Ingram

25 The Peggy Guggenheim Collection—Venice

PEGGY GUGGENHEIM WAS ONE OF THE twentieth century's great bon vivants. How fitting that her home base for thirty years was this airy palazzo on the Grand Canal. Today it's filled with a fabulous collection of modern art she acquired, including paintings and sculptures by such masters as Picasso, Kandinsky, de Chirico, and Mondrian.

Peggy's spirit lives on in these surroundings that resonate with the spicy times she and her artist friends had here from 1949 to 1979. You can imagine her stepping off the terrace into her private gondola for her daily ride, which she took religiously at sunset, wearing a flamboyant get-up and those signature butterfly-shaped sunglasses.

Born in New York in 1898, Peggy was the free-spirited rebel of the wealthy Guggenheim family. Her father died in the sinking of the *Titanic* when she was fourteen. When she came of age and inherited her fortune, she took off for Europe, and married writer Laurence Vail, who was nicknamed King of the Bohemians. They honeymooned in Capri, lived in Paris, and bopped around the continent, stopping in Venice where her lifelong passion for the place took hold.

By the time she was thirty-nine, Peggy was divorced, her two kids were in boarding school, and as she puts it, "I needed something to do." A friend suggested she open an art gallery.

Even though she knew nothing about modern art, she dove in, with Marcel Duchamp by her side to educate her. She made a vow to buy one painting a day and decided, taking Samuel Beckett's advice, that she would only buy the work of living artists. Duchamp and Beckett were not only friends who guided her along. They were just two of Peggy's myriad line-up of lovers she became famous for throughout her life. When asked in her later years, "How many husbands have you had, Mrs. Guggenheim?" she cracked back: "D'you mean mine or other people's?"

Her first gallery show in New York made a big splash—introducing the world to painters such as Robert Motherwell, Mark Rothko, and Jackson Pollack. It was Peggy's generous patronage of the American avant-garde that helped to bring international recognition to the movement.

"I have never been to a city that has given me the same sense of freedom as Venice," Peggy says in her autobiography. In 1949, when she was fifty-one, she settled there, buying the Palazzo Venier dei Leoni in the Dorsoduro *sestiere*. The eighteenth-century, one-floor building was perfect for her to sunbathe on the roof and display her sculptures in the garden. Little by little, more and more of her home became gallery space, and while she lived there she opened it to the public a few afternoons a week. She willed the palazzo to her uncle's Solomon R. Guggenheim Foundation, so today it's been expanded and stands as one of the world's most important small museums of contemporary art.

The Peggy vibe throughout the museum is palpable. A fantastic silver headboard designed by Alexander Calder graces what was her bedroom. A pair of paintings by the surrealist Max Ernst feature monstrous half-naked female images, draped in orange capes, interpreted as being inspired by Peggy. She was married to Max from 1942 to 1946. It was a tumultuous relationship, largely because Max was still in love with Leonora Carrington, a surrealist painter whom he'd left behind in France when Peggy helped him to escape the Nazis and come to America.

One of the first sculptures Peggy bought for the villa appears center stage on her terrace: *The Angel of the Citadel* by Marino Marini. This Etruscan-inspired bronze features an ecstatic rider on horseback—so ecstatic he has an enormous hard-on. Peggy loved peeking out from her sitting room to watch visitor's shocked reactions to the statue. And out of respect, because the terrace faced the Venetian prefect's home, she had the figure cast with a removable penis, so when nuns rode by on their way to get the patriarch's blessing, she'd remove it.

Peggy died at eighty-one and her ashes are buried in the museum's garden, alongside those of fourteen beloved Lhasa terriers she kept throughout her Venetian life. Nearby is an olive tree (a gift from Yoko Ono), and sculptures by such artists as Arp and Moore.

Along with the great collection, this place has wonderful docents. In contrast to most Italian museums, where employees typically slump on folding chairs and bark "No photo!" from time to time, here you'll find young, enthusiastic types. They're art students from all over the world on Guggenheim internships, thrilled to be in Venice, and delightful to talk to about what Peggy collected. Just as Peggy brought a fresh spirit of adventure to Venice, these docents keep her spark alive.

Peggy Guggenheim Museum: Daily 10-6, closed Tuesday.

www.guggenheim-venice.it

❧

Golden Day: Visit the **museum**, lingering a while in the **caffè** for a drink (hot cocoa on a wintry day is fab) or snack. Enjoy the Dorsoduro neighborhood, with a stop by **Cantinone già Schiavi** wine bar (Fondamenta Nani 992) and eat at **Ai Gondolieri** (Fondamenta dell'Ospedaletto, 041 528 6396, closed Tuesday), a romantic place for such specialties as Fegato alla Veneziana (liver and onions).

RECOMMENDED READING

Out of This Century: The Autobiogrpahy of Peggy Guggenheim by Peggy Guggenheim

Art Lover: A Biography of Peggy Guggenheim by Anton Gill

26 Palazzo Fortuny–Venice

VENETIANS CALLED THIS PLACE "The House of the Magician." It's where Mariano Fortuny, who became world famous for his outrageously gorgeous fabrics, gowns, and lamps, set up his home and workshop in 1907. There was a woman behind his success: Henriette Negrin, who he met in Paris in 1897, when she was a French widow, a model and a seamstress. She became his muse, collaborator, and wife—after they lived together for twenty-two years. You'll see Fortuny's paintings of Henriette here—some nude, others with her dressed elegantly with her hair swept up, along with photographs of their trips to Greece and Egypt, where Fortuny got lots of inspiration.

In the museum where they once lived and worked together, you enter the world of this eccentric, twentieth-century Renaissance man. Fortuny was born in Granada in 1871, to both a father and grandfather (on his mother's side) who were highly acclaimed painters in Spain. His father died when he was three, so his mother took him to live in Paris, and also traveled about, until they finally settled in Venice, because Fortuny was horribly allergic to horses, and this was the only place around without carriages.

After his early artistic endeavors in painting and photography, and success in designing sets and lighting for theater, Fortuny, at thirty-six years old, began his work on printed fabrics here with Henriette. He'd already had an attic studio in the thirteenth-century palazzo, and then bought the building that had been cut up into apartments and gutted it, turning it into a free-flowing creative space.

The walls of the first floor's large rectangular room are covered with Fortuny's patterned fabrics, creating a warm, exotic, colorful ambience. His paintings and lamps surround displays of his gowns and capes that were worn by such illustrious women as Eleanora Duse, Sarah Bernhardt, and Isadora Duncan.

Fortuny broke into the woman's fashion world in 1907 with his Delphos gown, inspired by tunics from ancient Greek statuary. It was simple and finely pleated, in soft, shimmering colors. Women happily tore off their corsets to put on the sensational dress that elegantly draped their bodies. He packaged it rolled up in a hatbox, so it was easy and light for travel.

The second floor of the museum gives you an idea of what life was like when 100 workers were there producing Fortuny fabrics, under Henriette's supervision. In contrast to what's below, it's stripped bare with only huge worktables. Off to the side is Fortuny's library and personal workshop, where you'll get a hit of the practical side of this free-spirited artist. It's packed with volumes of books about artists who came before him, lots of journals where he catalogued designs and colors, his paints and tools. Fortuny's preferred entrance to this palazzo was climbing through the skylight, straight into his workshop.

Fortuny's fabric designs, of intricate swirls, animals, and geometric prints, on cotton, silk, or velvet, clearly show his influences from Spain and travels to Greece and farther east. But ultimately, they're completely Venetian, reflecting the cultural melting pot of the city, with rich colors muted by the city's fog, or glistening in gold or silver sunlight. He was called "the magician" because nobody could figure out exactly how he produced these fabrics, and his techniques are still kept secret.

You'll be so tempted to reach out and touch them in the museum, but you can't. For a tactile experience, head to the **Fortuny Showroom** on Giudecca, or one of the **Venetia Studium** stores in Venice, where you can even buy a scarf, pillow, purse, or lamp to take home and keep a little bit of the Venetian magician in your life.

Palazzo Fortuny Museum: Campo San Beneto (San Marco), 10–6, closed Tuesday.

Showroom: Fortuny SPA, Giudecca 805, 041 528 7697 (next to Hilton Molino Stucky, which has a great terrace to stop for a cocktail and enjoy the view of the Venice mainland).

Venetia Studium Stores: Calle Larga XXII Marzo 2404, Merceria San Zulian 723, San Marco (www.venetiastudium.com).

❧

Golden Day: Visit the **Palazzo Fortuny** and have lunch or an apertivo at **da Fiore** (Calle del Scaleter, San Polo 202, 041 721 308, closed Sunday and Monday).

Villa Valmarana Ai Nani-Vicenza, Veneto

SPRINKLED OVER THE VENETIAN PLAIN are beautiful villas from the sixteenth to the eighteenth centuries. They're the jewels of superstar Renaissance architect Andrea Palladio and his followers, which recall the symmetry and grace of Greek and Roman temples.

You can visit some of them pleasantly from Venice or Padua by taking a boat ride down the Brenta Canal, which stops at the waterway entrances to the villas and a restaurant for lunch. That's a Golden Day right there.

But to get the full Palladio hit, go to the town of **Vicenza**. This is where Palladio was born and it's packed with his treasures, including the not-to-be-missed **Teatro Olimpico**.

A walk or short bus ride away from Vicenza's historic center takes you to Palladio's famous **Villa Rotonda**, and further along a favorite of mine: the **Villa Valmarana ai Nani**. "*Nani*" means dwarves, and the name originated with this legend:

Once upon a time, a couple who lived in this villa gave birth to a daughter, who was a beautiful dwarf. Loving their child dearly, they wanted to protect her from feeling different, so they hired dwarf servants and kept her secluded in the villa and walled garden. For many years she was clueless and content, but when she was fifteen she got curious about what was going on in the outside world. When her dwarf servants were sleeping, she climbed the stone wall, and up rode a handsome fellow on horseback. It was love at first sight for the dwarf-girl, but when she reached out to ride away with him into the sunset, for the first time she realized, "Oh no! I'm a dwarf!" Horrified, she hurled herself off the wall to her death. The servant dwarves heard her cries, woke up, and ran to find her. When they saw their dead mistress, they froze in grief.

That's why you'll see statues of seventeen *nani* atop the villa walls. They're all inspired by Venetian Commedia dell'Arte characters—such as the Doctor, the King, the Knight, and the Turk. When Giustino Valmarana, a theater fan, moved here in 1720 he incorporated the *nani* story as part of his redesign.

The legend probably originated in the seventeenth century, when dwarves were popular characters in royal courts. They were perfect playmates for children, entertaining, and considered good luck tokens. Many were the result of inbreeding, and they were treated like pets, often given away by their mothers, as they weren't considered part of the "real" family and wouldn't be inheriting anything. Cruel, but true.

Once you're past the *nani* and inside the walls, things get elegant: lovely gardens surround a *foresteria* (former farm-laborer's place) and butter-yellow *palazzina*. Inside the little palazzo is where superstar painter Giambattista Tiepolo created some of the most stunning works of his career.

Tiepolo was a Venetian master of Rococo, who frescoed this place with theatrical gusto, finishing the *palazzina* interior in only four months. Using a dreamy pastel palate, he created breathtaking scenes from classical myths and legends.

www.villavalmarana.com

When you enter, you're hit with his *Sacrifice of Iphigenia*, which packs the power of an opera climax. Center stage sits the Greek warrior Agamemnon, pleading to the heavens for mercy, as he holds a knife to his daughter Iphigenia's chest. The story goes that Agamemnon ticked off the Goddess Diana by bragging that he was a better hunter than she was. To punish him she silenced the winds, screwing up his fleet. A prophet appeared to Agamemnon and said he'd have to sacrifice his daughter to lift Diana's curse. In Tiepolo's unusual happy-ending version of the story, Diana (on the ceiling) has a change of heart and flies in to substitute a sacrificial deer for Iphigenia. On the surrounding side panels, Tiepolo painted new winds blowing through.

Action-packed love scenes fill the adjoining rooms. There are images from "Orlando Furioso," a Renaissance epic poem, where the gorgeous maiden Angelica makes Orlando absolutely *furioso*, because she can't help but attract the attentions of other men.

In the Foresteria, which was a guesthouse, there's one final Tiepolo masterpiece in the Olympus Room, where Venus is paired with her boyfriend Mars and Diana with Apollo.

The rest of the Foresteria was frescoed by his son, Giandomenico, who moved on to realism, and painted images from eighteenth-century life. There are scenes of peasants in the countryside, wealthy folks partying, a carnival—with both a monkey and an African servant serving chocolate!

Framed photographs of the Valmaranas, who still live here, are scattered about. One of their family's twentieth-century heroines was Amalia, who was a mover and shaker in the Italian women's movement after World War II. She helped to found the Catholic Centro Italiano Femminile, an organization that got women involved in the reconstruction of Italy, defending women's rights and helping them get health care.

There's a special charm to this small (for a villa) place that's been in the same family for over three hundred years. The comical statues, colorful garden, sweeping frescos, even the family photos, mix together magically in this exquisitely designed space.

Villa Valmarana: Open throughout the year, but different days and times depending on the season. Check www.villavalmarana.com for up-to-date hours and prices.

❦

Golden Day: Visit the **villa** and enjoy Palladio's masterpieces in Vicenza. For dinner, take a fifteen-minute drive to **Caldogno** and eat at **Trattoria Molin Vecio** (Via Giaroni 116, 044 585 168). It's built around a mill from 1520, surrounded by a lovely landscape and huge herb garden. Sleep at **Hotel Campo Marzio** (www.hotelcampomarzio.com), a boutique hotel close to the historic center.

TOURS

Boat tours of Italian villas are available from Venice or Padua at www.battellidelbrenta.it or www.ilburchiello.it.

28 Palazzo Ducale— Mantua, Lombardy

OF ALL THE 500 ROOMS IN THE humongous Palazzo Ducale, the two teeniest, hidden away on the ground floor, are the most enchanting. They are the *grotta* and *studiolo* of Isabella d'Este, aka First Lady of the Renaissance. Here's where she'd come to leave the world behind and read the classics, play her lute, or have her friends over to marvel over the paintings, antiques, and gems she'd collected.

It was all the rage for Renaissance palaces to have a *studiolo*. The idea behind it was to move away from the sterile, monastic retreats of the Dark Ages and into a space inspired by the ancient Greeks and Romans, where the appreciation of beauty was the path to transcendence.

The treasures that once filled Isabella's rooms have been sent off to museums, but there's still a tantalizing magic here. Her *studiolo's* deep blue walls, stars, and gilded woodwork create the ambience of an evening sky in paradise. In the *grotta*, polished cabinets of wood inlays form pictures of idyllic cities and palaces. Alabaster carvings of mythological figures grace the moldings. Right out the door is her secret garden, a square patch of trimmed shrubs and pots of laurel. I'd love to move in.

Isabella moved into the Palazzo Ducale in 1490 when she was sixteen and married Marchese Francesco Gonzaga. His powerhouse family dominated Mantua for 300 years, and the town is full of Renaissance buildings built during their reign. Francesco was a Captain General, off on fighting trips for long stretches, but came home enough so Isabella ended up having seven children. She was a faithful wife, while Francesco dallied about, even having a fling with the infamous Lucrezia Borgia.

Isabella let her husband's affairs slide and put her energies into ruling Mantua while he was away. She was already highly  educated, from growing up the daughter of the Duke of Ferrara, and then studied agriculture, architecture, and industry to get up to speed in other areas. Besides her brains, she had a natural talent for diplomacy, and could deftly swim in the shark tank of Renaissance politics. She did such a bang-up job that Mantua was raised in status to a Duchy.

While she was at it, she also made the palace a gathering place for poets, artists, and musicians, turning Mantua into a thriving cultural center. Leonardo da Vinci stopped by and made a sketch of her that now hangs in the Louvre. Titian painted her twice.

Her voracious appetite for beauty was where this almost perfect woman slid into naughty behavior. She insisted on wearing sables and elaborate costumes, even though the Mantua treasury couldn't afford it.

She left behind hundreds of letters and some are hilarious to read, showing her needy-greedy side. These are the ones she'd address to relatives of sick people whom she knew had precious collections. She'd begin with much sympathy, but soon enough stick it to them, all but begging to be informed immediately if their relative died, so she could get her hands on their stuff.

As an art patron she could be downright annoying. In one instance, she hounded the established master Perugino, demanding the painting she commissioned fit her standards exactly. The goddesses could not be naked. The theme had to be Chastity (Minerva and Diana) triumphing over earthly love (Venus and Cupid). It was Isabelle's blatant way of standing up against that ne'er-do-well husband of hers, pushing a "Purity is Power" line.

All through the early years of her marriage, Isabelle filled her downstairs *grotta* with her growing collection. When Francesco retired from the army, he came back to Mantua debilitated and addled from syphilis, but still managed to grump about how Isabella had become the boss, which she didn't let bother her in the least.

Isabella was forty-six when Francesco died, which was old in those days. She'd always had weight problems, so climbing the palace stairs to her rooms was getting to her. Just like empty nesters who trade in their family home for a condo, Isabella moved out of her upstairs palazzo digs and redecorated this ground floor space which would be her beloved haven until she died eighteen years later.

Engraved in the wall is her motto, from the Roman poet Seneca: *Nec Speranza, Nec Metu: Neither Hope, Nor Fear*. It was this forge-ahead attitude that fueled strong, independent Isabella, who in an age when many women couldn't even leave the house, undeniably triumphed.

Palazzo Ducale: Tuesday–Sunday 8:30–7.

www.mantovaducale.it

❧

Golden Day: Visit Isabella's *studiolo* and *grotta* in the **Palazzo Ducale**, and don't miss the upstairs Camera degli Sposi and

Hall of Mirrors. Eat nearby at **Ristorante Aquila Nigra** (Vicolo Bonacolsi 4, 037 632 7180, closed Monday), a converted Gothic townhouse. Sleep at **Casa Poli Hotel** (www.hotelcasapoli.it), a sleek boutique hotel about a ten-minute walk from the Palazzo Ducale.

29 The Royal Apartments in Palazzo Reale— Turin, Piedmont

CONSIDER MY FRIEND SOOZE, who always recounts this story to me in amazement: "When I told my parents I wanted to have a home wedding with just the immediate family, they painted the dining room."

Sooze was talking about a dining room in a split-level in Kankakee, Illinois.

Now multiply that image by about a zillion-million and you'll get what happened when brides moved into the Palazzo Reale (Royal Palace) in Turin. From 1719 until 1930, whenever a King took a wife, massive redecorating ensued. So when you visit this thirty-room section of the *gigantico* palazzo, you'll be walking through a history of interior design—from baroque to rococo to neo-classical. For some brides, only a few elements were changed, others added entirely new rooms. It's all richly layered with the history of the women who lived there.

And it's all so very French. Why? Because this is where the Royal House of Savoy, a France-based dynasty reigned over the Piedmont region beginning in 1494. They also went on to conquer and rule other parts of Italy, and held the monarchy until they were exiled from the country in 1946, all way too complicated to get into right now.

Back to Palazzo Reale. As soon as you approach it—a magnificent vision of pale blue-gray stone with gold touches—you'll understand why Italians nicknamed Turin "Little Paris."

There were two Parisian-born women who were powerhouses behind building it as part of their "let's beautify Turin" projects: Madama Reale I and her daughter-in-law Madama Reale II. During the seventeenth century, they lived in the Palazzo Madama (next door to the Reale) and ruled Piedmont in succession, because their Savoy King husbands died young. Both were beloved by the Torinese, governing like intelligent *mammas*, bringing art and culture to the city. The Palazzo Reale's most famous feature, The Scissor Staircase, an ornate criss-cross design by Juvarra, was one of the artistic triumphs of the days of Madama Reale II.

The apartments you'll be touring are basically from after their reign. Here you're surrounded by birthday-cake chandeliers, giant gold-framed mirrors, and all those stiff, fancy furnishings that you couldn't imagine a soul slouching on. Fantasies of gala affairs spring up. You can picture Spanish-born Maria Antonietta Ferdinanda's 1750 wedding party in the baroque ballroom where a tapestry depicting a scene from *Don Quixote* hangs in homage to her. Duchessa Maria Teresa, who came here as a fifteen-year-old bride from Milan in 1788, had a Chinese salon put in, at a time when Europeans were intrigued with the Orient. When Principessa Maria Adelaide of Hapsburg arrived in 1842, exquisite wood-inlay floors were created and walls covered with pretty brocades.

Cut to 1930 to 1933 when the rooms were redesigned for Marie José of Belgium and her husband Umberto II. The charm of it is that it brings up thoughts of a contemporary fairy tale. Marie and Umberto were living in these grand old-fashioned surroundings when my mother was three—maybe Gershwin's "I've Got Rhythm" was blasting on the radio. Their *sala da pranzo* (lunch room) is a gorgeous design of pale green walls and gold ornamentation. In the center is a table set as if any minute the King and Queen would walk in and sit down for a plate of foie gras.

But the truth is, Marie and Umberto never ate together. The marriage was politically arranged from the time Marie was a girl, and when they officially tied the knot, she, like everybody else, knew Umberto was gay. Umberto went off to "honeymoon" with his friends in Courmayeur, and then the couple moved in to the Palazzo Reale and lived completely separate lives.

Marie launched into entertaining philosophers, artists, writers, and musicians in her Blue Room. Not caring about royal protocol, she'd jump in her car and drive off to enjoy concerts and festivals in Turin. She separated herself from the whole Savoy family by speaking out against Mussolini—when he ordered her to Italianize her name to Maria Giuseppina, she refused.

In the meantime Umberto embraced the stiff traditions of his family, and loved redecorating the palace in grand style. He never visited Marie without announcing himself first, and always with someone accompanying him. Rumors flew that their four children had been conceived through artificial insemination, or maybe one of the guys Marie was hanging with.

World War II brought on great turmoil, and in 1946, when the monarchy was abolished, Marie was exiled with the rest of the House of Savoy. She went to Switzerland, Umberto to Portugal, and they remained apart for the rest of their lives.

www.turismotorino.org

Marie, who died in 2001, will always be remembered as the last Queen of Italy. Fondly remembered that is, for standing up against Fascism when all those around her were taking Mussolini's side. You may want to lag behind in the tour when you get to the Blue Room and picture Marie—a pretty blonde woman, sitting on her poufy couch with the fire blazing, surrounded by her artsy friends, having a grand time bucking the system in this beautiful place.

Palazzo Reale: The Palazzo Reale can only be visited on guided tours, which run every 50 minutes. Along with the Apartment of Princes (which many Italians call The Bridal Apartments) that lasts around forty minutes, there's one for the Royal Kitchen, recently opened and also great. All tours are in Italian, but you can rent an English audio-guide. Piazzetta Reale 1, Tuesday-Sunday 8:30-6.

❧

Golden Day: Visit the **Palazzo Reale's L'Appartamento dei Principi** and the **Royal Kitchen**. The **Caffè Reale**, opposite the entrance to the palazzo, is the prettiest caffè ever and wonderful to stop in if you're waiting for your tour. For a splurge and terrific meal, eat in royal surroundings at **Del Cambio** (Piazza Carignano 2, 011 546690, closed Sunday).

30 Oplontis–Torre Annunziata, Campania

To GET PEACE AND QUIET AWAY from the city of Pompeii, rich and fun-loving folk would come to nearby **Oplontis** for banquets and bathing or just to chill out amidst the villa's gardens. Here's where you'll find room after room of amazing frescos that out-shine most of what you'll see in Pompeii, and you'll get a good feel of what life was like in the suburbs before the whole shebang got covered in lava in that famous 79 A.D. eruption.

Unlike Pompeii, Oplontis (one stop away on the Circumvesuviana train line) is free of tourist crowds, so you can poke around in silence and let your imagination run free, picturing the intriguing woman who supposedly lived here, the Empress Poppea Sabina, Nero's second wife.

The Roman writer Tacitus described Poppea as bisexual and very ambitious. She married Emperor Otho to get close to Nero, soon became Nero's mistress, and then egged Nero on to murder his mother and divorce and execute his first wife. Poppea was a high-maintenance empress who insisted upon being carried about by mules shod with golden shoes, and needed to bathe daily in donkey milk, or, as some accounts say, the milk of 500 asses.

When Poppea married Nero, she gave birth to a daughter who died four months later. While Poppea was pregnant with their second child, Nero flew into a rage, accusing her of spending too much time flirting with gladiators. And then he kicked her to death. In another version of her story, made famous in the movie, *The Producers*, Nero jumped on Poppea. You may remember Leo Bloom screaming in fear to Max Bialystock: "I know you're going to jump on me—like Nero jumped on Poppea... Poppea. She was his wife. And she was unfaithful to him. So he got mad and he jumped on her. Up and down, until he squashed her like a bug."

But before all the horror stories, Poppea and her guests must have had luxurious times here at Oplontis. When you get here, you stand above the villa for a great view of the huge gardens, loaded with oleander. Inside are salons and dining rooms with intricate mosaic floors and walls frescoed to give a 3-D effect of marbled architecture. In the private baths, a painting tells the story of the Hesperides (daughters of the night) who lived in the garden of golden apple trees that Hercules visited when he was on one of his twelve assignments to gather fruits for King Eurystheus.

www.pompeiisites.org

The corridors are more subtly painted with enchanting birds against ivory backgrounds. These open to curved indoor garden rooms, where my favorite frescos have sumptuous paintings of fountains and ferns against an amber background, bordered by rich red. And then there's the huge rectangular outdoor pool that must have been dreamy to swim in with meadows in the distance back in those days.

On my last visit, one of the *signorina* guards had brought her dog to work, and the friendly mutt followed me around until an Italian tourist couple arrived with two daughters who were more thrilled with the pooch than the frescos. I left the group behind—the girls playing with the dog, as their parents wandered through just like I had, *oohing* and *ahhing* as they turned corners to be met with discovery upon discovery of beauty in this most enchanting, evocative place.

Oplontis: November-March 8:30-5, April-October 8:30-7:30.

✤

Golden Day: On your way in or out of Pompeii, take a stop at **Torre Annunziata** to visit Oplontis. In Pompeii, be sure to visit the **Villa of Mysteries**, where you'll find fabulous frescos that tell the story of the bride Ariadne's initiation into the cult of Dionysus. Relax and stay overnight, dining at **Zi Caterina** (Via Roma 20) and sleeping at **Hotel Forum** (www.hotelforum.it), which has rooms with balconies overlooking a pleasant garden.

31 *Villa Romana del Casale–Sicily*

ANCIENT ROMAN GIRLS IN BIKINIS? That's just one of the bizarre sights in this villa. It's a mosaic that covers the floor of the "Room of the Ten Girls," featuring a line-up of curvy, muscular young girls in two-piece suits pumping barbells and playing handball. Their outfits, which scholars say are actually their underwear, make them look totally contemporary, even though the mosaic is from the fourth century. It's a striking, entertaining change from the classical images we usually see of women in togas or lounging about nude in erotic scenes from those days.

The mosaic is just one of many in this villa where you'll find

the world's largest and most amazing display of mosaics from Roman times. It's smack in the heart of Sicily, in the rural, hilly province of Enna. Here's where the beautiful Proserpina, daughter of Goddess of the Harvest Ceres, was wandering around picking wildflowers when God of the Underworld Pluto pulled her down to Hades to make her his queen.

The massive 12,000-square-foot villa was built around the fourth century as a luxurious hunting lodge, which was surrounded by a farm estate. Not much is known about the original owner, except that he was a rich Roman, probably a member of the Empire's senate or imperial family. It's obvious from the set-up that he threw great parties.

There's a huge triumphal military arch at its entrance and a sprawling bath complex. Best of all are the floors of the public and residential rooms, which were created by North African mosaic artisans in a vibrant style that's distinct from what you'll see in Pompeii or Italy's medieval churches. Along with fantastic geometric patterns you'll find dramatic action-packed scenes that capture moments from myths to wild hunting expeditions to contests at the Circus Maximus.

Not much remains of the villa's wall decorations, but considering the floors, what a place this must have been. It was buried in a mudslide in the twelfth century, and not fully excavated until the 1950s. In order to keep the mosaics in the well-preserved state they were found and still have tourists traipse through, catwalks have been built. When you visit you'll be walking along narrow planks attached to the sides of the rooms to get an overview of the floors, which is actually a better angle to admire them than guests had back in Roman partying days.

Some of the most spectacular you'll see include the one in the "Corridor of the Great Hunt," which depicts rowdy scenes of animals (lions, leopards, and antelopes) being captured and carted off to Rome for shows at the Colosseum. In the corner of the room is a dark-skinned regal looking woman, who personifies India or Arabia, surrounded by an elephant, tiger, and phoenix in flames. Other rooms have whimsical scenes of cupids fishing, women dancing, and the Greek poet Arion playing his *chitarra*.

What would a rich Roman's villa be without a touch of erotica? In what's assumed to have been the master's bedroom a mosaic shows the voluptuous bare backside of a woman looking like she's giving a man on a throne a lap dance.

Villa Romana del Casale: July–November, daily 10-6. www.villaromanodelcasale.it.

᠅

Golden Day: Visit the **Villa** early in the morning, before crowds of tour buses arrive. Spend the rest of the day at **Piazza Armerina**, a medieval hill town nearby (3.5 miles/5.5 km away), which has a beautiful baroque **Duomo** and other impressive churches. Eat at **Ristorante Al Fogher** (Contrada Bellia, 093 5684123, www.alfogher.net), which serves Sicilian classics in refined style. Stay at **Hotel Ostello del Borgo** (www.ostellodelborgo.it), a converted Benedictine nun's monastery.

III

Gardens

Stroll through an Italian garden for a peaceful experience of *la dolce vita* (the sweet life). Here's where landscape architects tamed Mother Nature, harmoniously blending greenery, sculpture, and fountains.

Most Italian gardens are not about the flowers, but focused on an overall design, created specifically for the pleasures of the villa's residents. And the topiary! Like expert tailors, gardeners clip Cypress trees, boxwood, and ilex bushes into fashionable, clean shapes. Serene green, precisely arranged, is what defines the country's garden style.

Some of the most memorable to visit are gardens of the Renaissance or Baroque periods. These gardens were planned as carefully as the villas they surrounded, flowing artfully from the indoor spaces, merging with the natural landscape. They're comprised of sunlit paths, pergolas dripping with wisteria, belvederes for awesome views, and romantic niches fragrant with lavender. Fountains and statues add emotion to the mix.

Every garden you'll visit will have a distinct personality, reflecting the owner—whether it's the bursting, playful spirit of Niki de Saint Phalle or the idealism of Giovanni de' Medici.

Go and enjoy their pleasant fantasies...

INFO

Many gardens close down November–March, so be sure to check schedules. As many of the gardens are not marked, if you're an avid gardener and want a more in-depth experience, buy a guide before your visit or sign up for a tour.

32 Villa d'Este–Tivoli, Lazio

BEFORE YOU EVEN GET TO THIS GARDEN, you hear rushing water. Then you stand above majestic terraces filled with countless sculpted fountains, ponds, and grottoes. Water shoots up in grand columns, arcs out of a hundred animal heads, tumbles like a curtain over caves, pumps through a stone organ that plays a classical tune. On and on and on, it's High Renaissance Aqua-Theater.

Villa d'Este was Cardinal Ippolito d'Este's spectacular reaction to getting a booby prize. In the mid-sixteenth century, he lost out on becoming Pope. The powers that were in Rome shooed him away to suburban Tivoli and gave him the job of governor. Instead of living a life of luxury in the papal apartments, he was exiled to government housing: a plain ol' former Benedictine convent.

Being the rich Renaissance guy that he was, Ippolito embraced the "Man Controls Nature" philosophy of his day. Reaching back to the glory of ancient Rome, he built a massive aqueduct, diverting the plentiful waters of the Aniene River to his backyard. He pillaged the nearby Villa of Hadrian, using the former Emperor's marble and statues to make his home magnificent. He threw elaborate banquets, stocking his ponds with fish for his guests to catch and then hand over to servants to cook up. Folks came and marveled over the waterworks, calling it d'Este's "Garden of Miracles." *Living Well Is the Best Revenge* became his mantra.

Ippolito could have sulked and blamed his late *mamma*, Lucrezia Borgia, for his dreary Tivoli assignment. Lucrezia's father, Pope Alexander VI, had headed up a family of notorious Borgia villains who'd run the Vatican's reputation into the dirt. Lucrezia was the beauty of the clan, rumored to have worn a hollow ring filled with poison that she'd drip into cups of those the family found undesirable. Her first two husbands were gotten rid of by the Borgia men when they didn't cooperate with the family's evil plans.

The Duke of Ferrara (Alfonso d'Este) became Lucrezia's third husband, and father to Ippolito. Their marriage had glimmers of respectability. Sure, Lucrezia had her affairs—with the popular poet Bembo and, most naughtily, with the husband of that paragon of virtue, Isabella d'Este. But the Duke played around too and pretty much let Lucrezia's dalliances slide. To the outside world, the couple put on a classy royalty show. Lucrezia bore seven children and became zealously religious in her later years, until she died in childbirth at thirty-nine. Still, her *femme fatale* legacy would never disappear, which mucked up Ippolito's chance at becoming Pope.

Which is why at Tivoli he pumped up the fact that he was a d'Este. His whole paternal line had glorified themselves by wackily tracing their roots back to Hercules, so Ippolito filled his home and garden with allusions to the hero.

He had a villa room frescoed with a triumphant scene of Hercules in the Garden of Hesperides. According to legend, the strong man was challenged to go to this garden and pick an immortality-inducing golden apple that grew on a tree guarded by three "nymphs of the night," called Hesperides. All over Villa d'Este there are frescos including lemons, and lush pots of them in the garden, symbolizing those golden apples.

You'd hardly know this place was owned by a cardinal, or that it was even a former convent, as it has a smorgasbord of pagan images. Goddesses make their appearances in Ippolito's bedroom—there's a wall fresco of the gadabout Venus, and to balance things out, a chaste Diana on the ceiling. Ippolito put another version of Diana, as nature goddess of Ephesus, spouting water from multiple breasts, smack in front of the Water Organ. But conservative types that came in 1611 moved it to the more discreet corner you'll find it in today.

Minerva, Goddess of Wisdom and Rome, crowns the Rometta fountain, a mini-model of the Eternal City. It's at the top of the terraces, facing Rome. You can imagine Ippolito standing right there, amidst his happy guests—from cardinals to courtesans—as they romped about his playground. No doubt he'd take in the whole scene, look past Minerva towards the city that rejected him and smile.

Villa d'Este: Tuesday-Sunday 8:30-1 hour before sunset.

ぷ

Golden Day: Visit the **Villa d'Este** and the nearby **Hadrian's Villa.** It's best to go to the latter with a tour group, because like the Roman Forum, it's a huge, sprawling place and practically none of the ruins are marked. Have lunch at **Antico Ristorante Sibilla** (Via della Sibilla 50, 077 4335281, closed Monday), an elegant restaurant from 1730, set overlooking the river beside the Roman Temple of Vesta and Sanctuary of the Sibyl.

www.villadestetivoli.info

RECOMMENDED READING

Italian Villas and Their Gardens by Edith Wharton

Italian Gardens: A Guide by Helena Attlee and Alex Ramsey

The Park of the Monsters—Bomarzo, Lazio

IN 1564 WHEN HIS WIFE DIED, Prince Vicino Orsini dedicated this place to her. He called it his Sacred Grove. In 1954, Giovanni Bettini found it abandoned, cleaned it up, and renamed it **The Park of the Monsters**—better for marketing.

It's actually a combo of the two names, which is what makes it so uniquely alluring. It's set on a wooded hillside where you meander along gravel paths under sun-dappled light and then along the way, popping up in haphazard places, you come upon immense bizarre statues of mythological creatures.

There are about two dozen of these creations in all, most carved directly from the hill's rocky outcroppings, which explains the unplanned arrangement. There's a winged mermaid, a sleeping nymph, a sphinx, a colossal Ceres, a tortoise, a whole house that's set up purposely tilted to astonish you. The most famous of all is a giant screaming monster's head—so giant you can walk into its mouth, where you'll find a tongue turned into a picnic table. The inscription carved into this sculpture sums up the park's surreal atmosphere: *All Reason Departs.*

There's a lot of mystery surrounding what the heck Orsini was thinking when he created this place. Some look at the statues' tortured faces and say it was his expression of grieving for his wife, Giulia Farnese. But Orsini began this project before she died.

Their marriage was a good one. He was a military officer, gone a lot while Giulia took over the small town Bomarzo reins. He, of course, had his share of other women, during the marriage and after she died. As far as he knew, Giulia was a perfect, faithful wife. Twenty years after the Sacred Grove was completed Orsini built a temple in her honor that's the most logical structure in this whole place.

The Sacred Grove seems to be more of an expression of Prince Orsini's intriguing, artsy character. While everybody else in those High Renaissance days was building grand, structured gardens to flaunt their wealth, the Prince turned his back on all that, wanting to create something that was not at all pretentious. It's not even attached to his castle, but farther down the hill. Also, he didn't have the money to compete with the Farneses and the d'Estes, so instead of grandeur, he went for shock and awe. Wherever a stone jutted out of the hill, he'd have his workers sculpt it according to his whim. He was a creative type who wrote poems and surrounded himself with the literati. This was his place for contemplation and meditation. It was his dream world where he mixed images from classical Greek, Roman, and Asian times.

www.bomarzo.net

Like every other prince who had a garden, Orsini had illustrious guests come to visit. But he was always glad when they left, preferring the pleasures of simple country life and his shepherd girls. While other Renaissance gardens were kept up by families over succeeding generations, his was forgotten. Only the locals knew of it, and believed it was a haunted place.

In 1938, Salvador Dali, in the midst of a creative crisis, heard about the Sacred Grove, left Spain, and cut his way through a tangle of weeds to see this "sleeping garden." He became so inspired he made a film that included it and painted *The Temptation of Saint Anthony* that featured an image of an elephant— clearly inspired by one of the park sculptures.

Giovanni Bettini bought the park in 1954 and restored it back to life. A visit here is a relaxing, enchanting experience, where you enter into the mythological dream world of the Prince.

The Park of the Monsters: Daily 8-1 hour before sunset.

꿎

Golden Day: Wander around the **Sacred Grove**. There's a camp lodge-style snack bar there, where you can get a caffè and panino. Eat and stay a short drive north at *agriturismo* **Castello di Santa Maria** (www.castello-smaria.com), a beautiful former convent surrounded by olive groves that serves up exquisite meals.

34 Gardens Outside Florence–Tuscany

LEAVE THE VESPA ROARS OF FLORENCE behind and head to the surrounding hills to discover lovely small gardens with fabulous views. Here's where Florentines have come to relax since the days of the Medici.

These are two that you can get to easily from Florence, by taking a short bus ride and walking about ten minutes. If you're feeling energetic, you could even hike up to them from the city, just like folks in olden days.

● **Villa Medici–Fiesole**
Three terraces of simple grace make up Italy's first Renaissance garden.

In 1461, Giovanni de Medici, the son of Cosimo, bought this land because he loved the view of the city below. His dad thought it was a cockamamie idea: Why spend a bundle for a steep, rocky plot that you can't even grow anything on? The Medici were originally farming people, and Cosimo's beloved spot was his country villa, where he'd tend vineyards and olive groves, hang with the peasants, and have friends over to read Plato.

Giovanni, a Medici banker, was of the new generation. From reading Pliny's ancient Roman writings, he got the notion that a garden was a place to combine home, nature, and an awesome view. Forget about growing food. Forget about the walled medieval garden. His terraces would blend with the landscape and villa, like an outdoor room. This would be a beautiful place to kick back, enjoy entertainments, and contemplate the mysteries of life.

Giovanni's overeating and drinking got the better of him and he died of a heart attack in his forties before he had much time to enjoy this place. His nephew, Lorenzo the Magnificent, took it over and it became a meeting place for the Neo-Platonic Academy. Here was where Lorenzo would lead philosophical discussions centered around the idea that perfection and happiness could be attained right here on earth (not in the afterlife) through intellectual contemplation and the appreciation of beauty. Lorenzo's artist friends—Michelangelo, Leonardo da Vinci, and Botticelli—along with philosophers, poets, and musicians were invited. You can imagine Lorenzo in these gardens leading the group: "Play the lute! Read me a verse from the *Aeneid*! What's life's highest vocation? Tell me your ideas!"

The gardens have been relandscaped over the years, but the original structure and remnants of it retained. Tall cypress trees line the entrance and pots of lemon trees neatly arranged on the front lawn. Giovanni brought in lemons from Naples in homage to the mythological Garden of Hesperides. According to Greek legend, the earth mother Gaia gave this magical garden to Hera on her wedding day. In it was a tree bearing golden immortality-giving apples, guarded by Hesperides—nymphs of the night.

On a lower terrace, you walk under a pergola that's inter-twined with roses. Four old magnolia trees spread shade. Further along, you get the most stunning views of Florence. And in that garden are circles of trimmed boxwood hedges that replaced Lorenzo de Medici's herb garden.

These terraces were relandscaped in the early 1900s. That's when one of Tuscany's most beloved women, Iris Origo, was growing up here. Iris was born in Britain, and when her father died, she moved with her mother to this villa in Fiesole.

The legacy of Iris Origo lives on in southern Tuscany's Val d'Orcia. That's where she and her husband had a farm during World War II, where they courageously and gener-ously sheltered refugees. They transformed the property to a jewel-of-an estate called **La Foce,** that's now run by her daughters. It's comprised of a fifteenth-century villa and farmhouses that have been renovated into guesthouses you can rent.

The **Gardens at La Foce** are sublime. If you're in the area (near Montepulciano), stop by for a tour. In what had been a rugged place, Iris used memories of her past to cre-ate the garden's design. It's a mix of classic English style with influences of the Fiesole Villa Medici Renaissance garden she played in when she was a kid.

Villa Gamberaia—Settignano

This place is so pretty it makes me feel prettier when I step into it. Landscape architects come here to study it. Painting classes set up their easels on the grounds. It's a vision of exquisite harmony: Cypress trees are immaculately clipped into soft, rounded shapes and archways. Crisp boxwood shrubs line rectangular reflecting pools. Pink roses tumble from trellises. A baroque stone niche imbedded with shells and fossils holds a statue of Neptune. A greenest of green alley of grass stretches out to a low stone wall. That's your photo opp perch, with a glorious view of Florence in the background.

All this on only three acres! A graceful mix of Italian Baroque to Formal English styles.

The garden was first put together in the eighteenth century, when those grottoes were built. Then in 1895 came Romanian Princess Jeanne Ghyka, part of the wave of foreigners who descended on Florence in those days. She made the garden her pet project, tearing out the raised flowerbeds and replacing them with the oblong reflecting pools. She was a mysterious sort, only occasionally having guests in for tea, and neighbors knew little about her except that she lived with an American companion, Miss Blood. In 1925 a widow from Detroit who'd been married to a German baron took over and she, Baroness Von Ketteler, is the one who's responsible for the amazing topiary that gives this garden such a distinct character.

It was almost completely destroyed in World War II, and then bought by the industrialist Marcello Marchi, who restored it. Still run by his family, the villa's been converted to guest accommodations. To stay here is a dream. Or just get here in April, when the blooming pink azaleas are a quasi-psychedelic vision.

Villa Medici: Via Beato Angelico 2, Fiesole (055 59164/59417). The gardens can be visited by appointment only. From Florence: Bus #7 from the Stazione Centrale di Santa Maria

Novella, Piazza San Marco, or the Duomo, to Fiesole's Piazza Mino, then an uphill walk.

La Foce: The garden is open to the public every Wednesday afternoon. Guided tours leave from the Fattoria courtyard every hour from 3-7 (April-September) and 3-5 (October-March).

Villa Gamberaia: Daily 9-6 by appointment. From Florence: Bus #10 from Santa Maria Novella or San Marco to Settignano.

www.lafoce.com
www.villagamberaia.com
www.villasanmichel.com

❧

Golden Day: See the **Villa Medici Gardens** and explore the other treasures of **Fiesole**—the Roman Theater and Duomo. Lunch at the loggia of **Villa San Michele** (Via Doccia 4, 055 567 8200), a former convent with a facade designed by Michelangelo, that has become a romantic luxury hotel. Views from the restaurant are transcendent; the food refined and delicious.

TOURS

One Step Closer (www.onestepcloser.net) is a Florence-based tour operator that provides arrangements for guided garden tours.

The Tarot Garden— Capalbio, Tuscany

BURSTING OUT OF THE FOREST in this remote western corner of Tuscany is what artist Niki de Saint Phalle called her "Garden of Joy." It's a contemporary art park (opened in 1998), filled with twenty-two exuberant sculptures that represent her take on the major cards of a tarot deck.

The colors! The sculptures are made of a mix of day-glo mosaics, mirrored glass, and ceramics. They're curvy, over-sized mythical creations, some standing three stories high. They entice you to reach out and feel their textures, or walk inside and find yourself surrounded by sparkling colors and mirrors. Fountains created by Niki's husband, the Swiss kinetic sculptor Jean Tinguely, add to the exceptional magic. Olive and oak trees, myrtle and rosemary bushes, blend with the art. The garden has a playful ambience, infused with Niki's childlike spirit. She even put a bright spin on the Devil—a smiling winged woman poised on a pedestal with a flame between her legs.

Towering over the whole scene is *The Empress*, a shining, blue, mosaic sphinx with enormous multicolored breasts. Niki lived inside it while the garden was being built—hard to believe because it's so glittery in there. One breast was the kitchen, and she slept in the other. The nipples are windows. She said it was her "protective mother" for the project she worked obsessively on, relying solely on her instincts to lead the way.

Niki was a drop-dead gorgeous woman—lithe, with high cheekbones and delicate features. She was born in France in 1930, then moved to New York and modeled as a teenager, appearing on the covers of *Vogue*, *Harper's*, and *Life*.

When she was eighteen she eloped, and a few years later, moved with her husband and daughter to Paris. While studying acting there, she had a nervous breakdown. She'd been abused as a child by her father, and finally facing the trauma, started painting to work through it. She was self-taught and got encouragement to stick to her naïve style, showing her paintings in a Paris gallery in the mid-1950s. It was there she met and fell in love with the sculptor Tinguely. They both divorced their spouses and became life-long partners.

Niki's "Shooting Paintings" catapulted her to worldwide recognition in the early 1960s. They were created in galleries, bringing out the performance artist in her. She'd strut out in a white jumpsuit and black boots, whip out a twenty-two caliber pistol, and shoot at a blank board, where she'd imbedded bags filled with paint. Colors would explode and form spontaneous paintings. After three years of wowing fans from California to Amsterdam, she gave it up, saying, "I've become addicted to shooting."

Having worked the machismo stuff out of her system, Niki moved on to explore feminine archetypes. Inspired by a pregnant girlfriend, she created *Nanas*—huge pop-art styled fertility goddess sculptures. Expanding that theme, she rocked the art world with a room-sized Nana in Sweden. Visitors would enter through the sculpture's vagina and find inside a milk bar and screening room showing Greta Garbo films.

Ever since the 1950s when Niki saw Gaudi's Park Guell in Spain, she'd felt it was her destiny to create her own sculpture garden. In the 1970s she was given this land in Tuscany to begin the twenty-year project. She died four years after it was completed, in 2002. She was seventy-one and had suffered from emphysema, brought on by polyester fumes she'd inhaled while making those *Nana* sculptures. Her creations are exhibited all over the world, but the Tarot Garden is her greatest legacy.

To visit it on a sunny day, when bright light bounces off the sculptures, is spectacular. My favorite story of a traveler discovering this place comes from my friend JoAnn Locktov, who showed up heer in the midst of a thunder and lightning storm. Since there are loads of metal pieces in the garden's Tinguely fountains, the tour group she came with decided to stay in the bus, terrified they'd be struck by lightning. But JoAnn, a mosaics fanatic, was determined to get in no matter what. The guard who answered the door after twenty rings tried to stop her. JoAnn rushed past him and took in the marvels, running her hands over textured archways, awestruck by the rich designs. Caught up in JoAnn's enthusiasm, the guard turned on the fountains for her. She said to herself, "If this is where I was meant to die, it'd be okay."

The Tarot Garden: Il Giardino dei Tarocchi, open April-mid-October.

www.nikidesaintphalle.com

❧

Golden Day: Visit the **Garden** and spend time exploring nearby **Capalbio**, a tiny medieval hilltop village. Eat there at **Trattoria**

Da Maria (Via Comunale 3, 056 4896014), which also has a budget B&B attached. For luxury digs at the nearby seaside, stay at the **Pellicano Hotel** (www.pellicanohotel.com), a Relais Chateaux property.

RECOMMENDED READING

Travelers' Tales Tuscany edited by James O'Reilly and Tara Austen Weaver

36 Villa Cimbrone— Ravello, Campania

WINDING UP THE CLIFFS OF THE AMALFI COAST, mesmerizing views of lemon groves and vineyards tumbling to the shimmering sea take your breath away. Then you arrive above it all, in Ravello. A quiet path from the piazza of this romantic village opens to the fairytale **Villa Cimbrone** gardens.

You're drawn like a magnet down a shaded path to a statue of Ceres, Goddess of the Harvest, and then onto the Belvedere of Infinity. On the sheer cliff of this terrace it feels like you're floating in paradise.

Behind you, the terraced gardens are a bewitching mix of umbrella and cypress tree-lined paths, manicured lawns, arbors dripping with wisteria, nooks of purple petunias and daisies, a rose garden, and a tearoom. Sculptures of smiling cherubs and a curvy Eve in a cave add to the enchantment.

All this was created under the direction of Lord Grimthorpe (aka Ernest William Beckett), who came through Ravello on the Grand Tour, and fell in love with this spot that had been abandoned. In 1904 he transformed it into what it is today, blending Moorish and Renaissance designs with the remains of the Roman villa it once was. His guest list included Virginia Woolf, D. H. Lawrence, and T. S. Eliot, whom I imagine must have had a grand old time here.

www.villacimbrone.com

But the guest who came after Grimthorpe's reign, who I'm most intrigued by, is Greta Garbo. A plaque commemorates her famous month-long visit. In translation it reads: "Here in the spring of 1938, the divine Greta Garbo, fleeing the clamor of Hollywood, spent with Leopold Stokowsky hours of Secret Happiness."

If you'd like to believe that read no further.

The true story starts off like the ideal Villa Cimbrone romance. Garbo, the thirty-two-year-old glamour queen of

Hollywood got wooed by Stokowsky, a flamboyant fifty-five-year-old conductor. She thought "Stoky" would be the great love of her life. He invited her to meet him in Ravello, where he rented out the Villa Cimbrone just for the two of them.

According to a Swiss maid, Garbo arrived with one battered suitcase. All she'd packed were blue espadrilles, a bathing suit, lots of sunglasses, jars of jam, and a pair of pajamas, which the maid had to wash, iron and place at Garbo's bedside every evening.

Garbo's routine was morning calisthenics on the terrace, followed by a pool swim and strict vegetarian meals, except for the slathering of jam on her cornflakes and teatime cakes. She was in bed every night by eight.

Stoky had leaked to the press that Garbo was meeting him at the villa and hordes of paparazzi showed up, perching in trees, hoping to get shots of the wedding of the decade. Garbo hired policemen and guard dogs to keep them out.

As for the grand love story, in *Garbo, Her Story*, Greta says she was happy to be there at first and learn all about Italian art from Stoky. But when he talked about his plans for the future things took a nosedive. Stoky proposed they make a movie together—he'd do the music, star opposite her and they'd finance the movie with their own money. That last part of his proposal was the straw that broke the affair for Garbo, who was a notorious tightwad.

She says Stoky attempted to woo her back in Capri's Blue Grotto, but his sexual advance was unsuccessful; he got nervous and cried. Unbeknownst to the reporters, the love affair was finished. Stoky confessed to Garbo that he'd told the reporters they were going to get married. Graciously Garbo agreed to meet the press in the Villa library, if they'd agree to then go away. True to form, she played the interview close to the vest. When questioned about the relationship, she shocked the reporters with: "I have never had an impulse to go to the altar."

Years later, Stoky married the twenty-one-year-old Gloria Vanderbilt, heiress to a $20 million fortune.

Though Garbo didn't actually have "hours of secret happiness" here, this is undeniably a romantic place.

Villa Cimbrone: Via Santa Chaira 26, daily 9-6.

❧

Golden Day: Visit the **Gardens**, eat fresh seafood at **Villa Amore** (Via dei Fusco 5, 089 857 135), and sleep at **Villa Cimbrone**. The Vuilleumiers, a Swiss family who lived there for many years, now run it as a hotel, with 10 luxurious rooms, a swimming pool, and the gardens to yourself after visiting hours.

37 Parchi di Nervi– Liguria

CATCH THE SPIRIT OF GUTSY, GORGEOUS Anita Garibaldi as you walk along the seaside path named in her honor. Waves crash against rugged cliffs, as you look out to stunning views of Portofino and the Cinque Terre. Flanking the other side of the Anita Garibaldi Path are three villa lawns that comprise the **Parchi di Nervi**. They are shaded by palm trees and pines, filled with exotic plants and Mediterranean flowers.

The Genoa elite used to come here to escape the summer heat, but now it's the place to blend with the regular folk. Couples stroll arm in arm, kids run for the trees with bags of nuts to feed the squirrels.

The dramatic seascape and exotic nature of the gardens express the essence of Anita Garibaldi. She was Italy's wonder-woman who fought alongside her husband Giuseppe in the nineteenth-century revolution that culminated in giving them the titles "Father and Mother of Modern Italy."

I first encountered Anita on Rome's Janiculum Hill, where there's a statue of her brandishing a pistol as she rides a wild mustang, with a baby tucked under her other arm.

Anita's life story is the stuff of a blockbuster movie. She was born in Brazil and learned horsemanship from her father, who died when she was twelve. At fourteen, she was married off to a local older man, Signor Aguiar, aka "the drunken shoemaker."

While her husband was off at war, who should appear, but Giuseppe Garibaldi, sailing in from Italy with a passion to help Brazil fight for its independence. The moment Giuseppe set eyes on dark-haired Anita with her extraordinary almond-shaped eyes, he walked straight up to her and said, "Maiden, thou shalt be mine." Even though she was still married, Anita took off to fight by Giuseppe's side in Brazil and Uruguay, firing canons, teaching him gaucho guerilla warfare, and giving birth to their first son in the midst of all that. They married two years later, after Anita's first husband died.

In 1848, with four children in tow (between the ages of eight and two!), Anita and Giuseppe left South America to go to Italy and join the fight for unification. A year later, Anita died in Giuseppe's arms after a battle near Ravenna. She was twenty-eight and pregnant with their fifth child.

Giuseppe kept Anita's memory alive. When he rode in victory to the crowning of Emmanuel II as the first king of a united Italy, he wore a Brazilian poncho. And around his neck, Anita's striped scarf.

The Anita Garibaldi Passeggiata was created by Marchese Gaetano Gropallo in 1862, just two years after Italy's unification. It used to be a rustic path used by fisherman, but the Marchese fancied it up with lampposts and paving, so now it's an extended terrace to not only Gropallo's gardens, but also his neighbors, the Grimaldis and the Serras. The Villa Grimaldi rose garden is the most famous of the three and especially beautiful in spring. All are now owned by the state, house museums, and the grounds are used for outdoor ballets and theater in July.

Parco Villa Grimaldi, Via Capolungo 9, 8–dusk.

⁂

Golden Day: Take a train (fifteen minutes) from Genoa to **Nervi**, stroll the path and gardens with a stop for a seaside cocktail, and eat at **Il Bagatto** (via Marco Sala 77/79. 010 3202952), highly recommended by my friend Barbara Crawford of Visit Italy Tours.

RECOMMENDED READING

Anita Garibaldi: A Biogrpahy by Anthony Valerio.

38 Gardens of the Isole Borromee–Piedmont

THE TRADITION OF A GROOM GIVING his bride a wedding present was taken over the top by Carlo III Borromeo. In 1632, he decided to transform one of his family's Lake Maggiore islands from a barren rock into a baroque-a-palooza wonderland and dedicate it to his wife-to-be. Fisherman living there at the time were none too happy when they were pushed aside as Carlo burst in with architects, loads of dirt, and exotic plants to begin his project, but wife Isabella must have been pleased. Especially when Carlo named the island Isola Isabella in her honor. The name was later changed to the easier-on-the-tongue **Isola Bella**.

Carlo's project took generations to complete, but by 1700 there stood an opulent villa above a pyramid of ten terraced gardens. There are gushing fountains, fish ponds, and at the top level a curved stone theatrical backdrop with sculptures of gods, goddesses, and *putti*, crowned by a unicorn (the Borromeo family symbol), to complete the whole design.

Getting to Isola Bella by ferry from the town of **Stresa** is half the fun of this garden visit. On misty days the island rises from the water like a pearl on the lake. Nearby are the Borromeo-owned Isola Madre and the fisherman's island, Isola dei Pescatori. To have a dreamy day visit all three.

"There were white peacocks running around my daughter will never forget," my friend Rosanne told me about her June visit to Isola Bella. The garden's spring colors are a knock out—azaleas, rhododendrons, and camellias bursting into bloom.

The unique feature of the Isola Bella villa is its downstairs grottoes, all done up in elaborate stucco, fake stalactites, pebble and seashell mosaics—a fantasy of an underwater cave.

Among the elegant upstairs rooms is the Sala di Napoleone, named in memory of the general who found this place perfect for romantic encounters. He stayed in this room with his first wife, Josephine, back in 1797 when the couple finally got to take their honeymoon.

Napoleon and Josephine had married the year before in Paris. She was a thirty-three-year-old widow with two children, described as "the voluptuous Creole" from Martinique, whose husband had been beheaded in the French Revolution. Napoleon, twenty-seven, was just beginning to gain fame. Three days after their wedding he had to head to war in Italy and Josephine stayed behind.

Napoleon wrote Josephine passionate love letters (often two a day), with lines like "You are the eternal object of my thoughts. My imagination exhausts itself wondering what you are doing." Meanwhile Josephine was having quite the gay time in Paris, celebrating hubby's victories with handsome escorts. She barely responded to his letters, which drove Napoleon absolutely insane. He finally convinced her to come meet him in Italy, and I imagine since they'd been apart practically a year, a rollicking time was had in this *sala* and the nearby Giardino di Amore.

Ferrying on to **Isola Madre** you'll be in a less formal place, with English-style botanical gardens. It was named the "Mother Island" because it was where the Borromeo family planted their first gardens. The family's summer palace here has a big display of antique dolls in it, along with a puppet theater designed by Alessandro Sanquirico, who worked at La Scala.

Since there are no picnics allowed on those two islands, the **Isola dei Pescatori**, a tiny, touristy fishing village is where to stop for eating and drinking.

In *A Farewell to Arms*, Ernest Hemingway wrote about rowing to Isola dei Pescatori, not catching anything, but docking there and stopping in at a caffè for Vermouth. It's towards the end of the book when he's deserted the army and goes to Stresa to hook back up with the British nurse he's crazy about, who's pregnant with their child.

"I kissed her neck and shoulders. I felt faint with loving her so much," Hemingway writes in a scene that takes place at their Grand Hotel des Iles Borromees room in Stresa. It seems like even Papa Hemingway, not typically a romantic guy, allowed passion to overtake him in this beautiful place.

www.borromeoturismo.it
www.lagomaggioreonline.it

Gardens of the Isole Borromee: Open Mid-March through Mid-October, 9-5:30.

❧

Golden Day: From Stresa, ferry to the islands (www. navigazionelaghi.it). Eat at **Chez Manuel** (Via Di Mezzo 41, 032 332534, closed Monday) on **Isola dei Pescatori**. You can even stay there at **Hotel Verbano** (www.hotelverbano.it) or for a splurge head back to **Stresa** and, like Hemingway, stay at **Grand Hotel des Iles Borromees** (www.borromees.it).

RECOMMENDED READING

Napoleon and Josephine by Frances Mossiker

A Farewell to Arms by Ernest Hemingway

39 L'Infiorata

IF YOU'RE TRAVELING TO ITALY in late May or early June, you may stumble upon the amazing sights of *L'Infiorata*: streets in small towns paved with flower petals arranged to form painterly masterpieces. You'll find *L'Infiorata* in places like Genzano (south of Rome), Vernazza (in Liguria), Noto (in Sicily), and most notably, Spello (in Umbria). Locals go into a creative frenzy to create these temporary displays, in celebration of the Feast of Corpus Domini. The Feast commemorates a thirteenth-century miraculous event, in which a pilgrim-priest broke a Eucharist and it bled. These days the religious side of the *L'Infiorata* is overshadowed by all the colorful activity that goes on outside the paths that lead to the small town churches.

I'd never heard of *L'Infiorata* until my friend Anne Block, who runs **Take My Mother Please Tours**, told me that she's been taking groups to the medieval town of Spello for the *L'Infiorata* event for years and showed me fantastic pictures of it. The tradition began there in the 1930s, when a local elderly *signora* created a simple flower petal display in front of her house, to show her faith in the Corpus Domini miracle.

Now *L'Infiorata* has become a huge event in Spello. Local groups plan their designs all year and it's so popular that hotel reservations need to be made way in advance to get near it, which is why it's perfect to have somebody like Anne around to do the planning.

She gets there a couple of days before the big Sunday celebration, so there's time to tour nearby Assisi, see the beautiful Virgin Mary Triptych frescos in Spello's Santa Maria Maggiore church, and best of all get in the spirit of the town's *L'Infiorata* anticipation.

"Starting on Friday night, from the hotel windows," Anne told me, "you can peek into alleys where the locals are sitting outside in circles, busy breaking off flower petals, separating them by color."

On Saturday, those colors start to cover the streets, with teenagers working on their hands and knees under gazebos, filling in chalk-drawn designs with flowers, seeds, and leaves, fixing them with squirts of water, as there's no glue allowed. Younger kids run back and forth with deliveries, while mammas supply coffee and panini. A smell of wild fennel fills the air and, as this is Umbria, there's usually a pig roasting on a spit nearby.

By Sunday morning the teenagers who've worked non-stop through the night are tumbled over each other, exhausted. "Can you imagine the love affairs that must begin on that long night?" says Wendy Dallas, who's gone along with Ann on this adventure for five years.

With the creations complete, early on Sunday is prime time to stroll along and *ooh* and *ahh* before the tour buses arrive with crowds of gawkers. The flower paintings range from brilliantly colored geometric patterns to intricate mosaic-style portraits. One of the most memorable photos Anne showed me was from 2005. It was from the under-fourteen-year-old section and

www.infioratespello.it
www.infiorata.it

pictured Pope John Paul floating to heaven in a hot air balloon, while below him hands of all colors, from every nation, waved.

The morning continues with an excellent Spello band accompanying the Bishop's promenade along the flower carpet. After the church ceremony, out come the brooms, and as if it were a dream, the paintings are swept away.

Of course things don't end there. After all that planning and work, Spello celebrates with a huge outdoor party. There's music, dancing, and great food—some of it made with flowers.

L'Infiorata traditionally takes place on Corpus Domini, nine Sundays after Easter, but the dates vary if Easter comes too early.

TOURS

Ann Block, from **Take My Mother Please Tours**, has special tours for *L'Infiorata* (www.takemymotherplease.com).

IV

Beaches

Italians have mastered the art of a day at the beach. You've seen the photos: perfect lines of matching umbrellas and chairs, immaculately raked sand. It's summer theater with the sea as the show.

You pay a fee at these *bagni* (beach clubs), and your umbrella and chair is typically set up with flourish by an attendant. He may even come around and adjust your umbrella during the day, keeping you in the shade, so you'll feel like a real *principessa*. Fancy clubs have libraries, gyms, pools, and some even transform to discos at night. These places are packed in July and August, when Italians traditionally take their vacations. Show up then and you'll get seated in the back row—closer spots have been reserved by families for generations.

There are lots of free public beaches, but they're typically not maintained up to *bagni* standards. Which means some will be right next to the clubs, looking like poor trash-ridden step sisters. Don't despair—with so much coastline you can find beautiful free beaches in every region, and even gems of hidden coves you could have all to yourself.

What to wear? What you wish, of course. Just FYI: You may be startled at how Italian women of non-bikini-body types comfortably wear two-piece suits. The focus is on the fabulous sensation of feeling the sun on your body, so here you can throw concerns about sags or cellulite away.

Topless? No big deal, though it does depend on location. On the island of Sardinia, probably. On the coast of Tuscany, less likely.

I do hope that if you're in Italy between April and October, you take the time for a day at a beach. Settle in, taste the *granite* (fruit-flavored ices), and have a fresh seafood lunch with a glass of prosecco to make it all perfect. These are the places where you surrender to what Italians call *Il Dolce Far Niente: The Sweetness of Doing Nothing...*

INFO

To enjoy the best beaches of Italy, head to Sardinia. If you're looking for "The Summer Party Scene," the beaches around Rimini on the Adriatic Riviera are where it's at.

Legambiente (www.legambiente.eu) puts out an annual *Guida Blu* that ranks beaches in Italy.

Italian Naturist Foundation (www.fenait.org) lists Italy's beaches where you can go *au naturale*.

40 Sperlonga, Lazio

"A ROMAN SUMMER ISN'T A REAL Roman summer without a stay in **Sperlonga**," says my friend Gioia, an Eternal City native. She's been going there every August for twenty years. "It's where we all had our first boyfriends," she sighs.

Set high up on a seaside cliff, Sperlonga's historic center has the ambiance of an old Greek city: a pedestrian-only labyrinth of whitewashed stone buildings connected by stairways and arched alleys. Though now it's basically a tourist town, Sperlonga retains the quaint atmosphere of its fishing village days—pre-1957, before a road was built to reach this place. It's always attracted liberal, creative types like the Italian writer Natalie Ginzburg who had a home here. And because it's positioned halfway between Rome and Naples, it's a popular spot with visitors from both cities.

Stretching out below the town are immaculately raked beaches of golden sand and the tantalizing, rolling, cobalt sea. Modern beach establishments cover the area north of Sperlonga harbor, but to the south is where you'll find the treasures of free beaches and classic clubs, where rentals of umbrellas and chairs are about twenty euros. Gioia's advice is to head to **Lido Rocco**. "It has the best position, the widest beach, and the best restaurant—order the *spaghetti con vongole*."

www.sperlongaturismo.it

In the evenings, the Sperlonga *piazzetta* is a charming place to relax with a cocktail and enjoy a sunset view. And in traditional Italian beach town fashion, outdoor movies are shown—a different one every night to entertain the whole family.

For a break from the sun, walking south along the shore takes you to the ruins of a Roman villa, cave, and museum. Here's  where the Emperor Tiberius, who reigned from 14 A.D. to 37 A.D. would come to party, before he moved permanently to Capri. The cave had an island inside it that was his banquet room, and submerged in the surrounding waters were sculptures that told stories from Homer's *Odyssey*. You can see these enormous statues of such dramatic scenes as the multi-headed Scylla she-monster eating up Odysseus's crew or the blinding of the Cyclops Polyphemus in the museum.

❧

Golden Day: Get to **Lido Rocco**, have *spaghetti con vongole* (spaghetti with clams) for lunch, and stay in the historic center at **Hotel Corallo** (www.corallohotel.net), a cozy, three-star. Getting there by public transportation from Rome takes about two hours, via train to the Fondi-Sperlonga stop, and then by connecting bus.

41 Forte dei Marmi— Tuscany

COME TO THE PLACE THAT'S CALLED the Queen of the Versilia coast to luxuriate in one of Italy's chic-est beach experiences. Yes, it's in Tuscany, but erase all those quaint thoughts of cobblestoned streets and medieval architecture.

Forte dei Marmi is laid out in a flat grid, perfect for biking. Mid-century villas peek out behind clipped hedges, cypress, and palm trees. The town center is packed with designer shops, like Gucci, Prada, Versace, and Dolce & Gabbana. This is more like the Hamptons of Italy, where the elite meet to beach, dine, shop, and disco.

It has one of the mainland's best stretches of wide, fine sandy beaches, with shallow water that's perfect for the kids. If you go in season, you'll be mixing with well-to-do families who've been coming here for decades, along with the more recent trend of international jet-setters, who've taken their cue from folks like Miuccia Prada and Giorgio Armani, who have summer getaway homes here.

It wasn't always this way. Forte dei Marmi translates to "Fort of Marble," which is what that big brick building you'll see in the town's main piazza used to be. Back in the eighteenth century it was a storehouse for marble that was quarried from the Apuan mountains that backdrop the town. Now the jetty built to lug that marble out to ships is a promenade, flanked by beaches, and filled with glamorous tourists.

There are almost a hundred beach clubs to choose from to enjoy the Forte dei Marmi experience with starting prices of about fifty euro for your cabana, beach chairs, and umbrellas. A favorite for families is **Bruno** (V. Arenile 79 Riviera della Versilia, 058 589 972), which also has an excellent restaurant. If you want to go for the ultimate jet-set scene, head to **Twiga**, owned by the mega-businessman Flavio Briatore, renowned for dating models like Heidi Klum and Naomi Campbell. Here you'll find billowing Moroccan tents, chairs upholstered in leopard skin, and if you show up in the evening, a disco where you'll be dancing until the wee hours. Or you may go for one of Italy's top topless beaches, **Santa Maria** (V. Arenile 9), that's surrounded by pine trees.

This is a great place to settle into the scene for at least a few days. Nearby is the town of **Pietrasanta**, filled with artists whose sculptures, paintings, and handcrafted jewelry make for fun shopping opprtunities and gallery shows. Or you could visit **Carrara**, home to the famous marble quarry where Michelangelo chose his stone for the *Pieta*.

WWW. www.twigaclub.it www.versilia.org

❧

Golden Day: Get to **Forte dei Marmi** for the Wednesday market that has designer goods at discount prices, choose your beach. Or better yet stay longer, at **Hotel Augustus** (www.augustus-hotel.org) or rent a place (www.versilia.toscana.it). No matter how you play it, eat at **Trattoria Tre Stelle** (Via Montauti 6, 058 480220) for elegantly prepared seafood.

42 *Sirolo–Marche*

TWO GIANT POINTED ROCKS, called Le Due Sorelle (the two sisters), symbolize the Riviera del Conero. They resemble two nuns dressed in white habits rising from the azure sea, as if blessing the most stunning stretch of Italy's northern Adriatic Coast.

Bright white limestone is what makes this place so spectacular. Towering over the scenery is **Monte Conero**, that wows you as you drive along a winding panoramic highway above jagged cliffs. Deep green pine forests and yellow broom add bursts of color. All this wild beauty is the backdrop for pebbled beaches, coves, and a handful of sweet resort towns.

Best of these towns is **Sirolo**.

Below it you'll find four sublime beaches. My friend Alessandra is a fan of the largest, **Grotta Urbani**. It's shaped like a crescent moon, with an enticing cave at one end. Shallow water makes it perfect for families with children. The scent of pine trees backing up the beach mixes with the sea air. There are three beach clubs, a restaurant, and bar on the jetty. From Sirolo, you can catch a shuttle bus to get there, or walk downhill through the forest, which takes about ten minutes.

Sirolo's other beaches are only accessible by foot or boat from Grotta Urbani. Boat is better, as the paths are treacherous and steep. **Le Due Sorelle** is the gem of them all, with the view of the "two sisters" rocks. **San Michele** has a rustic appeal, with wildflowers covering its borders. If you're in the mood to sunbathe *au naturale*, head to **Sassi Neri**, the Beach of the Black Pebbles. Keep in mind all the beaches are pebbly, so bring your beach shoes.

Sirolo is a beautifully restored medieval village, that's a happening spot during its beach season. Along its narrow alleyways are lively restaurants and bars. Everybody hangs out on the wide piazza, a tree-shaded balcony at the edge of the village that overlooks the sea. In July and August, two theaters stage operas and concerts. The most unusual is the **Teatro Alle Cave**, a quarry that's been converted to an open-air 1800 seat theater. More traditional is the **Teatro Cortesi**, a 220-seat ornate building from 1873.

Sirolo is also the entrance to the Conero Regional Park, where you can hike to an archaeological site and find the Tomb of the Queen of Sirolo. Folks were amazed when this was excavated in 1989. They discovered jewelry, vases, and two carriages from the sixth century B.C., that must have belonged to this woman of mystery.

www.conero.it

❧

Golden Day: Choose your beach and enjoy the village of **Sirolo**. Stay at **Locanda Rocco** (www.locandarocco.it), a seven-room charming place that's recently been stylishly renovated, and blends into the town's thirteenth-century wall. Its restaurant is also excellent, giving modern twists to regional classics like *brodetto* (seafood stew). Be sure to taste the local dry red wine, Rosso del Conero.

43 *Positano–Amalfi Coast*

THANKS TO PASITEA, AN IRRESISTIBLE NYMPH who lured in Poseidon, the dreamy seaside village of **Positano** was discovered. It has six beaches to choose from. There's the large, busy **Spiaggia Grande**, where you can watch handsome fisherman glide in and out. A short walk away is the quieter **Fornillo** beach, where you can enjoy drinks on the porch of Il Pupetto.

But for the feel of discovering your own private hideaway and a delicious lunch, head to **Arienzo**. It's a small cove bordered with giant rocks, with views of fishing boats bobbing along the horizon, ferries headed for Capri and, in the distance, the Li Galli islands. Legend says these islands were once mermaids whom Ulysses turned to stone so they'd stop trying to seduce him off his course.

I'm not talking great sand. It's volcanic and coarse with lots of black pebbles. But like almost everything you touch around here, Positano's black pebbles have a story behind them. If you find one with a hole in it, it means the BVM passed through it, and it's blessed. You'll see many Positanesi wearing necklaces of these black pebbles.

The sand situation means you should bring along beach shoes and rent an umbrella and lounge chair. Then get totally comfy, lie back and get lulled by the lapping of the calm water.

Melody, an American who's lived in Positano for years, tipped me off that Ada's gnocchi at Arienzo is famous in these parts. As you approach the beach you'll see Ada, a fifty-some-thing-year-old *signora* with a radiant smile, bustling about in her walk-in-closet-sized kitchen.

The beach snack bar is set up on stilts, looking like something Thurston Howell III would have built on *Gilligan's Island*, perched to take in the view with eight inviting tables. A blackboard lists the day's specials, which along with Ada's gnocchi may feature spaghetti with clams, Caprese salad, fish caught that morning and grani-tas—flavored ices made from Positano lemons and whatever else is in season.

Around noon, locals start arriving on foot or pulling up on boats to enjoy Ada's lunch. Her gnoc-chi is light and beautifully textured, served with a delicate tomato sauce. The house red is rich and lively. On a visit there one warm October day, for dessert Ada served me a plate of ripe figs picked from a nearby tree, and poured me a glass of home-made limoncello.

Even if you don't find a pebble with a hole blown through it, at Arienzo Beach you'll feel blessed.

Arienzo Beach: To get here you can catch a small boat from Spiaggia Grande or walk down a zigzag path of steps from the Arienzo bus stop.

❧

Golden Day: Arienzo Beach and **Ada's** gnocchi for lunch. Stay at **Maliosa di Arienzo** (www.lamaliosa.it), a B&B nearby, with

www.positanolife.it

your private sea view terrace. Arrange for complimentary car service to **Mediterraneo** ristorante (www.ristorantimediterraneo. com) for a dinner of fantastic seafood and a Neapolitan guitarist who strums classics.

44 Parghelia-Calabria

"THE ENTERTAINMENT AT PARGHELIA is watching the tanned, pudgy, eleven-year-old local boys jumping off the rocks—it's hilarious!" my friend Tania told me about her favorite beach. She lives in Tropea, the prettiest town on Calabria's coast. In summer, Tropea's wide, white sand beaches (rated among the best in Italy) get packed with tourists.

That's when Tania takes a two-minute drive north to the little fishing village of **Parghelia**, and heads to the secluded **Spiaggia di Michelino**. Giant craggy rocks border it at one end. The pale turquoise water is so clear you can see all the way to the bottom of those rocks, and the light and sparkling sea playing against the intricate stone formations is hypnotic. It's a perfect place for snorkeling.

This beach is not in the least luxurious. There's no fee, no umbrella or chair rentals, no snack bar. From the shaded, woodland path you take to get there, birdsongs mix with the sounds of waves crashing against rocks. Just like so many other stunning places in Calabria, no big deal is made out of this rustic spot of natural beauty. The rocks give it a deep, old world mysterious vibe. Locals of all ages who come to relax here give it the authentic Calabrian flavor.

The Spiaggia di Michelino is part of a whole Tyrrhenian sea stretch called "The Coast of the Gods." Odysseus ran into loads of trouble in these waters. Just south of here, the she-monster

Scylla, a twelve-legged, multi-headed creature, snatched up his six best men and bolted them down raw. He got a bag of winds that steered him off course from Poseidon's son, Aeolus. That's how the Aeolian Islands, that lie off this coast, got their name.

From the Spiaggia di Michelino you can see the closest of the five Aeolians, Stromboli. With its smoking volcanic peak that erupts with a brilliant orange-red display from time to time, Stromboli adds a dramatic touch to the beach view.

Every time I look at Stromboli I'm reminded of the movie of the same name starring young, glamorous Ingrid Bergman. While it was being filmed, Bergman and director Roberto Rossellini fell madly in love, their affair causing a scandal as both of them were married to others at the time. Once again, a spicy romantic story seems inescapable wherever you go in Italy.

To be at Spiaggia di Michelino for a sunset—when shadows fall on the rocks, the orange ball slips into the deepening turquoise sea, and (if you're lucky) Stromboli shoots off its fireworks, is spectacular.

Spiaggia di Michelino: The beach is about a twenty-minute walk from Tropea. If you're arriving by train or driving, take a left from the Parghelia *stazione*, follow the road beneath an underpass, and keep going until you see steps that lead to the beach.

৵৬

Golden Day: Head to **Spiaggia di Michelino**, stopping on the way at the **La Piccola Rosticceria at Piazza Ruffa** to pick up Calabrian lunch goodies like *polpette di melanzane* (eggplant balls). If you want to stay over, check out **Porto Pirgos** (www.portopirgos. com), a luxurious converted villa with a seaside swimming pool.

45 *Santa Teresa di Gallura–Sardinia*

IT WAS QUEEN MARIA THERESA'S IDEA to name this town on the north coast of Sardinia Santa Teresa, to honor the Spanish mystic. Plus it happened to be her middle name. In 1808, her husband, King Vittorio Emanuele I, obliged. He happened to be ruling the island. This spot had been prime territory for smugglers, as its curved harbor made it naturally perfect for doing sneaky things. King Vittorio wanted to clean things up, so he had the town rebuilt in a neat grid plan and even offered free plots of land to respectable folks who wanted to move in.

These days **Santa Teresa di Gallura** is a pretty resort spot, more relaxed and less expensive than Costa Smeralda that lies to its east. The former famous-for-smuggling harbor is filled with ferryboats that go to the Maddalena Islands and Corsica.

And, on this island that has the best beaches in Italy, the **Rena Bianca**, that's steps down from Santa Teresa di Gallura, is prime. My friend Elizabeth spent two weeks here with her family recently, and loved Rena Bianca but she couldn't help scoping out surrounding spots. Though it was fun to watch windsurfers or go snorkeling on other beaches nearby, as far as classic beach-front, Rena Bianca was best.

It's sheltered from the winds by the harbor and has fine white sand, opening to clear waters that change in color from pale blue to turquoise to deep cobalt at the horizon. If you get there when the tide is right, the shoreline is tinged with pink from coral fragments that wash up. There's a restaurant, bar, and umbrella and chair rentals.

This is a beloved spot for Italian vacationers, which Elizabeth found out when she arrived there in August. "I never felt so white," she told me, as she and her blonde family placed their towels amidst the alligator-tanned Italians. August may not be the best time to go, as Elizabeth told me it was towel-to-towel packed—so much so that in order to get a good space, her husband would get up early and take the steps down to the beach to claim the family turf. But still, she found it divine, with her two boys, aged eight and ten, stay-ing in the water for the entire day while she and her husband read and drank prosecco. There also were a few topless *signorine* who made quite the impression on her boys. Elizabeth said, "a few topless." Her husband, remembering the vacation fondly, chimed in, "There were four."

www.comunesantateresagallura.it

If you're not up for the August crowds, come here another time during the May to September resort season. But August can be fun, as that's when there are celebrations honoring the town's foundation, with musicians in the piazza and evening classical concerts in churches.

֍

Golden Day: Relax at **Rena Bianca** and eat at **Pape Satàn** (Via Marmora 20, 078 9755048), where the pizza is out of this world and they also serve up fantastic seafood pastas.

46 *Scopello–Sicily*

"SCOPELLO IS ONE OF SICILY'S HIDDEN GEMS," my writer friend Maria Lisella told me. She lives in Queens, New York, and visits Italy often with her Sicilian-American husband. They're always getting off the beaten path to seek out unusual places. **Scopello**, a two-*via* fishing village on the west coast, is one of her recent discoveries.

It has a horseshoe-shaped beach that's free and tiny, made up of a mix of white pebbles and fine sand. Warm, transparent turquoise waters, framed by *faraglioni* (limestone towers), cover an amazing seabed, where colorful sponges and anemones cling to the rocks.

If you're up for diving to see *astroides* illuminating caves and tunnels or a World War II shipwreck, the **Cetaria Dive Center** in Scopello rents out equipment and is even kid-friendly, offering classes for those over seven years old. But just swimming around here is spectacular, and in spring and fall you may be joined by *stenelle*, a breed of dolphins who migrate through the area.

Though the town of Scopello is tiny, it's rich in history. Two medieval watchtowers and the *tonnara*, a twelfth-century tuna processing building that was in use until the 1980s, accent the surroundings. The piazza has charming B&Bs and restaurants, where you should definitely order the *tonno* (tuna). Not many

Americans get here, but it has become a popular spot for Italian and German tourists.

Adjoining Scopello is **Lo Zingaro National Park**, a fantastic seaside nature preserve. There are easy hiking trails set along the 4.5-mile/7.5-km rocky shoreline, where you get breathtaking panoramic views from the cliffs. Paths are surrounded by dwarf palms and wildflowers—from sea lavender to crocuses, irises, and orchids. It's also great for bird lovers, who'll enjoy watching eagles, peregrine falcons, partridges, and owls.

You may want to use Scopello as your base to explore the nearby hill town of Erice, the salt towers of Trapani, or the Temple of Segesta.

But best of all, as Maria puts it, "Scopello is the perfect place to end a vacation and let go of your tourist agendas. Just flop there, relax and swim."

᪣

Golden Day: Settle in for relaxing swimming and sunning at **Scopello** beach. For lunch, stop by the bakery in the piazza, **La Craparia**, and pick up a *pane ẓatu*, the town's signature *panino*, filled with eggplant, tomatoes, olives, and anchovies. A pretty bed and breakfast in town is **Pensione Tranchina** (www. pensionetranchina.com). It's owned by a Scopello native and his Chinese wife, who speaks English. The couple are passionate about sharing all they know regarding the region with travelers and they serve up delicious dinners of catch-of-the-day seafood.

V Beauty Treatments and Spas

Treat yourself to one of Italy's oldest traditions: taking the waters at a spa. That's SPA, as in *Salus Per Aqum = Health Through Water*. Spa, as in *AH...that feels soooo good*. If any "I'm in Italy, I should be at a museum" thoughts come up, shut them down. You're having a valuable cultural experience.

Every region of Italy has curative thermal springs gurgling below. The Ancient Romans, experts at enjoying sensual pleasures, built elaborate bath houses around these waters. They were social centers where spirits were lifted; aches and pains soaked away.

Today, these places are taken seriously by Italy's health care system. So say you're Italian and you have arthritis or some other ailment. Instead of popping pills, a doctor will write a prescription for you to spend time at a spa, where you'll go through a supervised program of soaking and massage.

Italians and visitors from all over Europe and Russia flock to these places. Many of them are grand old hotels. And there's a growing number (especially in Tuscany) of spas that are closer to the American model, offering yoga classes and acupuncture. American travelers haven't caught on to them yet, even though there are bargains to be had, especially in the early spring and fall off season. Hotel packages that include treatments cost a fraction of what you'd pay for the same thing in America. Well, not exactly the *same* thing: think Italian food and wine. Plus there's a gentler philosophy here—rarely are there hard core gyms or punishing diet offerings on the menu. And don't be surprised if you see a few folks smoking.

For the best bargains, head to the country and seek out Italy's *wild* spas—free places where you just walk in and soak with the locals. The most famous of them all is in **Saturnia**, southern Tuscany, a place named in honor of a Roman goddess, where you'll find a fantastic bubbling hot waterfall.

Wherever you end up taking the waters, you'll come out rejuvenated in body and spirit, just as the Romans did. So relax, slow down, enjoy...

47 *Hair Salons and Spas*

IF YOU'VE SEEN *ROMAN HOLIDAY*, the fantasy of impulsively stepping into a salon and becoming magically transformed à la Audrey Hepburn may stick with you.

I confess it happened to me. I wound up in a chair with a very enthusiastic Marco chopping and circling, telling me he was giving me "Hair for the pillow—Sexy!" When I got home my husband greeted me with: "Hey! Liza Minelli!" No offense to Liza, whom I adore, but it wasn't what I was going for.

So now I rely on my beauteous Italian girlfriends for advice, which I pass on to you.

If you're just in need of a shampoo and style, most of Italy's major cities and even small towns have Jean Louis David or Aveda salons. But for great cuts, beauty treatments Italian style, or massages to give you that boost while you're traveling, here are some places in major metropolitan areas.

Rome

* **Salus Per Aquam,** Via Giulia 4, 06 687 7449
  On Rome's most elegant street, flanked by Renaissance churches and palazzos, you'll enter a majestic courtyard, then zigzag up stairs to this ultra-luxurious spot. Not only can you

get a stylish cut, but they also have a spa with a Turkish bath
and rooms for facials, body treatments, and massages.

* **Contesta Rock Hair,** Via degli Zingari 10, 06 478 23717
In the under-touristed Monti neighborhood, this modern
shop is not just for rock and rollers as the name might
imply. It's a great place to get a chic, reasonably priced cut
and then stop next door at their boutique to buy some hip
clothes to match.

* **Spazio Beauty,** Via dei Chiavari 37, 06 686 9800
A simple "Beauty Place" off the Campo dei Fiori, where you
can get massages, body scrubs, facials, and waxing for reasonable prices.

Florence

* **Simonetta Pini,** Viale Antonio Gramsci 27r, 055 247 7713
Simonetta has a big following for her exceptional cuts, the
colorists are great, and you could also get your nails done.
To get the royal treatment there, contact Valentina at **One
Step Closer.**

WWW.
www.contestarockhair.com
www.onestepcloser.com
www.klab.it

* **Art 44 Tiziano Bollea,** Piazza Mino 24, Fiesole,
055 599 013
This modern shop in the main square of Fiesole
is where master cutter Tiziano reigns. He's an
expert on styling everyone from his loyal *signora*
clients, to fashion models and film stars who pull
him away to their photo shoots.

❀ **Klab,** Via de' Conti 7, 055 213 514
Conveniently located in the historic center is this huge,
modern fitness center where you can get massages and facials,
step into their tanning salon, get gym time on their equipment, or take a yoga, pilates, or aerobics class.

Venice

❀ **Hair Tecnart Salvo,** Calle dei Saoneri 2719 (San Polo)
041 716 765.
It's worth it to just take a peek at this place, that's incorporated into a ground floor of a fancy-shmancy palazzo. Come
here to get the most up-to-date cut by Salvo or Miky.

❀ **Bauer Palladio Spa,** Giudecca 3
In dreamy Venice, this place ranks up there as
one of the dreamiest. The Renaissance master
architect Palladio designed the building in the
sixteenth century as a sanctuary for unmarried
women. They learned lacemaking here, a craft
that kept them from heading out to the canals to
join in on the world's oldest profession. Their sanctuary has recently been restored to a luxurious hotel with a spa
that has a Turkish bath and eight treatment rooms for facials,
massages, or body treatments. All is top-of-the-line, with a
gorgeous view of mainland Venice from its relaxing room.

www.salvoemiky.com
www.palladiohotelspa.com

48 Bulicame–Viterbo, Lazio

MY WRITER-FRIEND JESSIE SHOLL LOVES the wild side of Italy. So when it comes to spas, her first choice is **Bulicame**, about an hour's drive north of Rome, outside the town of Viterbo. Bulicame isn't wild in the "jungle" or "rock 'n' roll" sense. In fact, it's a serene scene, attracting local families who come for relaxing afternoons. Like several *terme* in the area that are categorized as "wild spas," Bulicame simply appears in a grassy field: four thermal pools of different sizes and temperatures, surrounded by a smattering of Roman ruins.

What makes this wild spa experience extra relaxing? It's free. You park, walk in, and blend with the pleasure seekers.

In the Middle Ages, prostitutes bathed in these waters. That's what Dante writes in the *Inferno*. He's winding around the seventh circle of Hell, walking on fiery sand, when he sees a boiling red stream and shudders (paraphrasing): "AAAGGH! That reminds me of that brook in Bulicame, that's always full o' working girls!"

The poet doesn't mention who else was there: popes. Before the popes, the ancient Romans, and before them, the Etruscans. Over the centuries no civilization has missed out on the benefits of the warm sulfur springs here that are renowned for soothing the skin, aching bones, and working miracles on the respiratory system.

Bulicame is a no-frills set-up; you change in the car and bring your own towel. Steam rises from a nearby hill. To do things Roman style, start at the coolest pool, farthest from the hill and then soak your way to the hottest, which gets up to 140 degrees.

Nearby Bulicame are more upscale spas like **Pozze di San Sisto**, that's still on the wild side, but has been taken over by a non-profit organization and charges a fee. There you'll find changing rooms, showers, and a casual restaurant. The fanciest spas in the area are the Terme dei Papi, named in honor of the popes. They are charmless modern hotels right in the town of Viterbo, which come along with massages and body treatments. So out of all the many options, the *terme* that offers the style most in tune with those nature-loving Etruscans is Bulicame.

As long as you have a car, and are in the off-beat wild mode, complete your adventure by heading towards Rome for a visit to Italy's most bizarre town: **Calcata**. From the outside it may look like just another tiny medieval hilltop village. But once you enter its walls, you'll discover it's full of artists, from all over Italy and the world. This place was practically abandoned fifty years ago, until these creative types moved in, dug in their heels, and saved it from the government wrecking ball. Jessie got to know Calcata and the village's intriguing characters when she lived there with her husband, David Farley, while he was writing *An Irreverent Curiosity*—a fascinating and hilarious story about Farley's search to solve the mystery behind the theft of Calcata's famous relic: Jesus's foreskin.

Bulicame: The spas at Bulicame are a ten-minute drive from the town of Viterbo (Strada Provinciale Tuscanese and Strada delle Terme).

❧

Golden Day: Soak in **Bulicame**, then head to **Calcata**. Eat at **La Grotta dei Germogli** (Rupe San Giovanni; 761 588003; www.grottadeigermogli.org), a nouvelle Italian restaurant in a mosaic-lined cave. To spend the night, check out **I Sensi della Terra** (076 158 8003, www.isensidellaterra.it) for room and apartment rentals scattered throughout the village.

RECOMMENDED READING

An Irreverent Curiosity: In Search of the Church's Strangest Relic in Italy's Oddest Town by David Farley

49 Fonteverde Spa–Tuscany

A MARBLE THRONE DOESN'T SOUND VERY COMFY. But try sitting on one submerged in a pool of warm healing water, with hydro-massage jets soothing your back and the soles of your feet. Throw in a quintessential Tuscan view of vineyards and olive trees. It's good to be Queen.

The throne is part of **Fonteverde Spa**'s *bioaqum* pool. It's beautifully designed, all curvy with a sky-lit, glass-enclosed indoor section connected to an outdoor area where you'll find those thrones and marble beds to stretch out on Roman style. All over are jets designed to hit different parts of you from the waist down to (according to the brochure) *activate your energy*. All I know is it feels real good.

The idea here is to take ye olde Roman bath social scene and give it a modern twist with the hydro-massagers. They keep things uncrowded by having you sign up for pool time. Which is what my friend Kristin and I did, along with three couples. Everybody keeps to their own area and then we do-si-do. If you come here with your lover, this could be a perfect prelude to afternoon delight.

Back to Kristin and me, in recovery from a five-hour drive from Parma complete with traffic-jammed autostrada: we sit on our thrones and stare off at the beautiful view of San Casciano dei Bagni.

The Etruscans, who came before the Romans, discovered the forty-two springs in this southern Tuscany spot. Industrious nature-worshippers that they were, they built baths. They were also a mysterious sort who performed sheep sacrifices to their gods, then tore out the sheep's liver and studied it, believing the gods put prophecies in that organ. As in: *Long bile duct, the king will reign for many years!*

Reminders of Fonteverde's history are all around to enhance its Grand Tuscan Villa ambience. Etruscan and Roman sculptures line the hallway to the spa. A seventeenth-century portico, built by Grand Duke Ferdinando I de' Medici fronts the main building, and portraits of Medici family members who frolicked here stare out at us from the reception area.

Most of all, this place is focused on the healing waters those Etruscans discovered. There are seven pools that connect to the springs. Some have waterfalls and there's even one for pets who may need relief from arthritis or whatever is ailing them.

"All my life I grew up drinking this water to cure everything," the very beautiful spa employee, Federica Damiani, told me. "And my ninety-eight-year-old grandmother, she's cured her cataracts and arthritis with it."

We checked in for a few nights and every morning Kristin and I down a cup of the rotten egg smelling water from a spa fountain. It's the only thing here that doesn't taste heavenly. The fancy dining room does a fantastic job with Tuscan classics like Chianina steaks or tagliatelle with porcini mushrooms. There's even a wine-tasting room to try samples of the best vintages of the region.

www.fonteverdespa.com

We eat and drink guilt-free because we are detoxing with all this water! After an hour of *bioaquam*, we leave our thrones and head to a dimly lit room with a star-painted ceiling for *thalaquam*, where we float in a saline pool for twenty minutes. Then it's *salidarium* time: we lay down on a bed of salt crystals with a warm heavy blanket over us. Oh so sublime.

There's a lot of scientific study going into body-mind-soul balancing treatments at Fonteverde, which bring techniques from Eastern medicine in to the traditional Mediterranean spa deal. There are yoga classes, guided meditations, even an iridologist who shines a magnifying light in my eye and prescribes a whole list of herbs she says will give me a boost. A masseuse has me sniff crystal waters and oils pre-treatment. *Am I in California?* Then I get to the lunch buffet, which along with heaping helpings of good-for-you vegetables, has a lavish spread of Tuscan cheeses, frittatas, pastas (like spinach-stuffed ravioli), focaccia, fruit crostatas, and wonderful wines. Phew, I am in Italy.

I was skeptical over all the talk about the reactivating energy these waters and treatments would give me. That is, until I left and landed in Florence. For the whole week after my Fonteverde time, I was on the run, an unstoppable art fiend from dawn till dusk. Now I'm a believer.

Fonteverde Natural Spa Resort: Fonteverde is also available as a day spa, so if you're in the area, go take the waters and have a fabulous lunch.

50 *Grand Hotel Abano Terme–Veneto*

I CAME HERE FOR THE WINE THERAPY. Wine therapy is not downing a bottle, having a good cry, and healing your inner child. Wine therapy is a super ingenious body treatment invented in this place east of Venice. While all the region's winemakers are using the vineyards to produce such favorites as prosecco and amarone, these spa scientists have different ideas about the grape.

Which is why I am lying here as Lianna paints me with slick goo from toe to neck. The goo is made from fermented grapes and contains a *prezioso* ingredient: *resveratrolo*. *Resveratrolo* that will exfoliate me, anti-inflammatory me, re-collagenize me, and pump up my serotonins so my mood will be lifted. It's the "aroma-emotional path" of the **Grand Hotel Abano Terme** and I am on it.

"Your miracles, Abano, give speech to the mute," sang Claudius when he soaked in the waters here thousands of years ago. Roman emperors, thrilled to find 130 thermal springs in the surrounding Euganean hills, built baths. They slathered themselves with mud and sang the praises of its miraculous healing properties. They indulged in their own version of wine therapy, guzzling it and honoring Bacchus. They named this spot Abano, from the word *aponos,* without pain.

Now what you find here is *termalismo moderno,* modern thermalism that puts a cutting edge style on what Romans adored in olden days. Thermal waters pump through hydro-jets in curative Jacuzzis. Mud is treated like wine, maturing in tanks so it develops algae that has unique anti-inflammatory properties. And as for the grapes, it's all about extracting that miraculous *resveratrolo.*

The Grand Hotel Abano Terme is the only five-star amidst the many hotel/spas to choose from in Abano. Here the focus is anti-aging treatments. I winced as I put myself in for it, being from Los Angeles, land of the obsessive quest for eternal youth, where places like this can get awfuly pushy and expensive. But there's a kinder, gentler spirit to it here. The three-hour high-end wine therapy, that went from that *resveratrolo* to mud-packing to massage cost me about a third of what I'd pay for anything that would come close to it back in the States.

www.gbhotelsabano.it

Why haven't we Americans heard of this place, when the Germans and Russians are joining the Italians to fill it up? Because the town of Abano gets a grade of charm-minus. The forested hills that surround it are lovely, but it was built up for tourism in the 1970s. Its streets are lined with concrete-block multi-storied hotel/spas, like a low-key Vegas. Everything is neat and tidy, prettily landscaped with palm trees and other tropical plants. But there's zilch old world ambience or fabulous art like you'll find in abundance everywhere else in the Veneto region. The appeal here is the bargain deluxe digs, extraordinary spa treatments, and lovely service every step of the way. It's a great base to explore the treasures of Padua (ten minutes by train), or the hotel can arrange for you to get to prettier places nearby and go horseback riding or golfing.

The Grand Hotel Abano Terme is grand in an Empire Louis XIV meets Sheraton-of-the-1970s way. There are grand chandeliers all over the place, my room is humongous with all mod-cons and a beautiful bathroom done up in marble. The meals are lavish buffets, loaded with fresh fish, lots of nicely prepared vegetables, and the finest Veneto wines.

There are also corny details to add amusement. Right off the lobby is a formal glassed-in smoking room—in a spa! Opposite it is a matching room furnished with felt tables for card games, where I got a nostalgic hit thinking of my mother's bridge club, when I peeked in to see a senior-citizen foursome enjoying themselves. At dinner, there was a fashion show, where sleek-haired goddesses with legs up to their ears strutted around modeling furs—a big business for designers of the area.

The stellar thing about this place is excellent treatments for excellent prices. When I arrived home a week after my wine therapy, and met my friend Monica for a welcome back glass of wine, the first words out of her mouth were: "You're glowing!"

Grand Hotel Abano Terme: Specializes in anti-aging treatments. For special offers check www.abanograndhotel.it.

51 L'Albergo della Regina Isabella Spa— Ischia, Campania

SOAKING IN A JACUZZI OF WARM mineral-rich water until your fingers get pruney and your bones turn to rubber is a divine way to bliss out at **L'Albergo della Regina Isabella** in Ischia. Get a room with a private terrace, where from your outdoor tub you watch fishing boats float by and the only sounds are the lapping of the sea and the occasional church bell.

Queen Isabella of Spain came to these springs in the nineteenth century, pregnant and needing R&R. Before her visit the waters were named after Santa Restituta, a Christian martyr whose body washed ashore nearby in the third century, but the Queen's stay was apparently such a major deal they became known as Regina Isabella in her honor.

Women have left their mark all over Ischia. As you ferry in from Naples, you'll see the castle of Vittoria Colonna, a beloved Renaissance poetess, who surrounded herself with an elegant court up there. She later moved to Rome where she became Michelangelo's soul mate and he wrote poems to her, addressing her as "thou spirit of grace." In the town of Forio, Lady Susan Walton, who came to Ischia in the 1950s, welcomes visitors to her award-winning exotic gardens, La Mortella.

Anywhere you land you'll find places to luxuriate in hot bubbling pools and mud baths. My writer pal Maxine Albert (a woman of exquisite taste) insisted I head to Lacco Ameno and check into L'Albergo della Regina Isabella. The sprawling Spanish-style resort was built by film producer Angelo Rizzoli in the 1950s over the ruins of ancient Greek and Roman baths. It immediately became a hot spot for celebrities like Ava Gardner, Gina Lollobrigida, and Anna Magnani. These days it still has a mid-century retro vibe and is one of the island's most exclusive places, hosting an international film and music festival every June, with outdoor movies and concerts.

The atmosphere is a comfy combo of laid-back resort by day and old-world formality at night. In other words, you pad around in your robe to the downstairs seaside dining room for lavish breakfast and lunch buffets between ocean dips, spa treatments, and lounging on the dock with a good book. If you're feeling more energetic, you can stroll through the sweet town or the hotel can arrange a boat rental. Evenings get fancier, when ultra-attentive waiters fawn over you with French service, presenting refined dishes of fresh seafood.

The Regina Isabella Spa and Medical Center is rated as one of the best in the world because the waters of this particular area are highly radioactive. Radioactive sounded scary to me at first, but apparently this a good kind of radioactivity that makes the baths exceptionally therapeutic. Marine and volcanic mud is matured in pools for one year, and the staff of fifty top-drawer pros gives the huge facility a crisp clinical feel. You can get anything here from cures for respiratory or arthritis ailments to Reiki to anti-aging treatments.

After a mud facial, my skin felt soft as a baby's. The hot stones massage was sublime. "You slept for an hour," the *signora* whispered as I got up from the table in a most pleasant fog. I floated back to my room, stepped out on the terrace into that

www.reginaisabella.it

bubbling hot tub and watched the sun slide into the sea, turning the sky pink.

L'Albergo della Regina Isabella Spa: Piazza Santa Restituta 1, 081 994 322. Known for its ultrashape procedures, a non-invasive fat reduction and body contouring solution.

TIP: *If you're taking a day trip to Ischia from Naples, nearby there's* **Negombo Spa Park** *(www.negombo.it), a lush oasis featuring sixteen different pools, where you can check in for soaks and massage, or get in on a deal next door at the modern, sleek,* **Hotel della Baia**, *where low rates include entrance to Negombo.*

Masseria Torre Maizza—Puglia

I'M LYING ON A MASSAGE TABLE, feeling like Cleopatra, getting rubbed with warm olive oil. Here in Puglia, it's the most logical thing to use. All around are old olive trees, lots of them from 700 years ago. Their thick, gnarled trunks twist up like sculptures from shimmering green fields, with the calm Adriatic Sea as a backdrop.

Athena, Goddess of Wisdom, is the gal responsible for olives. She and Poseidon were fighting over who should rule the Greek region of Attica when Papa of the Gods, Zeus, stepped in and said, "Whoever brings the best gift to humanity gets the job." Poseidon stuck his trident into the earth and out popped a galloping horse. Pretty impressive. Then Athena stuck in her trident and out popped an olive branch, which must have looked puny by comparison.

But then the goddess talked her way through it: "This will grow into a tree that will live hundreds of years. There will be fruit on it, wonderful to garnish martinis. And the oil from that fruit will be what humanity will go crazy over. They'll light lamps with it, cure boo-boos, and no good kitchen will be without it. And by the way, this olive branch...will be the symbol of peace." No contest. Athena won. The capital of Attica was named Athens and the Parthenon built in her honor.

Thank you Athena, for this olive oil massage. And for peace. Centuries ago this place where I'm getting my rubdown was regularly invaded by Turks. It was a farm estate and the spa its watchtower, where folks hovered anxiously, looking out to sea for pirate ships. Now it's a most tranquil spot, where not only olive oil, but herbs and vegetables grown on the property are incorporated into their treatments. My friend Sheila is in the next room getting slathered with a creamy paste of fava beans. Sounds weird, but it's an age-old tradition in these parts. Post-slathering, she takes a steam in the Turkish bath (one good thing that came from those mean Turks), and comes out all aglow when we meet up for a Jacuzzi soak.

www.masseriatorremaizza.com

We go back in to get non-traditional (for an Italian spa) Kembiki Do facials. It's an ancient Japanese deal where the sweet technicians "reorganize the facial architecture" according to the write-up. This means such an intense massage they even put on rubber gloves to stick their fingers in our mouths to rub out marionette lines. I'm amazed looking in the mirror afterwards. Maybe I should try this at home.

Like many similar *masserie* (farm estates) in this stretch south of Bari, the Torre Maizza has been luxuriously renovated. Simple whitewashed stone buildings, that were servants' quarters and stables in the sixteenth century, are now spacious suites with arched ceilings, all airy and furnished in elegant style. Mine has a terrace that looks out on a manicured golf course. The walls are cleverly made just high enough so I can stretch out on a lounge chair *au naturale* and take in the sun that shines through palm trees.

All this white and perfect blue sky and sun makes Sheila and me feel extra energized. The air is perfumed with the scent of jasmine and myrtle bushes. Bougainvillea adds a splash of crimson to the buildings. There's an infinity pool a pleasant walk away that looks tempting, but we want to get to the private beach. We have the choice of taking a five-minute shuttle van or riding a horse there, but we decide on biking it, stopping on the way to gawk at those amazing old olive trees.

The sea is calm, shallow, and warm enough for a swim, even though it's October. There's a restaurant that blends right in to the beach, all white of course, and done up with chic bamboo furniture. They serve sushi, but we go for the salt-encrusted *orata*. And why not a glass of white wine from the nearby Locorotondo vineyards to match? We clink our glasses. We feel pretty.

Masseria Torre Maizza: 72015 Savelietri di Fasano, 080 482 7838. The Coccaro Beach Club, open to guests of Torre Maizza, is a happening spot on the Puglia coast in the summer.

53 Hammam–Palermo, Sicily

HOW DID MY FRIEND PETULIA DEAL with the hustle-bustle of Palermo? She stepped off the street into this luxurious and relaxing oasis for a few hours.

It's a dreamy callback to Palermo's Arabic past. In the ninth century, Moors from North Africa conquered Sicily, bringing their sophisticated culture to the city, which included the hammam, or what we call a Turkish bath. The Moors were shocked to see what the Romans were doing: "Bathing in their own filth!" Their cleaning style was a more intimate set-up of heated rooms, where they'd splash themselves with water, then scrub their skin and get massaged with perfumed oils.

This hammam has received rave reviews for giving visitors the calming pleasures of that thousand-plus year-old tradition. It was opened just a few years ago and designed by Andre Benaim, a Florentine who's internationally famous for his theater sets. He stuck to the classic cozy set-up, putting a sleek, magical spin on it. There are lots of candles surrounding two octagonal-shaped heated rooms of shiny white marble. One is domed with red brick and has openings that filter in a pale light. Between splashing yourself, you lounge around on warm marble slabs, going from the *tepidarium*, to the hotter, steamier *calidarium*. It's great for clearing up the respiratory system, sweating out stress, and getting your skin all set for a perfect tan. The pro staff sets you up with pretty water buckets, olive-oil soap, and a scrubbing mitt. All kinds of massages are available—from "comfort soul" to shiatsu.

In keeping with the Moslem way, the hammam is open on separate days for men and women. Over a thousand years ago, when the tradition started, women couldn't get near these places. That changed soon enough, and the bath became the prime spot for gals to socialize, as they could rarely leave the house. Mothers would go to check out prospective daughters-in-law, even kissing them so they could warn their son if the woman had bad breath. The hammam was especially popular in Turkey, where women would throw off their veils, smoke, laugh, and put on makeup. If a husband denied his wife the chance to go, she legally had grounds for divorce.

The scene is not at all as rowdy in this Palermo hammam. The experience ends in the relaxing room, where you curl up on colorful Moroccan pillows and get served herbal tea and sweets made with honey.

Hammam: Via Torrearsa 17/d, 091 320783. Women's days: Monday, Wednesday, Friday (April-November); Sunday, Wednesday, Friday (December-March).

www.hammam.pa.it

VI

Indulge Your Tastebuds

Transplendent flavors await. Not only in restaurants where you're treated to the main events of your Italian days—those course-after-course feasts—but in simpler, one-taste-at-a-time moments. These are the treasured times when you indulge with a focus on just one of the delicious things Italians create so artfully—be it coffee, gelato, chocolate, or wine.

You might pursue your passion for tasting by heading to the country and visiting a winery, where you could be welcomed by one of the new wave of Italy's female wine producers.

Or any day during your visit to any Italian city, from morning until night, you can indulge your tastebuds as you tune into delicious daily rhythms: the morning buzz of activity at the caffè, the leisurely afternoon pace you'll slip into as you stroll down the street with a gelato in hand. Finally there's the evening's relaxed pre-dinner interlude, when you settle in at a cozy wine bar. And Italian chocolate? That's a treat that gives a zing of pleasure anytime.

Savor these simple, one-taste-at-a-time moments, so easily found...

54 *Caffès*

"THE DEVIL'S DRINK" IS WHAT COFFEE was called when it first came to Venice on trade ships from North Africa in the sixteenth century. While wealthy Venetians were having a gay old time getting hopped up on it, pious peeps ran to Pope Clement VIII and urged him to ban it. The Pope figured he should at least have a taste first. He took one sip, declared it would be a sin *not* to drink this delicious gift from God, and blessed it. Now Italians drink 14 billion cups of coffee a year.

Caffès are happening places in Italy. In a Verona caffè in 1983, Howard Schultz looked around at everyone enjoying themselves so much that he went home to America and created Starbucks.

As far as Italy's caffè styles, you have many to pick from for your postcard writing, people watching, Devil's Drink break.

If you're in the mood to go **fancy**, you can splurge in one of Italy's historical caffès, some of which have been around for 300 years. Every Italian city has at least one of these classic places, where you're seated in a jewel-box of a salon and waited on by tuxedoed waiters. All have lists of illustrious travelers who have come before you—from queens to writers like Oscar Wilde to stars like Elenora Duse. They are also great stops for evening cocktails, and offer delicious sweets and snacks. You'll pay a lot less if you stand at their counters, but come on, you're on vacation, so you might as well settle in. You're not going to end up some old lady eating cat food and muttering, "Oh, if I only hadn't spent 10 euros for that cappuccino at the Florian..." Go for it.

If you're feeling more like having the Italian **bohemian** experience, there are caffès that have rich traditions of being gathering places for artists and intellectuals, which are typically also popular with locals.

And finally, if you want to go to a place that's legendary for serving the absolute **best coffee** in each city, I've listed them below. After you elbow in with the natives at the bar for your drink, you can buy a bag of beans to bring home.

Rome

* **Fancy: Antico Caffè Greco,** Via Condotti 86 (near Spanish Steps)
  This caffè was founded by a Greek man in 1760, thus the name. Amidst the elegant surroundings, check out the photo of Buffalo Bill, whose 1906 visit caused a sensation.

* **Bohemian: Antico Caffè della Pace,** Via della Pace 3 (near Piazza Navona),
  From 1891, there's a theatrical atmosphere here—both in the interior dark wood bar and on the patio flanked by ivy-covered walls. In the evenings it becomes a hipster gathering spot.

* **Best Coffee: Caffè Sant'Eustachio,** Piazza Sant'Eustachio 82, or **Tazza D'Oro,** Via degli Orfani 84 (both near Pantheon)

Florence

* **Fancy: Caffè Gilli,** Piazza della Repubblica 39r
  This began as a confectioner's shop in 1733, and moved

here in the early 1900s. Now it's the place to have your espresso in airy *belle époque* surroundings and buy their *delizioso* chocolates.

❋ **Bohemian: Gran Caffè Giubbe Rosse,** Piazza della Repubblica 13/14R
A *caffè storico letterario* (historic literary caffè) where the Italian futurist movement blossomed in the early twentieth century. It's traditionally been a meeting place for intellectuals from around the world, and hosts book signings, art exhibits, and performances.

❋ **Best coffee: Caffetteria Piansa,** Via Borgo Pinti 18r (near Santa Croce)

Venice

❋ **Fancy: Caffè Florian,** Piazza San Marco, closed Wednesday
Opened in 1720, this is Italy's oldest and most divine caffè. Casanova enjoyed coming here because it was the only place at the time that admitted women. When the evening orchestra starts up it feels like you're in a dream world.

❋ **Bohemian: Caffè dei Frari,** Fondamenta dei Frari 2564 (San Polo)
Since 1870, this cozy spot attracts the range from students to local *nonnas*. They also serve beer on tap and cheap wine by the glass.

❋ **Best Coffee: Caffè del Doge,** Calle dei 5 (Rialto) and Ponte del Lovo (San Marco)

Naples

❁ **Fancy: Gran Caffè Gambrinus,** Via Chiaia 1-2
Since 1850, here's where you can sit ensconced in a stunning
art nouveau atmosphere, and enjoy a Viennesse orchestra on
Saturday nights.

❁ **Bohemian: La Libreria delle Donne Evaluna,** Piazza
Bellini 72
A lively caffè, tea salon and book shop, run by the wonderful Lia Polcari. It's headquarters for the Evaluna Association
that, since the 1970s, has been publishing books by women
authors and hosts classes in such things as photography, writing, and shiatsu massage.

❁ **Best Coffee: Mexico,** 72 Piazza Garibaldi

Turin

❁ **Fancy: Baratti & Milano,** Piazza Castello 29
Since 1858, hot chocolate, thick as pudding, is what to order
here, and they've got great housemade chocolates, like *gianduiotti* (hazelnut chocolate) and liqueur-filled goodies to bring
home. My friend Emanuela, a Torino native, called it "the
caffè for *principessas*" when she was a child.

❁ **Bohemian: Caffè al Bicerin,** Piazza della Consolata 5
Since 1763, this teeny, welcoming place has served *bicerin*,
Torino's famous drink of espresso, chocolate and whipped
cream. Though founded by a man, it has been operated by
women since its start. For the last twenty years, charming

Maritè Costa, the blonde woman with the chic bob you'll see poking in and out, has owned and managed it.

❀ **Best Coffee: Lavazza**, San Tomasso 10

RECOMMENDED READING

Café Life series (Rome, Florence, and Venice) by Joe Wolff

55 *Gelato*

THE FLORENTINES CLAIM GELATO WAS INVENTED by the Medici's family architect, Bernardo Buontalenti, in 1565, when he churned it up during a banquet for Francesco I. Coincidentally, 1565 happens to be the same year Francesco married the seventeen-year-old Austrian Duchess Joanna, so I fantasize this was where the great tradition of hubby offering wife ice cream to bring a smile to her face began.

This is just my imagination, because the facts are that Joanna was miserable all through the marriage—homesick for Austria and fed up with Francesco's philandering. He's suspected of poisoning her; she died in childbirth at age thirty, and Francesco quickly married his mistress.

Still I think it's in the best interest of gelato folklore to imagine they had one happy gelato moment together before the crash and burn.

There are countless places for happy gelato moments in Italy, with just a couple of caveats. Be sure to check for a sign that says *Produzione Propria, Nostra Produzione, or Produzione Artiginale*, which mean "homemade" in Italian before you go in. And never buy from a shop that has tubs of yellow banana or bright green pistachio gelato, which means somebody tossed some artificial coloring in there.

Like all Italian food, gelato flavors vary with what's in season and whatever's growing in the region. I've found amazing *cipolle* (red onion) in Tropea, truffle-flavored gelato in Alba, and *carciofi* (artichoke) in Venice. Be adventurous.

Here are some suggestions for the best:

Rome

* **San Crispino,** Via della Panetteria 42 (near Trevi Fountain)
Many call this "Best in the World," beloved for its purist's style: just cups, no toppings, scoopers dressed in lab coats. Try the house specialty, a mix of fruits, nuts, and Marsala wine.

* **Giolitti,** Via Uffici del Vicario 40 (near Pantheon)
So popular even Pope John Paul II got regular deliveries. Always crowded with tourists and natives, do as the locals do and get it *con panna* (with fresh whipped cream), then enjoy a stroll to the nearby Santa Maria Maddalena, the only pure Rococo church in Rome.

* **Old Bridge,** Via dei Bastioni di Michelangelo 5 (near Vatican)
Stop by here for generous scoopage and fantastic flavors to take the edge off the wait in line for the Vatican or Saint Peter's.

Florence

* **Gelateria dei Neri,** Via dei Neri 20-22r (near Santa Croce)
A *signor* who once ran the revered Vivoli now runs this little place nearby, with not only great fruit flavors but delicious profiteroles.

* **Caffè delle Carrozze,** Piazza del Pesce 3-5/r (near Ponte Vecchio)
  The location may seem too good to be true, but this is the first suggestion out of locals' mouths when I've asked "Where's the best gelato?" From what I've tasted they're absolutely right.

* **La Carraia,** Piazza Nazario Sauro (just over Ponte Carraia on Oltrarno side) and Via Benci 24/r (near Santa Croce)
  Another local favorite where the prices are low and quality is tops.

Venice

* **Alaska,** Calle Larga dei Bari 1159 (Santa Croce)
  Owner Carlo is a fanatic who gets his gelato ingredients fresh from the Rialto market everyday and is always churning up flavors of the season, along with great renditions of standards.

* **Il Doge,** south end of Campo Santa Margherita
  In a lively location, typically filled with a younger crowd, here the Crema del Doge, flavored with bits of orange is great, along with the standards and specialties of the season.

RECOMMENDED READING

Gelato: Finding Italy's Best Gelaterias by Michael McGarry

56 *Chocolate*

"LET THEM EAT CHOCOLATE," was the kind proclamation of Madame Reale. There she was, thirty years old, widowed during her first year of marriage, with a three-year-old boy to raise and the Piedmont region to rule from her palazzo in Turin. This was back in 1678 when the French House of Savoy governed the region.

Chocolate came to Italy through the Spanish explorer Cortez, who found it in South America. In Madame Reale's day it was a precious novelty served only to royalty and  priests. When a Turin baker asked her permission to make chocolate for regular folk, I imagine she figured, "Why not?" She probably frequently needed the seritonin fix to deal with the hassles of being a female ruler and wanted to pass on the high to keep her popularity ratings up with her underlings.

The baker began making hot chocolate—a drink called *bicerin* that's still "what to order" in Turin caffès today. A love affair with chocolate began and Turin became Europe's top producer, even inventing a machine that made the world's first candy bars.

Italy's chocolate-making tradition has continued ever since, and you can thank Madame Reale as you visit these establishments:

⚜ **Rome: Moriondo & Gariglio,** Via del Piè di Marmo 21-22 (near Pantheon)
This fairy tale-styled shop near the Pantheon was founded by a family from Turin over a hundred years ago. Sales *signorine* wear old-fashioned lace caps and box up bon-bons, marzipans, or fruit glaces into beautifully crafted boxes at an old world pace...so don't say I didn't warn you.

⚜ **Florence: Vestri,** Borgo degli Albizi 11r (near Santa Croce)
There's a lively energy at this tiny shop where *molto bello* owner Leonardo doles out treasures that include chocolates made with flavors like Earl Grey and chile. The gelato here is *fantastico*, which you should order *affogato*, topped with their to-die-for hot chocolate sauce. Candies are packaged in Tiffany-blue boxes and make great gifts.

⚜ **Tuscany: The Chocolate Valley**
The most exciting developments in Italy's chocolate scene are happening in an area bordered by Florence, Pisa and Montecatini, where since the 1980s artisans have taken on chocolate production like meticulous Tuscan winemakers. It all started with Robert Catinari in **Pistoia**, and now includes **Slitti Cioccolato e Caffè** in Monsummano Terme, and Paul De Bondt who teamed with Cecilia Iacobelli to create a success story in Pisa. The most well known among them is **Amedei**, whose factory outside Pontedera has become so successful it sells to specialty food shops in the States.

www.amedei.it
www.debondtchocolate.com
www.robertcatinari.it
www.slitti.it
WWW.

The creators behind Amedei are Cecilia Tessieri, a brilliant chocolate maker, and her brother Alessio, who takes care of the business side. They were children of Tuscan candymakers with no chocolate experience, who decided to give it a go over twenty years ago, experimenting with great dedication. In 1991, they brought their findings to the pinnacle of the chocolate world, Valrhona in France, and tried to partner with them. Valrhona flatly turned them down.

Insulted but not discouraged, Alessio set out to find the best beans he could to make Amedei chocolate. In Chuao, Venezuela, where a perfect microclimate supports excellent cacao, Alessio took a risk. He offered the farmers three times as much as what Valrhona had been paying them. Now all of Chuao's cacao goes to Amedei. It's what's called Sweet Revenge.

❀ **Venice: Vizio Virtù,** Calle del Campaniel (off Campo San Toma, San Polo)
Award-winning Mariangela Penzo is the master chocolatier of this shop that opened in 2006. Her scrumptious artistic creations include chocolate flavored with pumpkin, artfully designed candies, and hot chocolate, which makes this a fun place to snuggle into on a chilly Venice day.

❀ **Perugia: Home of Baci**
This artsy town in Umbria is home to the famous **Perugina** chocolate company that's now owned by Nestlé. Perugina goodies abound around here, and hard-core types may want to head out to the suburban factory for chocolate-making classes, along with tours, a gift shop, and museum.

Baci, Perugina's most famous chocolates, were invented in 1922 by Luisa Spagnoli, and were an immediate hit when first introduced that Valentine's Day. Luisa, the wife of

Perugina's founder, fell in love with the much younger
Giovanni Buitoni, who also worked at Perugina.
She'd write secret love notes on the chocolates she
sent to Buitoni for inspection. When she died he
renamed her chocolates Baci (which means
kisses) and had them packaged with romantic
musings, in memory of those notes. Which is
why when you unwrap one, you'll find such
Luisa sayings as: *Non esiste salvaguardia contro il senso
naturale dell'attrazione* (There is no safety-net to protect against attraction).

WWW. www.perugina.it www.bonajuto.it www.laboratoriodonpuglisi.it

⚜ Modica: Sicily's Chocolate Center

This pretty baroque town in southeastern Sicily is famous for
its Aztec-style chocolates that are granular, like what you'd
find in Mexico. Its origins go back to seventeenth century
Spaniards who brought over the tradition of grinding cocoa
beans to a paste that's mixed with cane sugar, cinnamon, or
other spices. Top shops are **Bonajuto** (Corso Umberto I
159), that's been around since 1880, and **Laboratorio Don
Puglisi** (Vico De Naro 9), a newer place created by former
pasty chef Lina Lemmolo. Don Puglisi is in a building that
was a *casa di accoglienza*, in other words, a house for women
with criminal records. Lemmolo staffs her shop with these
gals, and their lives have been turned around by chocolate-
making, giving them focus, and a sense of dignity and
accomplishment.

⚜ Turin: Where It All Began

Grace Kelly loved *gianduiotti*, the chocolate-hazelnut candies
of Turin, so much she used them as her wedding favors when

she married Prince Rainier. The creamy candy was invented during a nineteenth-century recession, when cocoa imports were limited. Clever candymakers figured out how to blend the little they did have with the plentiful nuts that grow all over the region.

Peyrano (Corso Vittorio Emanuele 76), near Turin's train station, has been around for almost a hundred years and serves up fantastic *gianduiotti* and dark chocolate that's roasted in olive wood. The award-winning newcomer on the scene is **Guido Gobino** (Via Lagrange 1), whose small shop with a sleek tasting room offers the master's inventions of mint or orange chocolates, and *cremini al sale*, a new hit on *gianduiotto*, perfectly blended with sea salt.

www.peyrano.com
www.guidogobino.it

International chocolate festivals are held in Perugia (October) and Modica (March) each year. For information, go to www. eurochocolate.com.

RECOMMENDED READING

The Great Book of Chocolate by David Lebovitz

Wine Bars

ONE OF THE BEST WAYS TO BLEND into the Italian social scene is to go to a wine bar. They're down-to-earth places, where along with great wines, delicious nibbles are offered, differing from region to region. They make perfect pre-dinner stops or may even fill you up for the evening.

Wine bars are also the best places to buy good *vino* to take home. Most will ship you a case if you fall in love with one of their vintages.

Here are a few favorites:

Rome

In ancient Rome there were *enoteche* at every corner, but as the city transformed, the tradition slipped away. In the 1970s a wine bar revival began in the Eternal City. These days, *enoteche* fill up with working people meeting friends after a long day. Along with your wine, you'll enjoy such delicious Roman treats as *suppli* (deep-fried rice croquettes stuffed with cheese) or pecorino cheese wrapped in chestnut leaves.

* **L'Angolo Divino**, Via dei Balestrari 12, closed Sunday and Monday afternoon

A romantic spot behind the Campo de' Fiori clamor, where you can get great snacks like *tuna carpaccio* or a delicious meal by candlelight along with choice, reasonably priced wines.

❃ **Il Goccetto**, Via dei Banchi Vecchi 14, open 1-3, 5-11, closed Sunday
It's always packed with locals, many filtering out to the sidewalk, aka the smoking section. Order up at the front counter, then tuck yourself into the cozy backroom, and have owner Sergio pair a cheese plate to match your wine.

❃ **Cul de Sac**, Piazza di Pasquino 73
One of the first of the new wave of Roman wine bars, this place has a list of 1,500 vintages. Get there before 9 P.M. to score an outside table and enjoy small plates that easily add up to a meal. I recommend the *involtini alla Romana* (rolled stuffed veal).

And, while we're talking about *vino* in Rome, check out the **Wine Academy of Rome**, that you'll find at the top of the Spanish Steps. There are regularly scheduled tasting events here, and you can even stay in one of their four guest rooms, take classes, and dine well.

www.wineacademyroma.com

Florence

What with all those wonderful vineyards surrounding the city, Florence has a long-standing tradition of wine shops that would always serve their customers glasses of *vino* and snacks. These old-style wine bars are called *fiaschetteria*, from the word *fiasche*, meaning straw-covered chianti bottles. I'll date myself with the sweet memory of turning those bottles into candlesticks to add a romantic touch to a dorm room. Whether you get to a *fiaschetteria* or newer place, you'll be drinking some of the best wines in Italy and eating delectable Tuscan cheeses, salamis, and panini.

❀ **Casa del Vino**, Via dell'Ariento 16/r (San Lorenzo), closed Saturday afternoon and Sunday
This humble place, tucked behind the San Lorenzo Market, hasn't changed since I first walked in twenty years ago. Then I stood alongside the workmen, had a tumbler of wine and anchovy panini, and got an ecstatic feeling that I'd discovered a hidden treasure. It's in every guidebook now and gets crowded with tourists. But the Migliorini family, who's owned it for seventy years, keeps things traditional.

❀ **Enoteca Pozzo Divino**, Via Ghibellina 144r, (Santa Croce)
Though the building is from the thirteenth century, this just opened recently, and is a fun place to really learn about Tuscan wines, and also for tastings of olive oil and balsamic vinegars. The owners, Pino and Antonella, host wine talks, arrange wine tours, and there's an art gallery in the downstairs tasting room.

❀ **Le Volpi e L'Uva**, Piazza de' Rossi 1r, open 11-9, closed Sundays
The sommelier and his partners who run this place are committed to be like *volpi* (foxes) and seek out new, high-quality, small wine producers. Get in on their discoveries that you'll enjoy with gourmet nibbles: delicious cheeses and cured Tuscan meats.

Venice

In the place that does everything differently, here wine bars are called *bacari*, the snacks (including fab seafood) are called *cichetti*, and a drink of wine is called an *ombra*, which means shade. That's because back in the old days, wine sellers in San Marco would move their carts to the shadow of the Campanile to keep their wine cool, and workers would take a wine and panini break there. In warmer months, you'll want a *spritz*—sparkling water and Aperol or Campari.

* **Cantinone Già Schiavi,** Ponte San Trovaso
  On a quiet canal in the Dorsoduro *sestiere*, near a gondola workshop, this classic family-run spot is where old-time regulars go elbow-to-elbow with foreigners. I had my first *baccala mantecato* (whipped *baccala* on toast) here and they've hooked me ever since.

* **Bancogiro**, Campo San Giacometto di Rialto 122, open 11-9, closed Sunday night and all day Monday
  On the east side of the Rialto Bridge, this converted medieval bank is a comparative newcomer on the *bacari* scene. You can sit at outside tables for a Grand Canal view and enjoy innovative *cichetti*, like *carpaccio di branzino* (raw sea bass).

* **Cantina Do Mori**, Calle dei Do Mori 429 (San Polo), closed Sunday
  One of the oldest in Venice, here you perch on a wine barrel with copper pots hanging over you, and have a selection of 600 wines to choose from, along with fabulous *cichetti* such as braised baby artichokes with lemon.

TOURS

Context Tours (www.contexttravel.com) offers wine walks
in each of these cities. These are fun ways to discover the
best places, learn about wine from an expert, and perfect
to join in on if you're travelling solo.

58 *Women-Owned Wineries*

LUCILLE BALL LIFTING UP HER SKIRT, jumping into a barrel, and stomping grapes with the peasants might be the first image that comes to mind when you think of Italian women and winemaking. As entertaining as that is, cut to the twenty-first century's more sophisticated and inspiring phenomenon: Italian women have jumped into the art of winemaking and joined the ranks of the country's top producers, winning awards and high scores in wine journals.

It all started in the 1980s, when gutsy Italian women began to move away from their traditional roles. Instead of simply helping out on their family's farms and with marketing, they enrolled in winemaking schools, often where they'd be the lone  female in their classroom. In 1988, an organization called *Le Donne del Vino* (Women of Wine) was formed, and now it has over two hundred members from all over Italy.

Che coincidenza that ever since that time Italian wines have become some of the most beloved in the world. Not only have women brought fresh insights into production, they've also pumped up the marketing, traveling internationally as multilingual ambassadors for Italy's major export. Big wineries like

Antinori, Lungarotti, Planeta, Argiolas, and Zenato all have women running them or in top-level positions.

If you're planning on visiting wineries, keep in mind that most aren't set up Napa Valley-style with elaborate tasting rooms and souvenir shops. Once again, a woman, Donatella Cinelli Colombini (profiled below), was on the forefront of Italian wine tourism, founding an organization in 1993, called Movimento Turismo del Vino. It now includes over eight hundred wineries which host events throughout the year. The most famous is Cantine Aperte on the last Sunday in May, when these wineries open their doors to the public. For now, even if a winery's tasting hours are posted, it's best to call ahead to confirm or make an appointment.

Here are a few of the many places where women reign:

Tuscany: Val d'Orcia-Brunello

South of Siena, the landscape opens to rolling hills graced with stately cypress trees, stone farmhouses, olive groves, and vineyards. Here's where Brunello di Montalcino, one of Italy's most prestigious wines, is born.

* **Casato Prime Donne, Donatella Cinelli Colombini**
  This place is exceptional for two reasons: It's the only winery in Italy (maybe anywhere) that has an all-female staff, and it produces award-winning Brunello that made history as the first to be designed by an all-female panel of experts.

  Trailblazer Donatella moved on from her family's renowned wine business in 1998 to create two Tuscan wineries. Both have brought her great success, including the Best Wine Producer in Italy award from the Italian Sommeliers Association.

A visit to her Casato Prime Donne, a converted six-teenth-century hunting lodge, is not only a wonderful tasting experience. The grounds have been transformed into an open-air museum, inspiring peaceful wandering. Paths amidst the hilly vineyards have rest spots with contemporary artwork or engraved quotations from winners of the Casato Prime Donne award, given annually to a female who has promoted women's roles in society. Among previous awardees are the Cabrinian nuns and the ballerina Carla Fracci. The engraved quotation on Fracci's signpost says: "Look around, you are in the moral center of the world."

Guided tours in English are available Monday-Friday, and by appointment on Saturday and Sunday.

* **Fattoria Resta, Anna Lisa Tempestini**
"Earthy and soulful," is what I'd call Anna Lisa's Martin del Nero Rosso Orcia wine. I would describe her the same way. Her passion for sharing her passion of the Val d'Orcia, a place she's called home for twenty years, is deep. In only half a day with her, I felt plugged into the spirit, and flavors of this place.

Though she grew up in cities, Anna Lisa is a country girl at heart. She was born in Chicago and moved to Florence with her family when she was four. Her love for wine began when she was nineteen, working in the PR department of Florence's Chianti Consortium and slipping next door to taste top DOCG wines. Yearning to work in the vineyards, she quit her job and headed to the Val d'Orcia.

www.cinellicolombini.it
www.fattoriaresta.it

I meet her twenty years later, with a husband and three kids, living in a converted monastery that overlooks her very own vineyard. We taste her wonderful wine, her olive oil, there's even some balsamic vinegar she's working on. As Anna Lisa is part American, she especially enjoys visitors from the States, and she's sought after for her custom-designed winery tours and cooking classes. "Each tour is an adventure for me, as well as my guests," she said.

My tour included lunch at the **Vineria Le Potazzine**, in the heart of the nearby medieval hilltop town of Montalcino. Wine bottles surround us as we dig into homemade *pici* with *sugo di cinghiale* (thick spaghetti pasta with a sauce of tomato and wild boar). We taste a rich, delicate Le Potazzine Brunello, made by Anna Lisa's girlfriend Gigliola and her husband. *Potazzine* are the little, colorful birds that flit about these parts, and also a word used as a term of endearment for children. As we're sitting there, Gigliola's two young *potazzine* burst in from the school bus. They're wearing matching grape-colored turtlenecks. Full of energy, the girls spin around, kiss their parents, then settle down for lunch. That's just how idyllic life can be around here.

By appointment. Winery tours and cooking classes also available.

Piedmont: Le Langhe-Barolo

West of Alba, the northern Italian town that's famous for its white truffles, is a graceful wide valley of lush vineyards—Le Langhe—where Barolo, the "King of Wines" is produced. It was a woman, Marchesa Giulia Colbert, who made Barolo famous in the nineteenth century. She wanted somethiing better than the wine that was being produced from the grapes growing around her Piedmont castle. So she called in a French wine expert to make wine similar to a Bordeaux. She was so happy with the result, she sent cartloads of it to the King of Savoy in Turin. It became a hit there and all over the courts of Europe.

❖ **Marchesi di Barolo, Anna Abbona**

Anna has been married for twenty-eight years to Ernesto Abbona, whose family has owned this prestigious winery since the early twentieth century. She's a glamorous VIP of the wine world and when I met her she graciously took a break from a meeting with producers to sit with me in the dining room, which she also oversees. By the way, you must make a reservation to have lunch here to enjoy Piemontese special-ties such as *brasato*—veal braised in Barolo. "My husband is home resting from the weekend," she said. "We women are stronger!"

The winery is a grand butter-yellow complex that sits across from the Barolo castle where Marchesa Giulia Colbert once reigned. It origi-nated as the headquarters for the Opera Pia Barolo, a charitable foundation Giulia created to help the town's needy, which the Abbona family keeps going. On a tour, you get to see the original barrels used in Giulia's day, and there's an incredible wine library, with a bottle of Barolo from 1859 as well as shelves that hold vintages from 1938 on up—totaling 35,000 bottles.

www.marchesibarolo.com
www.pira-chiaraboschis.com

Call for appointment and restaurant reservation (017 356 4400).

⚹ **Pira & Figli Estate, Chiara Boschis**
"The Barolo Boys and One Girl" was written on a t-shirt for
a promotional tour for Barolo in the 1980s. That one girl was
Chiara Boschis, who was put in charge of this place in 1990.

Chiara says that since her parents never treated her any
differently than her brothers (who taught her winemaking),
working in the male Barolo world has never been a problem.

Chiara's an exceptionally attractive woman who makes a
silky and refined Barolo. It's won many awards and turned a
spotlight onto this small winery that puts out a limited production. The winery offers accommodations in a renovated farmhouse on the outskirts of Barolo—a perfect agriturismo base to
explore the abundance of delicious wines in the region.

Movimento Turismo del Vino: www.movimentoturismovino.it

TOURS

Terre di Emozioni (www.terrediemozioni.com)—Land of
Emotions in English—is an Italian tour operator that
offers explorations of the wineries of Piedmont.

RECOMMENDED READING

Barolo, by Matthew Gavin Frank; also excerpted in *The Best Travel
Writing 2008* and *The Best Travel Writing 2009* edited by James
O'Reilly, Larry Habegger, and Sean O'Reilly

Adventures in Wine edited by Thom Elkjer

VII

Shopping

One of the reasons Italian vacations are so relaxing is because we allow ourselves to slow down and look at beautiful things. Not only masterpieces in museums, but in shop windows where artisans' craftsmanship is on display. These handicraft traditions have been passed down for generations. Shopping becomes more than piling up souvenirs. You're brushing up against history.

Shopping is also your chance to interact with the natives. You may feel pounced upon when you enter a small store and the owner greets you, enthusiastic to help. You're probably looking at something they've made, or a display they spent hours creating. It's as though you're a guest in their home. So always ask before you touch.

The magic word for Italian shoppers is *saldi = sale*. The second weeks of January and July are generally when *saldi* begin in stores all over Italy. They last a month or so, but you'll get the best stuff if you show up early. And there are **designer outlets** all over Italy, where you can score pretty good bargains. New outlets are popping up all the time, so check out the web site (**www.factoryoutletsitaly.com**) to keep up.

Bargaining is expected when you're shopping at outdoor markets. It's also O.K. to try in a small shop, especially if you're buying in quantity. I use the tried-and-true bargaining style: carry only small bills, go through the show-interest-then-walk-away-get-called-back game. A line that rarely fails is: "I wanted to buy this for my mamma..."

However you play the shopping game, savor the experience, whether you walk away with just a memory, a treasure, or both.

RECOMMENDED READING

Made In Italy by Laura Morelli

Born To Shop by Suzy Gershman

Lo Scopri Occasioni by Theodora Van Meurs (available in Italian bookstores, lists discount places in Italy, written in English and Italian)

The Fearless Shopper by Kathy Borrus

Shoes

WE HAVE SALVATORE FERRAGAMO TO THANK for being the grand-papa of modern Italian shoe fashion. These days his widow Wanda is queen of the company he began in 1938. She's so beloved by Italians they've even named a rose in her honor.

The Ferragamo story is legendary. Salvatore was a man of humble beginnings, the eleventh of fourteen children, born in 1898 in the mountain town of Bonito, outside Naples. He apprenticed with a cobbler there, making his first pair of shoes when he was nine for his sister to wear at her confirmation. He took off for America when he was seventeen, and set up a little shop in Santa Barbara, California, that caught the eye of silent film stars like Mary Pickford. Within a few years he was a Hollywood sensation. Besides designing for movies like *The Ten Commandments*, actresses clamored for his creations to wear off the set. What's always separated Ferragamo's shoes from the pack is that he never wavered from his conviction to combine glamour with comfort. He was so obsessed he even took anatomy classes at the University of Southern California, so he could learn all about the foot.

As for Wanda, she met Salvatore in 1939 when he'd moved his successful business from California to Florence. Always remembering his roots, he was sending money back to help out his Bonito hometown. A doctor from Bonito wrote to Salvatore, telling him he should visit and see all the good his donations had done. When he arrived, Wanda, the doctor's nineteen-year-old daughter answered the door. Since her mother had died, Wanda

 was the lady of the house, and she shyly thanked Salvatore for all his wonderful work. Salvatore turned to his sister who he was traveling with and said, "I am going to marry this woman."

Three months later, Wanda wed Salvatore, who was twenty-two years older. They had six children, lived in Florence, and the retail business thrived, along with Salvatore being named "Shoemaker to the Stars," designing for such beauties as Marilyn Monroe, Ava Gardner, and Audrey Hepburn.

In 1960 Salvatore died of cancer. Wanda was thirty-eight, had no business experience, and could have sold the company. But instead, she took it on, with her eldest child, nineteen-year-old Fiamma, becoming the new creative force. Fiamma, who'd quit high school to learn shoemaking from her father, went on to design the award-winning Vara pump—that fabulous square toed, chunky 3-inch heel number with the grosgrain bow. As the rest of the family joined the business, Fiamma continued to design. Sadly, she died of breast cancer in 1998.

Now the **Ferragamo Museum**, in the lower level of his Florence store, pays homage to Salvatore with fantastic displays, molds he made for the stars, videos, and photos of celebrities showing off their shoes—from Carmen Miranda to Katharine Hepburn to Andy Warhol. It's in a medieval palace that Ferragamo bought in 1938. It even has an original well in a back room, called the Pozzo di Beatrice, named after the girl Dante went gaga over when he first laid eyes on her on the Florence bridge that's steps away from the palace.

Shopping upstairs from the museum is a treat, especially in the boutique, where you'll find limited edition copies of such beauties as the heels Ferragamo designed for Marilyn Monroe for *Some Like It Hot.* You've got to at least try a pair on and have sales people measure your feet like when you were in grade school, and fit you to your exact width.

Ferragamo Museum and Store: Piazza Santa Trinita 5r, open 10-6, museum closed Tuesday.

The list of fantastic ready-to-wear shoe shops in Italy is endless, while finding places that custom-make shoes as Ferragamo did in the old days is becoming rarer and rarer. But here's are a few where you'll find artisans still going at it with Ferragamo's passion:

* **Petrocchi,** Via dell'Orso 25, Rome. Closed Sunday and Monday.
  Bruno Ridolfi has taken over the shop his uncle started in Rome's 1950s *la dolce vita* heyday. He handcrafts classic designs for men and women made with leather that's "like buttah."

* **Giovanna Zanella Atelier,** Calle Caminati 5641 (Castello), Venice
  Giovanna was a student of the famous, eccentric Venetian shoemaker, Rolando Segalin. Her creations show his influence—including wacky styles of curved pointed shoes and ones that look like gondolas. But she's branched out to

include designs that you would wear more often, and can custom-design shoes for you. You may just want to snatch up what's on the shelves of her adorable boutique—from sneakers to evening wear, and even hats and dresses.

❧

Golden Day: Visit the **Ferragamo Museum** and store, stop for wine and a truffle paste panino at **Procacci** (Via de Tornabuoni 64, www.antinori.it), a gem of a six-table place from 1885 that also sells wines, olive oils, etc.

60 *Leather*

WHAT IS IT ABOUT US WHO swoon when we run our hands over a smooth leather handbag and then stick our noses inside for a sniff? Probably it's best not to analyze. It's probably better to just go to leather heaven on earth: Florence.

As you walk through the streets in the Santa Croce district you're hit with intoxicating smells and sights—everything from luxurious coats to purses and belts in appealing styles and colors. Here's where leathermaking in Florence all began, in the days of the Renaissance Artists' guilds, when this was the primo Arno riverside spot for tanning cow hides.

Florence

* **Scuola del Cuoio,** Piazza Santa Croce 16

This store and workshop was once a monastery built by the Medici, tucked behind the Santa Croce church. And by the way, when you stop by to see all the wonders of Santa Croce, notice (as you exit) the statue of Florence Nightingale, who was born here and named after the city.

Shopping at the Scuola del Cuoio has a step-back-in-time feeling, where you can watch artisans at their hallway wooden work stations crafting leather boxes

www.leatherschool.com

or, with torch in hand, magically bordering them with gold filigree. Everything for sale is cut and sewn right here, using leather tanned from Tuscan experts. There are desk sets, wallets, lovely designed purses, and jackets. They have expert tailor services on hand who'll mail your jacket back home after it's fitted perfectly, or you can work with them to have one custom-designed just the way you like it.

❁ **Madova,** Via Guicciardini, 1r, Oltrarno

The Donnini family has been creating leather gloves in Florence since 1919. Their tiny shop, just over the Ponte Vecchio, is crammed with beauteous cashmere and silk-lined leather gloves, that you'd pay twice the price for back home. Customer service is ultra-attentive. You place your hand on a green velvet pillow and the shopkeepers measure and fit you. For a moment, you feel like a queen.

www.sirnipelletteria.it www.giotti.com www.madova.com www.leatherschool.com www.

❁ **Giotti,** Piazza Ognissanti 3-4r, Lungarno North

Directly across from the Excelsior (stop in there for a cocktail!), the Biagiotti family began this stylish shop in the fifties and they carry an amazing selection of high-quality leather designer-look-alike purses at great prices.

Rome

❁ **Ibiz,** Via dei Chiavari 39 (near Campo dei Fiori)

Elisa Nepi, a young Roman artisan, is the designer of every chic thing in this fun shop. She also (bless her) keeps her prices for handcrafted wallets, purses, and belts reasonable. Her parents started the business in 1972, making satchels for local workmen that became popular with backpackers. In 2002, Elisa was all set to fly the coop and become a physical therapist. But when she flunked her university exam, she decided to put her hands into the business and has brought the shop into the fashion limelight.

* **Sirni,** 33 Via della Stelletta (near Campo Marzio)
The Sirni family has been in the Rome leather business for over a hundred years. In this sophisticated, tiny shop, Mamma Rosanna (along with her son and daughter), handcraft exquisite luxury bags, some done up in crocodile or ostrich leather. Roman women adore Sirni for their customized services; you can have them make a purse for you with every compartment you'd ever desire. It'll take a month, since it's a small workshop, but to have something beautifully styled by these folks is worth the wait.

* **Palazzo Fendi,** Largo Goldoni (near Spanish Steps)
You've got to stop in to this shrine to leather and fur. It all began with Adele Casagrande who created a little fur shop back in 1918. She married Edoardo Fendi in 1925 and then encouraged her five daughters to join the business. The Fendi daughters brought a whole new energy to the company, that's turned it into a worldwide famous business.

Venice

* **Raggio Veneziano,** 30124 Campo della Guerra (San Marco)
Anna Maria Urbani and her husband get the finest leather from Tuscany to make purses here, which range from chic cocktail designs to handsome portfolios for men.

* **Fanny,** Calle dei Saoneri (San Polo)
Here you'll find everything from polka dot to fur-lined funky gloves, in every color imaginable. Snatch a pair up to take the Venice chill away.

❧

Golden Day: In Florence, visit **Santa Croce** and shop at the **Scuola del Cuoio**. Eat at **Cibreino** (Via dei Macci 188, 055 2341100, closed Sunday, Monday and August. No reservations, cash only.) This adorable trattoria is the budget branch of the revered Cibreo.

Ceramics

LEAVE IT TO THE ITALIANS TO turn a bathroom tile into a work of art. Vibrant colors and timeless designs turn their ceramics into irresistible treasures.

The craft took off during the Renaissance, mainly in small towns close to hills full of perfect-for-pottery clay. These are the towns to shop in—where you'll see artisans following centuries-old traditions and can pick up ceramics for much lower prices than in big city stores.

The major ceramics towns (over thirty) are scattered up and down the boot and have been officially designated "Cities of Italian Ceramics."

I have to warn you about some of them (such as Deruta and Vietri sul Mare). These places are packed with shop after beautiful shop. In other words, do not take along a not-interested-in-ceramics partner or child. Or plan ahead to have them enjoy themselves at a restaurant as you blissfully poke about. They also generally have ceramics museums, which are great to stop by before your shopping excursions to get an idea of the traditions being followed in each town.

Just like pasta shapes, ceramic styles differ from region to region. Along with every style there's a fascinating back story. One of the all-time most startling comes from Sicily.

If you've ever wandered around the island, you'll have seen planters on balcony ledges that were shaped and painted to look like Moors' heads—mustachioed, dark-eyed, turbaned guys. The legend of the Teste di Moro goes that around the year 1000, in Palermo's Kalsa neighborhood, there lived a beautiful virgin. Like all young Sicilian girls, she was forbidden to leave the house and could only watch the world from her balcony as she tended her garden.

One day, a handsome Moor passed by, looked up, and declared his love at first sight for the young maiden. She instantly fell for him, gave up her precious virtue, and passionate lovemaking ensued.

But then the girl discovered the horrid truth: the Moor was married with children and on his way back to his family. To get her revenge, on their last night together, she slit his throat and cut his whole head off. She put the head on her balcony, scattering basil seeds into it. The plant grew so lush that every girl in town wanted to have a planter just like it. Since cutting off real Moors' heads was awfully inconvenient, ceramic ones were made, and a new design for Sicilian pottery was launched.

Whether you're shopping for a planter or plate, keep an eye out for authenticity. Like Italian D.O.C. wines, ceramics that conform to government standards for following Italian traditions are stamped: Ceramica Artistica & Tradizionale. If it's not stamped and you're determined to get something handmade, check for an unglazed ring at the bottom, which means it's been traditionally fired, and look at the decoration. If the brushstrokes are uneven, it's handpainted. Whatever you do, don't make the mistake my friend Tita did, when she bought a bowl in Positano and didn't discover a "Made in Japan" stamp on it until it was shipped home.

It's impossible to narrow down places for you to shop for ceramics, because Italy is so rich with them they'd fill another book. But do keep in mind such off-our-beaten track ceramic towns, such as **Castelli** in Abruzzo, **Faenza** and **Bassano del Grappa** in the Veneto, and **Caltagirone** in Sicily. In the meantime, I've provided some suggestions...

UMBRIA

Deruta

Italy's most famous ceramic town is chockablock with hundreds of shops. Among the designs you'll find are the *bella donna* (beautiful woman), created in the sixteenth century, featuring profiles of beautiful women. You'll also see *albarelli* (old-fashioned pharmacy jars) decorated in Raffaellesco style, with golden dragons and mythological beasts. These got their name from the artist Raphael, who copied the images from frescos in Roman villas that were excavated during his Renaissance days. Among the loads of high-quality shops, are:

* **Bettini Germano**, via Tiberina 320
  Popular with locals and tourists as *the* place to go for everyday ceramics at great prices.

* **Ubaldo Grazia**, Via Tiberina 181
  One of the oldest family-run businesses in the world, Grazia started out in the sixteenth century making pottery for churches and now their clients include department stores like Neiman Marcus. The shop is huge and my friend Patty tipped

www.terrecottederuta.com
www.ubaldograzia.it

me off that to the left as you enter there are seconds available for discount prices.

Gubbio

In this serene, magical hill town, you'll find a style called *bucchero*, influenced by Etruscan pottery, with a black background and copper-colored decoration. Gubbio is also known for *lustreware*, pottery painted with vivid colors that has an iridescent sheen. Check out:

* **La Fornace del Bucchero**, 10 Federico da Montefeltro
* **Magnanelli,** Via XX Settembre, 31

Orvieto

Along with *bucchero*, Orvieto's styles feature unusual colors like *verde ramina*, which resembles the green oxide of copper church bells. Right next to the magnificent Duomo are these two shops:

* **Mastro Paolo**, 36 Piazza Duomo
* **Ceramiche Giacomini,** 34 Piazza Duomo

AMALFI COAST

This region's lemon trees, flowers, fish, and cobalt sea appear in the *maioliche* found in such towns as:

Vietri Sul Mare

This major ceramic center is known for its beautiful decorative tiles, which are exported worldwide.

* **Ceramica Artistica Solimene**, Via Madonna degli Angeli 7
The Gaudi-style exterior of this huge warehouse sets this
shop apart from the cutesier places in town. The selection is overwhelming, including adorable tableware
featuring animals—from chickens to pigs.

Ravello

* **Ceramiche d'Arte Pascal,** Via della Repubblica 41
In this gorgeous shop right off the piazza, the work
of top artisans includes giant platters which are absolute masterpieces.

For a list of places certified by the Association of Italian Ceramic Cities:
www.ceramics-online.it.

www.ceramichedarte.com

❧

Golden Day: Go to **Gubbio**, not only to shop for ceramics, but
to enjoy this gem of a peaceful medieval town. Eat at **Ristorante
Federico da Montefeltro** (Via della Repubblica 35, 075 927
3949) and stay at **Hotel Relais Ducale** (www.mencarelligroup.
com), a restored Duke's palace.

62 *Jewelry*

As you can tell from the statues of ancient Roman empresses, crafting jewelry has been going on in Italy for a very long time. The tradition not only includes gold and silver, but micro-mosaics, glass beads, and even eye-catching *plastique* costume pieces. Artisans still carve shells or coral to create intricate cameos.

These days, Italian women are enchanted by Dodo jewelry. It all started in 1995, when the Pomellato company created its first Dodo bird miniature gold charm, with a portion of the price going to the World Wildlife Fund in Italy to protect endangered species. Every year since, there's been a new animal, and each symbolizes a sentiment. For example, the Dolphin's is "Take Me With You," and the Frog's is "Kiss me, I am your prince." You can feel just like a native, stopping by one of their shops (found in big cities and major department stores) and creating your own necklace or bracelet with your choice of animals.

Here are some suggestions for beautiful bauble shopping:

Rome

* **Studio Giolleria R. Quattrocolo,** Via della Scrofa 54 (near Campo Marzio)

    This antique jewelry shop has pretty displays of gold, coral, cameos, and gems. But most unusual are the micro-mosaic pieces, created to replicate souvenirs from the days of the

Grand Tour, with scenes of ancient ruins, mythological figures and landscapes.

* **Diego Percossi Papi,** Via Sant'Eustachio 16 (near the Pantheon)
Sophia Loren and Naomi Campbell are fans of Percossi's shimmering, colorful creations. He uses a unique cloisonné enamel technique, incorporating precious and semi-precious gems and pearls into his beautiful designs.

* **Massimo Maria Melis,** 57 Via dell'Orso
You can watch Massimo's staff of goldsmiths crafting exquisite pieces in the back of this tiny shop. He uses twenty-one carat gold incorporated with gems, antique coins, engraved stones, or bronze fragments for designs that are crafted using techniques inspired by the Etruscans.

www.quattrocolo.com
www.massimomariamelis.com
www.faustomariafranchi.com
www.fratellipicini.com

* **Fausto Maria Franchi**, Via del Clementino 98/100 (near Palazzo Borghese)
This award-winning designer creates modern-styled jewelry of silver, gold, and gemstones that has a stunning, sculptural look.

Florence

* **Fratelli Piccini,** Ponte Vecchio 23r
All the jewelry shops on the Ponte Vecchio used to be vegetable and fish stalls. Then the Medicis decided to build the Vasari corridor over the bridge to connect their two palaces. "That stench!" they said to the merchants, kicked them out,

and replaced them with goldsmiths. These days, according to Florentines, the only place to shop among the bridge's many choices is Fratelli Piccini, owned by the same family since 1903 and now run by Laura.

❀ **Angela Caputi**, Via S. Spirito 58r (Oltrarno) and Borgo SS. Apostoli 44/46
This bold designer has been creating fantastic *plastique* cos tume jewelry since 1975. It's high fashion, exotic pop art— fun and colorful.

❀ **Aprosio & Co**, Via S. Spirito 11 (Oltrarno)
Ornella Aprosio creates ultra-feminine crystal and glass bead jewelry, including unique pieces in the shapes of insects.

❀ **Museo Bottego del Maestro Alessandro Dari**, Via S. Niccolo 115/r (Oltrarno)
As I walked by the fifteenth-century building that's home to Dari's shop, I was drawn inside by the sounds of a classical guitar. The player was the master goldsmith Alessandro Dari himself, sitting there in a muscle shirt, surrounded by cases of his jewelry that are inspired by Florentine architecture.
His rings and pendants, shaped like domes or castles and studded with gems, are extraordinary.

www.alessandrodari.com
www.aprosio.it
www.angelacaputi.com
www.

Venice

❀ **Gloria Astolfo,** 1581 Calle Frezzeria, San Marco
There are so many Murano glass jewelry shops in Venice, they all start to blur together. But Marcella and Victor Hazan

steered me to seek out this one that's totally original, with exotic beaded designs that have a playful feel to them.

❧ **Esperienze Di Sara Visman**, San Marco 473B
Visman's Murano glass jewelry is strikingly simple, with colors and designs inspired by Miró and Kandinsky.

Naples

❧ **Giovanni Ascione e Figlio,** Galleria Umberto, 081 421111, by appointment only
Torre del Greco, outside of Naples, is the world's biggest producer of handcrafted cameos. The Ascione family's workshop there (since 1855) is the oldest in town. You can see an amazing display of their cameos in this Naples showroom and shop. They also make elegant, art-deco-styled jewelry using mother of pearl, turquoise, and tortoiseshell.

www.esperienzevenezia.com
www.ascione.it

Amalfi

❧ **La Sirena Di Bellogardo Andreina,** Via P. Capuano 37
My friend Risa (a shopper extraordinaire) discovered this low-key place on Amalfi's main drag, that she said was different from the other cameo shops she'd passed by, that all looked like places you'd find in a mall. Here there was a small selection of pretty hand-carved cameos, signed by the artist. She bought one that had a more sensual take on the classic woman's profile. It's pentagon-shaped and the young woman's eyes are closed, her hair entwined with grape leaves. They're one-of-a-kind pieces, or I would have bought one exactly like it, too.

❧

Golden Day: In Rome, shop at **Diego Percossi**, visit the **Pantheon**, and eat at **Armando al Pantheon** (Salita Dei Crescenzi 31, 06 688 03034, closed Saturday night and Sunday).

63 *Fragrances*

ITALY SMELLS GREAT. Not only the food, gardens, forests, and sea. There's the perfume they make.

The whole perfume-making deal started with monks in the Middle Ages who gathered flowers and herbs from the countryside and turned them into health and beauty potions. Their secret recipes are still used, so as you shop you can get in on the alchemy.

Rome

Within a few blocks from Piazza Navona, you have your choice of three places:

* **Ai Monasteri,** Corso del Rinascimento 72

  A simple two-room spot where dark polished wood cabinets are stocked with varieties of monk-made beauty products, along with chocolates, honey, liqueurs, and marmalades made in abbeys all over Italy. It's been around since 1864 and still run by the Nardi family who started it all when they teamed up with the Benedictine Order.

  Favorites are Antica Acqua di Colonia perfume, a bergamot-and-musk blend created for the 1900 World Exhibition, and soap scented with violets of Parma. Everything is beautifully packaged and reasonably priced, though the white-smocked sales gals are none too friendly.

- **Officina Profumo Farmaceutica di Santa Maria Novella,** Corso del Rinascimento 47
  If you can't get to the original store in Florence, you can pick up goodies at this elegant spot or at least treat yourself to sniffs with the assistance of glamorous shopkeepers.

- **Erboristeria,** Corso Vittorio Emanuele II 140
  A chain that specializes in organic beauty products, including a blissfully light almond massage oil and even scented stationery.

Florence

- **Officina Profumo Farmaceutica di Santa Maria Novella,** Via della Scala 16 (near Santa Maria Novella)
  Don't miss this place. Here gorgeously frescoed ceilings, sculpted columns and arches, stained glass windows, and a staff dressed in chic black takes a shopping experience to a mystical level.

  www.smnovella.it

  The shop was a fourteenth-century Gothic church of Dominican friars, which was turned into a *farmacia* to sell their potions in 1612. Today scent scientists reproduce the monk's recipes and their creations are shipped all over the world. Even though you can now buy their products in Beverly Hills or Soho, nothing beats getting to this source.

  Santa Maria Novella potpourri, a blend of ten different herbs and flowers from the surrounding hills, comes in monogrammed satin pouches and makes a perfect gift. The top perfume choice is Acqua di Colonia, a citrus and bergamot blend created for Catherine de Medici when she went off to Paris to marry Henry II. There's also Acqua di Santa Maria

Novella (aka anti-hysteria water), which was created when tight-corset-wearing gals needed relief from the vapors. Today it's touted as a cure for digestive problems.

❁ **Lorenzo Villoresi,** Via de Bardi 12/14 (Oltrarno)
This ultra-chic shop was created by the forty-four-year-old, cutting-edge Tuscan master, who brings his university studies of psychology and extensive travels in the Middle East to creations of soaps, lotions and perfumes. Villoresi will custom design a scent for you (as he's done for Madonna), or you can stop in to buy sleek pre-packaged items. By Appointment.

www.lorenzovilloresi.it

Capri

❁ **Carthusia,** Via Federico Serena, 28, Via Camerelle 10
This pretty shop embodies the bewitching purity of Capri, with light polished wood floors and white archways, staffed by beautiful salespeople in lab coats.

The legend goes that back in 1380 a Carthusian monk got caught off guard by the arrival of Queen Giovanna D'Anjou of Naples, and ran off to gather flowers all over the island for her. Three days after she left, the monk smelled the vase's water, found it delightful, and went to an alchemist to figure out how to reproduce it. In 1948 a monastery prior discovered the monk's recipe, and got the Pope's blessing to begin the commercial production of Carthusian perfumes.

Everything here is made from Capri's flowers, such as Fiori di Capri, a combo of wild carnation, lily of the valley and oak. And the current award-winning perfumemaker of

Italy, Laura Tonatto, has stepped into the Carthusia picture, creating *Ligea La Sirena,* a light scent inspired by the legend of a mermaid who tried to lure Ulysses to Capri's shore.

૪ૐ

Golden Day: In **Capri**, stroll the **Gardens of Augustus**, continue on the path to **Carthusia**, eat at **Ristorante Villa Brunella** (Via Tragara 24A, 081 837 0122) and stay at their beautiful hotel with a fantastic view (www.villabrunella.it).

64 Lingerie

WINDOW DISPLAYS OF ITALIAN LINGERIE WILL stop you in your tracks. And then you just might purr. There's a range of fantastic styles to content your inner kitty cat—from cutesy to romantic. Or if you're looking for something especially allur- ing, Italy has what it takes to give you the power of Venus's golden girdle, which she'd whip on to attract mortals she had the hots for.

You'll see Intimissimi shops all over. The fun, quality, affordable brand is now carried by Victoria's Secret, but you'll get a bigger variety of selections in Italy, and a chance to elbow in with the natives who adore this company. In the same price bracket, is **Yamamay**, another chain store which gets its name from a Japanese silkworm, and offers flashier designs.

But the real treasures you'll find are luxury Italian lingerie, where silk, satin, lace, and embroidery are combined to make masterpieces. The most famous brand is **La Perla**, which began in 1954 when Ada Masotti, a Bologna housewife, started a part- time business in her home, making corsets for wealthy women. Her son, who was a cardiologist, took over the business and now it's a multi-million dollar enterprise, turning out exquisite cre- ations, with boutiques in big Italian cities and worldwide.

Another top designer is **Flora Lastraioli**, a Florentine company that was founded in 1932 by a family whose great-grandmother was the embroideress for the Grand Duke of Tuscany in the nineteenth century. And there's newcomer **Guia La Bruna** from Torino, who grew up around her grandfather's lingerie company. Guia went on to study design in Paris and brings an elegant vintage look to her styles, incorporating fur and lace. Her company's sales escalated when Charlotte, in *Sex and the City*, lounged around in one of Guia's violet-and-black lace nighties.

All these luxury labels are usually carried in Italian department stores (Coin and Rinascente). Many you can now find in stores in the States. But the most enjoyable shopping experience will be at lingerie boutiques. They're sweet shops that carry these well-known luxury brands, wonderful up-and-coming designers, and the sales help are typically kind and attentive.

Rome

Brighenti (Via Frattina 7, near Piazza di Spagna) is a two-floor old-world wonderland and the prettiest lingerie shop I've ever seen. Crystal chandeliers hang over rooms of dark polished wood, layers of gorgeous lace bras and panties fill shelves and cabinets. Upstairs are racks of gelato-colored silk negligees, displayed with matching jewel-ornamented mules. The dressing rooms, frescoed in pale turquoise and gold, entice you to try something on, and the prices are surprisingly not astronomic.

Florence

The stores listed in the Lace and Embroidery section (**Loretta Caponi** and **Giachi Grazia Ricami**) carry fabulous negligees and robes. But for an lingerie-only experience, head to **Genni** (Via Dei Cerretani 29r, near San Lorenzo).

Naples

You'll find two old-fashioned shops on the chic Via Chiaia that stock colorful selections: **Carmagnola** (Via Chiaia 261), that's been around since 1904, and **Elena Abet** (Via Chiaia 124), from 1840.

TIP: *For La Perla discount wear, head to **The Mall Outlet** (www.outlet-the-mall.com) outside of Florence where you'll also find many other top Italian designer shops. You can arrange for a private driver or van transportation from Florence through their website.*

⁕

Golden Day: In Rome, shop at **Brighenti**, head to the nearby **Via Condotti** if you're up for more shopping fun, then eat at **Palatium** (Via Frattina 94, 066 9202132, closed Sunday) for Roman specialties with a modern twist. Or have a prosecco at the elegant **Caffè Antico Greco**, then hurry back to your digs to try on your frou-frou.

65 Embroidery and Lace

WHY HAS THIS TRADITION LASTED FOR SO LONG? Isn't it way more practical to do this by machine? Thankfully, patient Italian women, dedicated to making life pretty, have kept the tradition alive.

Embroidery and lacemaking began over a thousand years ago as nuns' work, with busy-as-bees holy women decorating priests' vestments and altar cloths. Embroidery came first, in 1000, when Arabs taught it to Sicilian women and then the craft spread to the mainland. Lacemaking eclipsed embroidery in the frou-frouier Renaissance, when the rich nobility wanted it on everything from their tables to their shoes. Lace became as valuable as cash—farm estates were traded for it, wealthy girls' dowry trunks were stuffed with it.

Demand became so great all over Europe in the seventeenth century that middle-class women began to take on the work—it was a good, honest way to make a living back then. Many got sent to lacemaking schools (run by nuns) at age five. They'd start out cutting thread and move on to master a specialty pattern, stitching the same design for the rest of their careers. The work was intense, studios were dimly lit. Many went blind.

Most of the *signore* who craft embroidery and lace today are in their eighties. They learned from their grandmothers, many who were employed in workshops set up during World War I, so women could make a living while the men were off fighting. If you have the chance to watch one of them crafting a small piece that takes hours to create, you'll never balk at the prices for handmade doilies or embroidered tablecloths again.

Here are places where you can get the real thing:

Burano-Venice

The island of Burano has been world famous for lacemaking since the 1500s. The Venetian legend goes that it started when a man who was heading off to sea gave his beloved an intricate piece of seaweed. Pining for him, she took out her needle and copied the design. The more practical story is that these island women were experts at mending their husband's fishing nets, so when lace making came along they took to it naturally.

Now Burano, a twenty-five-minute vaporetto ride from the Fondamente Nuove in Venice, is covered in lace shops. Though many sell machine-made pieces from China or Eastern Europe, the handmade tradition lives on in places such as:

- **Scuola di Merletti** (Lace Exhibition and School), Piazza Baldassare Galuppi 187, closed Tuesday
  Displays of antique lace, a workshop where you can peek in to observe experts, and a store that sells quality originals, makes this a great place to start your Burano shopping expedition.

- **Merletti d'Arte Martina**, Via San Mauro 307
  Come here for lace blouses, in beautiful colors and stylishly designed. And check out their wonderful selection of table linens.

- **Creazioni Monica**, Fondamenta dei Assassini, 686
  Here you'll meet Emma Vidal, an eighty-something-year-old artisan who will proudly tell you about the tray cover she made for Pope Paul VI, that's on display at the Vatican.

Florence–Tuscany

* **Giachi Grazia,** Via Borgo Ognissanti 6r
An adorable, shoebox-sized shop that stocks Grazia's antique designs of luxurious silk lingerie with accents of lace, children's wear, and reasonably priced embroidered tea towels and table linens. She hs been embroidering since the age of eight, and also has a workshop and stores in Chianti.

www.lorettacaponi.com
www.gandolfilaces.com
W W W .

* **Loretta Caponi,** Piazza Antinori 4r
Wow! Seven glorious rooms in the former Palazzo Aldobrandini show off Loretta's awesome hand- and machine-made pieces—from table linens, outfits for newborns that make grandmamas melt, and elegant lingerie. Nicole Kidman and Madonna are fans.

Rapallo–Liguria

* **Emilio Gandolfi,** Piazza Cavour 1
In the elegant Italian Riviera town of Rapallo, you'll find Gandolfi's family-run shop from 1920, with women in the backroom stitching away, turning out refined embroidery and lace that's shipped all over the world. The tradition had its heyday in the nineteenth century, when 8,000 Rapallo women were employed as lacemakers.

Isola Maggiore–Umbria

Taking the ferry to this small island in Lake Trasimeno turns a shopping experience into a fun, step-back-in time adventure. Isola Maggiore is a mini-Burano, with a main street lined with senior citizen *signoras* sitting on rickety chairs making lace. Elena

Guglielmi was the first to open a workshop here in the early 1900s, creating a style called *irlandesi*, that was inspired by her Irish servant.

❋ **Lace Museum**, Via Guglielmi 1, 075 8254233. Easter-October 10-1, 2:30-6, closed November-Easter.
Start here to get to know the island's lace tradition and shop for beautiful handmade creations.

TIP: *Every two years (the even ones) in Tuscany, on the second weekend of September, the town of Sansepolcro becomes the City of Lace, and there's an international showcase of lacemakers.*

᛭

Golden Day: Visit **Isola Maggiore**, by taking the *traghetto* from **Passignano** on the north shore of Lake Trasimeno—it's a twenty-minute ride. Eat and stay at **Hotel Da Sauro** (075 826 168), that serves lake-caught fish, such as eel and trout. The hotel is a rustic 10-room family-run place, near a private beach.

66 *Paper*

IT'S A MYSTERY TO ME HOW T'SAI LUN, a Chinese eunuch, was sitting by a river one day in 150 A.D., saw some plants and a rag floating on the water and thought, "A-ha! I can make paper!" But somehow the genius put two and two together and became China's hero, because they were fed up with drawing on silk.

Cut to the thirteenth century, when Arab traders—who'd wrangled the Chinese to get the secret paper formula—brought it to Venice. Italians went crazy over the discovery. "Alleluia! We're fed up with those stinky sheep skins!"

It was as amazing as the unveiling of the first PC. Europe rejoiced over the new paper world. Guttenberg really appreciated it, because the one Bible he wrote out the old way required skins from 300 sheep. "Let's put it on paper. I'll make a printing press," he said.

And so the Italians, many in Florence, became bookbinders. And being Italian, they wanted to make their books pretty. So they covered them in tooled leather or paper they decorated with wood-block stamps. And they didn't stop there. "What about those pages with all those words.... How about some designs!"

And that is why you'll be wowed by the designs on Italian paper that artisans reproduce to this day. Most of them come from Renaissance times, such as lilies, which are the symbol of Florence. All that marbled paper got popular around 1750, when a company in Bassano del Grappa, north of Venice, produced it and sent it all over Italy.

Here's where you can pick up beautiful handmade paper:

Florence

* **Abacus,** Via De' Ginori 28-30r (near San Lorenzo Market)
  One of the best bookbinding and restoration shops in Florence, they have a line of journals and photo albums covered in tooled leather that look like antiques.

* **Giulio Giannini & Figlio**, Piazza dei Pitti 37r (Oltrarno)
  The Giannini family started out as bookbinders in 1856, then went on to become printers, publishers, and finally top decorative papermakers. This is a big shop with many varieties of designs, lots of marbled paper, and also classy leather desk sets. If you're interested in the secrets of the craft, they offer classes in papermaking.

* **Il Torchio**, Via dei Bardi 17 (San Niccolò)
  Since most of this tiny store is taken up by the workshop, here's a chance to get a look at all the hard work that goes into their fab line of marbled journals and picture frames. This is a friendly, woman-owned business and since it's slightly off the Oltrarno beaten track, the prices are a bit lower than most.

www.aabacus-bookbinding-legatoria.it

Venice

❀ **Cartería ai Frari,** Calle Larga 2948 (San Polo)
Elisabetta Casaburi has been handcrafting decorative paper products for twenty years and just opened this shop in the fall of 2008. She brings a fresh hit to the craft, with playful designs. I like her Moon Journals that are covered in neon pink, yellow, or turquoise paper that's roughly textured, resembling craters.

❀ **Il Pavone**, Fondamenta Venier dei Leone 721 (Dorsoduro)
Here rich colors are blended as brilliantly as those on a *pavone's* (peacock's) tail, then hand stamped on to paper. You can buy sheets of paper (suitable for framing) stamped with patterns from geometric designs to gold-flecked floral prints. Their stationery, decorated with fancy lettered initials, makes for a great gift.

❀ **Paolo Olbi**, Calle della Mandola 3653 (San Marco)
Here's where you'll find the most classic Venetian designs. Olbi is a self-taught artisan, who makes such beautiful things as journals covered with intricately hand tooled leather or Byzantine patterned paper, stationery decorated with etchings of Venetian landmarks, and pens made of Murano glass.

Amalfi

The Valle dei Mulini, adjacent to the coastal town of Amalfi, was a major center of paper production from medieval times until the mid-twentieth century, when a flood wiped out the mills. Amalfi has a paper museum where you can walk through an old factory and get the scoop on how the whole production process went.

And there's:

* **Eva Caruso Paper Shop,** Supportico Sant' Andrea 10 (next to Duomo)
  Eva is a beautiful young artisan who presses flowers and leaves into her papers and makes pretty textured stationery. I love her soft leather journals that she accents with bright flower-shaped pieces.

Museo Della Carta: Via delle Cartiere 24, March–October 10-6:30, November-February 10-3:30.

www.museodellacarta.it

❧

Golden Day: In Amalfi, stop by **Eva Caruso's** shop, see the **Amalfi Duomo,** and eat at **Trattoria Da Gemma** (Via Fra Gerardo Sasso 9, 089 871 345, closed Wednesday).

Milan

SHOPPING IN MILAN IS STEPPING INTO THE FUTURE. Newborn styles, fresh from the showrooms of megastar designers, fill the city's fabulous shop windows. It'll take a while for these fashions to appear in stores back home, so whatever you buy here will be sensational for a couple of seasons.

The city is a teeming cauldron of energy, a fashion kingdom that rose to power in the 1970s. Here Italy's old-time traditions of tailoring and craftsmanship are transformed into a spectacular industry.

And everybody looks so good! Women walk down the street as if they've just stepped off a fashion-show runway. And then there are all those handsome soccer players, as Milan is home to Italy's two top teams.

You'll inevitably begin your Milan explorations at **The Galleria**, the city's heart. It's the world's oldest mall, rising in neo-classical splendor between the **Duomo** and **La Scala** opera house. The very first **Prada** store is the highlight here. Though Milanese call it the "Tourist's Prada," it's still a beautiful place to peek into: two floors of exquisite stuff created from the vision of Miuccia Prada, the reigning Queen of Italian Designers.

Miuccia's grandfather founded Prada in 1913, making leather bags and suitcases. At first, Miuccia (born in 1949) couldn't care less about her family's old-fashioned business. She went to university for a Ph.D. in Political Science and then on to theater school for five years and performed mime in the streets. Yes, you read correctly: Miuccia Prada was a mime. During that phase, she was also an outspoken Communist and rallied hard for women's rights.

In 1978 she inherited the company, which was on the financial skids. The same year, she married Patrizio Bertelli. He took over the marketing, while encouraging Miuccia to design. What she ultimately came up with in 1985 turned Prada's fortunes around: a simple, sleek, black nylon handbag. You never know. Since then, her runway shows have been media sensations, with styles that range from austere to outrageous. Always a lover of the avant garde, Miuccia spreads the mega-fortunes of her company around, with a foundation that supports and exhibits contemporary artists.

The Galleria is fun for a look at Prada and people watching, but for a caffè, I say head to the nearby **Trussardi** (Piazza della Scala 5). It's a sleek, ultra-modern place where you can blend in with the locals.

I hope you have time to head a few blocks from the Galleria to the **Quadrilatero della Moda**, the *zona* that's the high-fashion heart of Milan. If you don't, **Rinascente** department store is right around the corner from the Galleria, with seven floors of everything. Best of all is its rooftop food halls and **Obikà** mozzarella bar, which has a terrace that puts you eye-to-eye with the top of the nearby Duomo.

It's crazy when people compare the Quadrilatero della Moda to Fifth Avenue. This is way more chic, with no H&M in sight. This is the Mount Olympus of Italian designers—**Dolce & Gabanna**, more **Prada, Moschino, Versace**, etc. It's all tucked into a few blocks, centered around Via Montenapoleone, with cobblestoned

streets so clean you could eat off them. The **Armani** superstore
(Via Manzoni 31) at the edge of it, is five floors of modern elegance, a great caffè, and Nobu restaurant. Prices here are in the
stratosphere, but it's still fun to window-shop.

Heading a few blocks away you get to the **Brera** district,
bordered by Via Manzoni, Via Fatebenefratelli, and Via
Bonaparte. Here's where you'll find antique shops and boutique designers—such as the crisp looks of **Patrizia Pepe** and,
a favorite, the romantic, flowing creations of **Luisa Beccaria**
(Via Senato 18).

The place designers love most of all in Milan is **10 Corso
Como**, that's owned by the sister of the head of Italian *Vogue*.
It's about a ten-minute walk from Brera. When you get there,
the mosaic sign up top and narrow entrance gives you the feeling that it's a private club. Then it opens up to this dreamy
courtyard where there's a garden restaurant, and upstairs photography galleries and a huge art bookshop. Best of all is the
warehouse-sized dazzling store packed with designer goodies—
from clothing to housewares. There's even a three-room B&B.
A few blocks away, is the **Corso Como Outlet** (Via Tazzoli 3,
open Friday-Sunday), where items are discounted, but still not
inexpensive.

The best bargain you'll get in Milan will not be while you're
shopping, but at the evening's 'Appy Hour. From six to nine
every night, bars all over the place spread out lavish buffets. For
the price of one cocktail, you can fill up on snacks that will add
up to dinner.

❧

Golden Day: Shop and stop for caffè where your desires lead
you. Get to the roof of **Rinascente** (Piazza Duomo) at sunset,

settle into the terrace of **Obikà** mozzarella bar. A good choice for 'Appy Hour is the **Hotel Sheraton Diana Majestic** (Viale Piave 42), that also puts on a fabulous Sunday brunch.

TOURS

Select Italy (www.selectitaly.com) offers great guided shopping tours of Milan that they can custom-design to your tastes. They also can arrange for special entrances to stores during sales weeks, and private visits to designer showrooms.

68 *Antique Markets*

IT'S WORTH IT TO PLAN YOUR TRIP so you'll be in Arezzo the first
Sunday of the month. That's when this Tuscan town's historic
center overflows with Italy's biggest outdoor antique market.
Five hundred vendors spread out an eclectic mix of treasures
to satisfy your inner huntress. There are carved armoires, can-
delabras, and giant urns. And suitcase-friendly treasures from
vintage linens to jewelry, cordial glasses, faded postcards, and
comic books.

Besides Arezzo, loads of other small towns and cities regularly have weekend antique markets, that aren't as big as
Arezzo's but still grand. No matter where you land, it's
an entertaining shopping experience. There's the
magic of being in a piazza that's transformed into
looking like countless *nonnas* have snuck in before
your arrival and dropped off their pretty possessions,
each piece unique and holding memories of the past.
The vendors are colorful characters—from antique
fanatics to teenagers who'd rather be watching the soccer game and are easy to bargain with.

Most antique markets also have flea market type set-ups at
their borders, so if you need cheap socks, there you go.

A few suggestions among the many:

www.arezzofieraantiquaria.com WWW.

- **Arezzo Antique Market,** first Sunday of every month and preceding Saturday
Besides the best market, right here is Piero della Francesca's stunning *Legend of the True Cross* fresco cycle in the church of San Francesco. Or go on the *Life Is Beautiful* tour, which takes you to spots around town where the movie was shot.

- **Florence: Oltrarno Flea Market in Piazza Santo Spirito,** second Sunday of every month
The Brunelleschi-designed **Basilica di Santo Spirito** is a perfectly pure backdrop for this market. Along with antiques, there are stalls where Florentine artisans sell their latest creations.

- **Rome: Ponte Milvio Antique Market,** first weekend of the month
The neighborhood surrounding Rome's oldest bridge is one of the city's hippest. Historically, it's where Emperor Constantine won the battle that began the Christian era. These days you'll see the bridge's lamp posts covered in padlocks. It's a craze begun in 2006 by the bestselling book *I Want You,* that's inspired lovers to write their names on padlocks that they chain to the bridge. Then they toss the keys into the Tiber, symbolizing their eternal devotion.

- **Near Padua: Piazzola sul Brenta,** last Sunday of every month
This is Italy's second biggest antique market, held in a piazza that fronts the splendid **Villa Contarini**, which you can tour

while antiquing. En route take the opportunity to visit some Palladian villas.

❋ **Near Parma: Antique Trade Market of Fontanellato,** third Sunday of every month
At this castle surrounded by a water-filled moat, along with 300 vendors, you get a chance to see recently restored Parmigianino frescos. It's an 18 km drive from Parma, and bus service from town is available.

❋ **Naples: Villa Communale Antique Market,** last two weekends of every month
Surrounded by gardens, close to the picturesque bay, here's a place where you may find antique crèche figures and if you're lucky, an impromptu puppet show.

❋ **Sarzana, Liguria: National Antiquarian Exhibition,** every August
This annual event transforms the pretty walled town of Sarzana into what's called "The Attic in the Street," with hundreds of stalls. Even if you come here when the fair's not on, there are wonderful antique shops, chic restaurants, and bars.

❋ **Fossano, Piedmont: Città Antiquaria,** fourth Sunday of the month
Pros call this the best antique shopping spot in Italy. It's a huge indoor exhibition center, arranged to look like an old fortified town, where you'll find antiques, paintings, and crafts from all over the world.

www.cittantiquaria.net

List of Italy's Antique Markets by region: Mercantini d'Italia at www.mostre.it/ mercantini.

ಜಿ

Golden Day: Get to the **Arezzo Antique Market** and see *The Legend of the True Cross* fresco cycle. Eat at **Ristorante Logge Vasari** (Piazza Grande 18, 057 5300333), to enjoy rich, innovative versions of the region's traditional specialites.

RECOMMENDED READING

The Antique and Flea Markets of Italy by Marina Seveso, translated by Oonagh Stransky

VIII

Active Adventures

Mother Nature poured a heaping helping of beauty on Italy, then spread glorious days of sunshine on top of it. You could sit back on a terrace and admire its seas and lakes, rolling farmlands, volcanoes, and majestic mountains. But it's even better to get up and into it for a knock-out sensorama experience.

Outside the cities, you'll have the chance to be hiking in Italy's golden light that poets have praised. You'll stop and smell the lavender. Or maybe you'll be diving into cool waters off the coast of Ponza, in a cove you discovered as you were circling around it by boat. You could be in the Dolomites, warming up with a sip of fiery grappa after an exhilarating day on the ski slopes.

Inevitably, the countryside brings with it the chance to experience the natives' warmth and generosity. As in one May afternoon in Puglia when I was riding a bike past a cherry tree grove. I stopped to take pictures and a ninety-something-year-old farmer walked over, took two handfuls of just-picked cherries from his bucket, and put them in my bike basket.

That's just a for instance of the sweet surprises that will likely come at you when you get into exploring Italy as an active adventurer.

Biking

I GET AN "I'M FREE!" rush whenever I take off on a bike. That feeling, plus the Italian atmosphere, equals pure bliss. Italians bike with passion. You'll see everything from *nonnas* cycling through village markets to super athletes who compete in the Giro d'Italia Feminile, one of the world's most famous women's bike races.

There are loads of ways to blend in with Italy's cycling culture. You can be the chic *signorina* gliding into the piazza in **Ferrara**, nicknamed "The City of Bicycles," where about a third of the population gets around on two wheels. You can take off for a day ride through the **Chianti** region, surrounded by vine-  yards. If you're feeling all woman warrior, you can get an endorphin rush mountain biking through the **Dolomites**.

For an easy, whimsical experience, go to Lucca, Tuscany:

Going to Lucca and not biking along the top of the town's old wall is like going to Paris and not visiting the Eiffel Tower. The thick wall took over one hundred years to build back in Renaissance days. After all that Lucca was never attacked, but now the top of the wall is being put to fun use.

This 3-mile/5-km loop, shaded by tall trees, makes for a flat easy ride, with views of Lucca rooftops down below, backyards where the locals don't mind you clicking photos of their laundry waving in the breeze, and fields of wildflowers. It's perfect for families. Even my friend Cheryl's five-year-old did the ride with no problem.

If you're feeling more adventurous, Group Biking Trips:

Choose your region, and take off for a week-long biking adventure. There are many companies out there offering trips for all levels of riders.

Not an experienced long-distance biker, I signed up with **Backroads** to go to Puglia, attracted by the words: "Puglia is Italy's flattest region." I loved it so much I went back the next year to southern Sicily where there were more hills. Both were fantastic weeks. We were pampered by excellent guides, with ingenious routes that took us through farmlands and small towns for lunch and gelato breaks. Backroads supplied the bikes, great snacks, and a support van rode alongside so if we pooped out we could hop in. I had the freedom to lag behind and talk with the local farmers or speed up and join the more athletic of the group. Accommodations were in farmhouses or fortresses that had been converted to luxury hotels, with nightly feasts. There was loads of good eating, but with all the exercise, I didn't gain a pound.

Backroads also custom designs itineraries if you want to do something really fabulous like set up a private trip with your girlfriends for a reunion or big birthday.

If you're independent and up for a bigger challenge:

Here again you also have lots of choices of companies, such as **Randotrek**, that helps to arrange self-guided biking tours of

www.backroads.com
www.randotrek.com

Italy, providing bikes, maps, and a service to move your luggage from hotel to hotel.

TIP: *Team Estrogen (www.teamestrogen.com) has the most fabulous selection of biking ensembles, so you can be stylish and comfy on the long trips. And thank you Diana from **Backroads** who told me, "Don't wear panties with those bike skorts, the padding works better without them."*

❧

Golden Day: In **Lucca**, rent a bike at **Antonio Poli Bicicletta** (Piazza Santa Maria 42) to circle the town's wall. Eat at **L'Antico Sigillo** (Via Degli Angeli 13, 058 391 042), a casual family-run place that serves delicious pizza and pasta.

RECOMMENDED READING

Lonely Planet Cycling Italy by Ethan Gelber

Hiking

EXPERIENCING ITALY ON FOOT IS THE perfect way to savor every detail, get peace of mind, and a good fragrant hit of nature while you're at it.

You don't even have to be a gung-ho hiker to do it. In Rome you can get your endorphins going with a half-hour uphill walk from Trastevere to the **Janiculum Hill** or in Florence wind up to the **Piazza Michelangelo** and beautiful San Miniato church. Both reward you with fabulous city views, and are easy ways to get a break from the tourist crowds.

If you're up for real hiking, you can:

Enjoy the Coast

The most popular hiking place in Italy for American travelers is the **Cinque Terre** on the northern Ligurian coast. There, the **Sentiero Azzuro** (Blue Path) connects five enchanting seaside villages. You can do the one-way walk (starting at Riomaggiore) in five to six hours, then take a ferry or train back to your starting point. But a better idea is to settle in for at least a few nights for beach and boating time.

Two of my gal friends rave about **Manarola**, which they say is the best village of the five to stay in. "I thought I was over hostels," Lauren told me. But she makes an exception for

www.hostel5terre.com

Hostel Cinque Terre (018 792 0628, reservations a must), that has a fantastic rooftop terrace and rooms with private baths. Hope (a girlfriend of many exclamation points) sings the praises!!! of **Trattoria dal Billy** (018 792 0628, reservations a must), a seven-table restaurant where Billy's mamma cooks up such great things as fried shrimp or pesto. By the way, pesto is absolutely what to order in these parts, where it was invented.

Guidebook writer Rick Steves made the Cinque Terre famous so these days it's best to avoid it in summer high-tourist season, and no matter when you come, reserve your digs well in advance and be prepared to pay a fee (three euro) to get on the hiking trail. As far as how challenging a hike it is, the first leg (from Riomaggiore to Manarola) is flat enough to be done with a baby stroller, and then things get progressively steeper and harder as you go along. It's all glorious.

My favorite coastal hike is the **Sentiero degli Dei** (Path of the Gods) above the Amalfi Coast. Here steep paths, that were once used for mules to bring goods to the mountain villages, take you through lemon groves, forests, and vineyards. You get great views of the candy-colored villages below that stretch out to the tantalizing sea horizon.

But even with a map, parts of the Sentieri degli Dei are not easy to follow, so to the rescue comes **Francesco Carpegna**, an energetic, silver-haired ex-New Yorker who's lived in Positano for twenty years and created a company called **Walking with the Gods**. He can be booked to lead your hike and along the way he'll fill you in on the many legends that surround this amazing stretch.

Mountain Towns

Umbria and Tuscany have loads of well-marked trails, with good maps available at small town tourist offices. A favorite starts in

Spoleto, leading you up to where Saint Francis gave his famous Sermon to the Birds.

National Parks

There are over a hundred to choose from, including the **Gran Paradiso** (in northern Piedmont and Valle d'Aosta) that has everything from glacier walking to paths specially designed for the disabled. A two-hour drive east from Rome takes you to **Abruzzo**, where wolves and bears are kept in ingeniously designed zoo reserves. My friend Maria loves hiking **Lo Zingaro**, in Western Sicily, a park with trails along rocky seaside cliffs that lead to quiet pebbly beaches.

www.parks.it

Group Hikes

If you're up for a week of hiking with a group in a particular region, **Country Walkers** offers choices all up and down the boot, with excellent guides, accommodations, and meals included. "Not having to make any arrangements makes it a great vacation," Mona Lou McConnaughey, who's been on several trips with the company told me.

Another Country Walkers veteran, Jill Clark, went along with her sportier husband through Tuscany and loved that there were side trips to wineries and artisan workshops. "It was my first time in Tuscany, and it was wonderful to get into places we never would have seen if we were traveling on our own."

These are perfect trips for families. With everything so well taken care of, nobody can whine to Mommy, and bonding goes on among the different generations, often leading to life-long friendships that began on the shared adventure.

TIP: *Club Alpino Italiano offers hiking maps for Italy (www.cai.it).*

❧

Golden Day: From **Positano**, hike the **Sentiero degli Dei** to **Montepertuso**. Have a delicious lunch at **Il Ritrovo** (089 875 453), where Salvatore cooks up dishes such as ravioli with tomatoes and basil that come straight from his garden. Sleep in Positano at **La Rosa Dei Venti** (www.larosadeiventi.net), where you can relax on your balcony after all that hiking.

TOURS

Walking with the Gods (www.walkingwiththegods.com) leads guided hikes in Sentiero degli Dei.

Country Walkers (www.countrywalkers.com) offers guided hikes throughout Italy.

RECOMMENDED READING

Walking in Italy by Sandra Bardwell
Songbirds, Truffles, and Wolves by Gary Paul Nabhan

Skiing

FOR THE MOST DELICIOUS AND LEISURELY ski experience, you've got to come to Italy. The day typically begins around ten-ish, with a stop at a caffè, and then along your ski path you can stop at restaurants and *refugios* (wooden huts) where for lunch you could go gourmet (lobster) or rustic (pizza from a wood-burning oven). Top it off with the best of the region's wines or prosecco, and then you're back on the slopes until late afternoon. Why push it when the après ski scene—spas, shopping, and evening jazz or disco-is such fun?

You can score a bargain package of this routine by going in for a *settimana bianca* (white week), which Italy's ski resorts regularly offer.

Where? With all the mountains and volcanoes, there is skiing in every region. Doing Sicily's Mount Etna could be exciting or you could take off on the slopes of Abruzzo's national parks. But the best is on those glorious mountains at the top of the boot, where you can ski from November to mid-April.

Bormio, Lombardy

When Sara Chamberlin, from Milan, had to pick the perfect place for her girlfriend's bachelorette party, she chose Bormio. This place near the Swiss border in the western Dolomites is not only great for skiing, but it has an equally *splendido* attraction:

natural thermal springs. Picture it: outdoor steaming pools you can relax in after ski time, right in the midst of snow-covered mountains.

The **Hotel Bagni Vecchi** is the place to be based to get the best of them. "It's amazing, there's nothing else like it in the world," Sara said. The twelve-room converted convent is built right into the mountain. Its spa has thirty areas, some that incorporate original Roman bath structures, others are tiny natural caves, and you can even go into one that's built into the mountain, directly where the water springs from.

The skiing is fab, with a 5,000-foot vertical drop and twenty-four lifts. The runs are good for beginners and intermediates, without many super-challenging ones, so head to nearby Santa Caterina and Livigno if that's what you're looking for.

In spring folks come here to mountain bike, golf, or use it as a base to ski at nearby Stelvio Pass, where there's always snow. Whenever you come, ski or bike to **Baita de Mario** for specialties like *pizzocheri* (buckwheat pasta with cabbage and fontina cheese), *breasola*, and the rustic red wine of the region: Valtellina Superiore.

www.bagnidibormio.it
www.bormio.ski.com
www.baitademario.com

The town of Bormio has a chic pedestrian-only center of zigzag cobblestoned streets filled with fun shops and both Romanesque and Renaissance architecture. And how about a grappa tasting? You'll have much more than a skiing vacation here in Bormio.

Alta Badia, Alto Adige

Here's a Tyrolean Italy. You'll hear German, Italian, and Ladin—a language that's existed since before the Romans came,

which about twenty thousand natives still speak. The area originally belonged to Austria until after World War I, so a lot of the
architecture is chalet-style—old farm huts, which blend in with
the green meadows and rugged eastern Dolomite Mountains.
On menus you'll find unusual dishes like venison carpaccio, and
a full-bodied, bright red wine called Lagrein.

What's wonderful about Alta Badia is that there is so much ski
area. It's made up of six rural hamlets, so you can ski from
place to place, with hundreds of runs to choose from.
It's perfect for families-with a renowned ski school
that teaches all ages, a nursery to take care of the little
ones while you're getting snow time, and cross-
country paths. There are also sleigh rides and horse
shows. This all sounds very folksy, but there's a
sophisticated edge-three Michelin starred restaurants
in the area.

www.altabadia.org

"And you should see the men! They have beautiful
blue eyes…. I even saw George Clooney there, at Rosa Alpina,
playing cards and drinking wine with the hotel people," says my
friend Marzia, who comes here from Rome. Marzia e-mailed me
a photo to prove it, full of many exclamations!

❧

Golden Day: In **Alta Badia** (www.altabadia.org), base yourself in
the village of **Corvara** at the **Hotel Posta Zirm** (www.postazirm.
com), which has a Feng Shui-designed spa with a huge pool. Eat
at **Club Moritzino di Moritz Craffonara** (Piazza La Ila), where
Marzia recommends the five-course dinner with fresh lobster:
"Eating seafood up there at 4,000 meters is amazing!"

Boating

WITH 4,536 MILES/7,300 KM OF COASTLINE, gorgeous lakes, and all those enchanting islands, Italy has opportunities *amundo* for

boating adventures. Getting out on the water gives you a chance to change your perspective and take in the landscape like an old-time explorer. Rentals of everything from canoes to 40hp boats can be arranged without a license, but if you'd rather not boat on your own, there are plenty of natives available who will take you around—stopping at choice spots for swimming, fishing, and snorkeling. A few primo places to boat are:

Ponza, Lazio

My Roman friend Gioia gets ecstatic talking about renting a *gozzo* (old-fashioned wooden fisherman's boat) to circle this small island. Ponza, part of the Isole Pontine chain, has long been beloved by Italians, but it's still virtually undiscovered by Americans.

It's coastline is an enticing mix of chalk-white cliffs, emerald grottoes, tiny bays, and mysterious tunnels, surrounded by clear, deep turquoise waters. Most of its beaches can only be reached by boat and the sea is perfect for snorkeling and diving.

A sublime boat ride east from Ponza takes you to **Palmarola**, a tiny, craggy island covered in dwarf palms, where you can drop anchor and have lunch at **Cala del Porto**.

"Just avoid weekends in July and August, when Ponza's mobbed," Gioia says. This is the perfect place to enjoy a three-day (at least!) idyllic break from the mainland. It would combine well with a trip to Rome.

Lake Como

It's heavenly to get on a boat and admire the shoreline view of Lake Como's elegant gardens and villas, backed by the snow-covered Alps. In **Domaso**, on the north end of the lake where winds are best for sailing, you can arrange to rent a sailboat through **Como Lake Boats** or a motorized rubber dinghy from **Blue Easy Rent**. In the southern town of **Lezzeno**, below Bellagio, **Matteri Cantiere Nautico** is a family-run boat building and rental business that's been around since 1860. Among their many selections is the traditional boat of Lake Como, the *Lucia*, named after the heroine of *I Promessi Sposi*, a classic nineteenth-century historical novel.

www.comolakeboats.it
www.blueeasyrent.it
www.matteri.com

Elba

Up for a week of sea kayaking to explore the hidden beaches, intricate rock formations, and fishing villages of Elba? Barbara Kossy of **California Canoe & Kayak** arranges group trips to this bewitching island off the coast of Tuscany. It's what she calls, "Soft adventure, the cross-country skiing of kayaking."

Travelers are based in the cozy town of **Marciana Marina**, and each day explore a different part of the coast by kayak. "It's a great social experience," Barbara said, "not only within the group, but lots of times we're joined by kayakers from Italy and other parts of the world as we go along." There's also fun to be had swimming, at group dinners, and hiking through olive groves and vineyards. And there's a row out to **Isola Paolina**, named for Napoleon's sister, aka "Elba's first female nudist."

Best of all, you get to experience the island as the natives do. Leading the trips is Gaudenzio Coltelli, owner of **Sea Kayak Italy**. He grew up on Elba and knows every inch of the island. As far as kayaking here goes, you couldn't dream up a better guide.

www.calkayak.com
www.seakayakitaly.it

❦

Golden Day: Get to **Ponza** by taking an *aliscafo* (fast ferry) from the coastal town of Anzio. Rent a *gozzo* and stay at **Gennarino a Mare** (www.gennarinoamare.com), a hotel on stilts that also has an excellent restaurant.

73 Yoga and Pilates

IMAGINE IF INSTEAD OF RUSHING BACK into traffic after your yoga class, you're in bell'Italia strolling through a mountaintop village...or swimming in a pool with vineyards surrounding you... or taking a walk through a meadow full of wildflowers.

Masterful minds from the United States and United Kingdom are one step ahead of your fantasies. They've followed their bliss and created programs that cover all the bases when it comes to combining yoga or Pilates with the pleasures of Italy's peaceful surroundings.

Each of the programs below is open to beginners or long-time practitioners, classes are small so there's lots of individual attention, and prices are affordable.

Whether you want to stop by for a few days on your own or sign up for a week with a group, check out:

Sunflower Retreats Holidays–Casperia, Lazio

Casperia is an un-touristed medieval village (population 350) in the Sabine hills north of Rome. The retreats here are "divine," according to Adrienne Storey, who's been here six times, and cries every time she leaves and goes back to London. Sunflower was created by Hatha yoga teacher and holistic practitioner Lucy Bremner, and her husband Alan Scheda, a Casperia native. In the ten years they've run the retreats, they have revitalized

Casperia—renovating homes, employing locals, and promoting eco-tourism

Along with morning yoga classes, their packages include B&B accommodations in houses scattered around the village, a guided walk in the mountains, and bikes for the week. You can add on excellent massages and reflexology treatments, go horseback riding, head to the hot springs for a soak, take cooking or Italian lessons. Master guest teachers come through offering workshops in Tai Chi and Reiki.

The freedom to create your retreat however you want it to be is what makes this so appealing. Adrienne calls it the "perfect chill-out vacation." There you are in the "time stands still" ambience of Casperia, with fresh mountain air, the smell of pine all around, wonderful restaurants, friendly natives. You can hang out in the village, take solitary walks up in the hills, or pal around with the other retreatants. Alan and Lucy are on hand to make everything easy—whether you want to add on yoga and meditation classes or get a lift to the train station to head out for a day in Rome or Assisi.

www.sunflowerretreats.com
www.yogaborgo.com

"From the first time I went to Casperia it felt like coming home. It's like one big happy family," Adrienne says.

Yoga Borgo—Passano, Umbria

Ten acres of woodland and meadows surround this former convent in northern Umbria. It was converted into a yoga retreat by Sada Sat Kaur and Sada Sat Singh, who each have over thirty years of experience teaching Kundalini, a practice that focuses on releasing psychic energy at the base of the spine. They're also experts in the Yoga of Sound, meditation, homeopathy, refloxology, and tantric numerology—all of which you can study or experience with them here. It's open year round, whether you want to just drop by for a peaceful stay, take morning classes and enjoy their vegetarian meals, or focus on meditation. Wandering around the property and relaxing in the hammocks is sublime, or you can head out to explore the nearby towns of Assisi, Perugia, and Arezzo.

Pilates and Cooking Classes at Cascina Papaveri—Piedmont

High on a ridge in Italy's northwest gourmet mecca is this luxuriously renovated farmhouse with a state-of-the-art Pilates studio. Hosts Robin and John Sims, former ergonomic designers, welcome guests who come to learn Pilates and experience the culinary delights of this area that's famous for its wine and truffles. They call in master teachers, including Tannis Kobrinsky, a sought-after Los Angeles trainer. I've taken class with Tannis, and she makes Pilates fun while at the same time stays completely focused on your every move. Gals who have gone on her group vacations have only one complaint: "I wish it were longer."

Cascina Papaveri packages include two daily Pilates sessions (one group and one private), all meals, afternoon cooking classes in the farmhouse kitchen, wine tastings, and trips to nearby towns (like Asti) to enjoy markets and food festivals. There's time for massage, swimming in the pool or relaxing in the sauna and steam rooms. The program is flexible, and you may just want to hang out on the property, surrounded by five acres of organic vineyards and vegetable gardens. Papaveri means poppies, and this place is covered with them in May and June.

www.cascinapapaveri.it

IX

Cooking Classes

Taking a cooking class in Italy is getting a backstage pass to the country's soul. Everything comes together in the kitchen: a cook's passion, the freshest flavors of the season, enticing aromas, sounds of garlic sizzling, and wine glasses clinking.

Each class will give you an opportunity to experience a different type of cuisine, depending on what region you land. In Rome you may be stuffing artichokes, in Naples stretching out pizza dough. You can sign up for a one-day class or join in on the many week-long programs offered, where the itinerary typically includes visits to wineries and food artisans. Whether you're an experienced cook eager to learn every detail or more the type who wants to sit back and watch some culinary magic, Italian kitchens welcome you.

Often classes revolve around recipes that were taught to your teachers by their *nonnas*. You follow along, becoming part of the tradition, by watching and learning through your senses of touch and smell. It's an experience that takes you far beyond what you'd get if you were creating a dish from a written recipe.

It's a joy to get swept up in a cook's enthusiasm. That could mean prowling the Rialto market in Venice, intensely focused on the color of fish eyes or swooning over the smell of just-picked basil in Ravello.

Whatever form your class takes, there will be that glorious moment, when you sit down at the table to enjoy the fruits of your labor and toast, *"Buon appetito!"*

RECOMMENDED READING

The World Is a Kitchen: Cooking Your Way Through Culture edited by Michele Anna Jordan and Susan Brady

The Southern Italian Table: Authentic Tastes from Traditional Kitchens by Arthur Schwartz

Cooking with
Daniela–Rome

"I FELT LIKE I WAS WITH MY SISTER," Margaret Vos says about the cooking class she took with Daniela del Balzo. Margaret, who lives in Minnesota, rendezvoused in Rome with her twenty-five-year-old son Jacob. They both love to cook and thought signing up for a one-day class would be a fun way to get to know the Eternal City. Plus they'd have recipes to take home with them. The "clicking like they were sisters" part was a magical surprise.

Daniela is an extraordinarily welcoming woman, who sets up her class as if she was taking her students along with her for her typical Roman day: shopping at the local market and cooking in her apartment. She also speaks perfect English, having spent time in the States going to college and working there in the culinary side of the hotel business.

Her passion for cooking is boundless. She learned the traditional way—from her mother, grandmother, and great-grandmother, during her childhood in Naples. Then, after a successful twenty-year career working for Alitalia, she decided to go back to school to focus on her love for cooking. She studied at Italy's renowned Gambero Rosso Cooking School, the French Culinary Arts School & Le Cordon Bleu, and the International Cooking School of Naples. Now she teaches and runs a catering and personal chef business. She's fifty-something, married to a Roman, has two teenaged boys, and a mother-in-law who lives two floors above her. Putting all those work and life experiences together, Daniela has created a class where she teaches Roman classics with professional flair, always adding a Neapolitan touch from her ancestors.

The class begins where every cook in the neighborhood starts their day: the **Testaccio Market**. Even though Testaccio is not far from the historic center of Rome, it's under the tourist radar, and the market is an authentic bustling scene. "Everywhere we went with Daniela it was so personal," Margaret said. "It made me really think about how I rush into the supermarket, buy vegetables, and don't say a word to anyone who works there."

They met Daniela's butcher, who specially prepared veal in paper-thin slices and "her" artichoke sellers from Australia, who Daniela knows to be expert at cleaning and cutting the vegetables so they're just right to stuff and make artichokes *alla romana*.

Loaded down with bags, they headed up the Aventine hill to Daniela's apartment and tied on their aprons to continue class in her modern, renovated kitchen. "She was so gracious," Margaret said. "She showed us her whole big apartment, the antiques that had been in her husband's home for generations. Plus as we cooked we got into conversations just like I'd have with a girlfriend back in Minnesota." They covered the nitty gritty about balancing work and home, and raising kids. Daniela even recommended a Roman spa to Margaret, the Aquamadre, that turned out to be a great experience.

It was relaxed hours of chopping, picking herbs from Daniela's garden, and hovering by her side at the stove as she taught them how to make Roman specialties like *bucatini all'amatriciana* and *involtini alla romana*. In the latter dish, since it was autumn, Daniela got inventive and filled the veal rolls with pureed pumpkin, along with parmigiano and slices of lightly smoked pancetta. For dessert, they cooked up a Neapolitan sweet that Daniela had learned from her grandmother, using fresh ricotta and chocolate.

Lunch in the garden, surrounded by pots of lemon trees, rosemary bushes, and herb plants, had Margaret and Jacob feeling far away from the city. And as they enjoyed each course, served with Lazio wines, it certainly didn't feel like school. It was a perfect experience of a classic Roman day.

TOURS

Context Travel (www.contexttravel.com): For Cooking with Daniela in Rome and classes in Florence, Venice, and Naples.

RECOMMENDED READING

Williams-Sonoma Rome by Maureen Fant

Tuscan Women Cook—
Montefollonico, Tuscany

IOLANDA MARCOCCI, AN EIGHTY-NINE-YEAR-OLD *NONNA*, has been making *pici*, the thick spaghetti specialty of southern Tuscany, since she could stand up. To watch her expertly roll out dough on the wooden board her mother once used is a marvel. The moment comes in your **Tuscan Women Cook** class when you're invited to "give a hand" at rolling *pici* and you may feel like it's someone handing you a chisel and asking you to "give a hand" at sculpting the *David*. Iolanda inevitably moves in to redo your attempts.

She's just one of the three teachers at this cooking school where local grandmas reign. While Iolanda's a rough-around-the-edges type who prowls her five-foot stocky frame around the kitchen holding on to her paring knife she calls "*mi amore*," you'll also get a lesson with Dania Masati, a flirty blonde who flits about in stiletto heels and Prada ensembles like an Italian movie starlet. Dania's a Michelin-starred chef and cookbook author who owns and operates **La Chiusa**, a luxury hotel and restaurant that was once an olive press. She takes you strolling through her herb garden and then back to her restaurant's kitchen where you'll learn to prepare her signature exquisite *ragu*. To round out the instructor trio, there's Bruna, trim and precise, who turns a mound of flour and egg into delicate strands of tagliatelle, like a demure magician. Each class has a family party vibe, with wine flowing while Christina, the local pharmacist's daughter, translates.

Tuscan Women Cook was created by Bill and Patty Sutherland, charming Texans who fell in love with the small town of Montefollonico in the 1980s, and ended up buying and renovating a farmhouse there. Wanting to share their discoveries of the wonderful chefs, winemakers, and craftsmen they'd come to know, they got this school up and running in 2003. It's a week-long program that winds up fulfilling every aspect of a traveler's *Under the Tuscan Sun* fantasy.

www.tuscanwomencook.com

The Montefollonico location is ideal: smack in the middle of the Chiana Valley, where rolling hills of olive groves and vineyards present a landscape right out of the Florence galleries. Along with three morning classes followed by lunch, there are visits to nearby towns of Pienza, Montepulciano, Bagno Vignoni, a full-day excursion to Florence, and a tasting with one of the region's most good-looking winemakers.

Dinners are relaxed affairs that stretch late into the evenings, at restaurants where the bounty of the surrounding farmlands is transformed to flavorful dishes—from simple grilled Chiana beef to rich duck spiced with wild fennel.

You stay at **Hotel La Costa**, a former farmhouse that's now a Montefollonico landmark, where you can relax on the terrace with views of Lake Trasimeno and Cortona in the distance or cool off with a dip in the hotel pool.

The two-*via* village of Montefollonico (population 700), where the school is based, is so charming you may want to extend your stay after classes are over. This is the kind of place where faces become familiar after only a few days and you'll be greeted with cordial *buona seras* by the *signoras* who gossip on stone benches in the tiny square.

If you do stay longer and want to experience life on an organic working farm, head to **Agriturismo Reniella** (www.reniella.com), where hardworking, fun-loving British transplants Bob and Elfride Vaughan offer a large apartment or B&B accommodations. Or to get pampered in luxe surroundings with gourmet food, check into **La Chiusa**, (www.laristorantelachiusa.it).

TOURS

Tuscan Women Cook (www.tuscanwomencook.com): Programs run May–October.

RECOMMENDED READING

The English Patient by Michael Ondaatje
Under the Tuscan Sun by Frances Mayes
War in Val D'Orcia by Iris Origo

76 Monday at the Market–Florence, Tuscany

THE MERCATO CENTRALE DI SAN LORENZO is a place so revered by the Florentines that it's overseen by the same art commission who looks after the Uffizi galleries. It's a vast glass and cast-iron structure from 1865, one of the oldest and biggest markets in Italy. Two floors of mouth-watering temptations: wheels of fragrant pecorino cheese, tubs of grapes, shelves glowing with bottles of olive oil, stuffed pig heads.

It's as overwhelming as a Florentine gallery. I've loved wandering through here on my own during previous visits—picking up wine and cheese and olives. But this time I have Judy Witts-Francini by my side. I'm not wandering. This is honing in on the finest treasures to be found here.

Judy's been shopping here since 1984. That was the year she left her job as a pastry chef in San Francisco and moved to Florence. She arrived not knowing a soul and didn't speak a word of Italian. It was at the Mercato Centrale where she learned the language—talking to the vendors, hearing their recipes, eavesdropping on conversations.

Twenty-five years later, Judy is part of the Mercato Centrale family. She's been taking the curious like me on tours through here for over a decade, teaching cooking classes, and leading culinary vacationers through Tuscany and other parts of Italy she's come to know and love.

She's a bubbly woman and we have an easy-going fun time together. Though she's lived in Florence for almost half her life, the spirit that shines through Judy is of her native California. She's taken on Italy like an enterprising pioneer, becoming a culinary expert and creating a company called **Divina Cucina** (Divine Kitchen). Its logo is an angel holding a wooden spoon that you'll see in restaurant and shop windows all around Florence. They're places this woman-in-the-know recommends.

"Taste this," she says, as we stand in front of the counter of one of her friends' shops. It's twelve-year-old balsamic vinegar that wakes up every taste bud. That's just the opener to one refined taste after another: twenty-five-year-old balsamic, pecorino cheese with truffle honey, olive oil fresh from the press. There is red pepper jelly—Judy's recipe that's now bottled and sold here.

Upstairs I meet the man she tells me taught her how to cure olives, and the oldest *signora* in the market, a bird-boned woman in a pale blue ratty sweater, who sits on a rickety wooden stool next to her crate of apples.

There aren't many like that *signora* left around here. "They've moved out to the country," says Judy. The faces here make up the changing face of Florence—immigrants from Sri Lanka and Eastern Europe, who are keeping the tradition of the city's beautiful food alive.

As we head out of the market for our lunch at nearby Mario's, we make a final stop at **Pork's**, one of the restaurant stands on the lower level. This one has been run by a Sicilian family for over twenty years, Judy tells me. I meet the Pork's matriarch, Benita, a 70-something woman with dyed jet-black hair piled high in a fifties bouffant style on her tiny head. "She's my market mamma," Judy says.

Benita stands proudly in front of her case of food: *eggplant caponata, arancine.* If I'd come here on my own I probably would have passed this stand by, thinking "it's not Florentine."

I stay in Florence for the week and go back to the Mercato Centrale on my own. Benita, at her stand, gives me a welcome back kiss. I sit down at one of her tables for lunch. The *caponata* is out of this world. I see a couple of American tourists stop by, look at the Sicilian menu, shake their heads, and move on.

I savor every bite of Benita's *caponata.* It's as though Judy has pulled the curtain open to this place for me. After my morning with her, I'm here at the Mercato Centrale, feeling so in the know.

TOURS

Divina Cucina (www.divinacucina.com) offers Monday at the Market Tours, Culinary Adventures in Tuscany and Beyond, and restaurant advice (www.divinacucina.com).

RECOMMENDED READING

Secrets from My Tuscan Kitchen by Judy Witts-Francini

77 Cooking with Micaela, Parma–Emilia-Romagna

PIEDI DI DIO (GOD'S FEET) IS HOW Italians describe the smell of Parmigiano-Reggiano cheese. When Micaela, my cooking teacher, unwraps a giant chunk, I bow my head and inhale. Divine! Out next comes the prosciutto—salty, rich, woodsy. Here I am, with Parma's culinary stars—the *delizioso* products that turned this town into a gourmet mecca. I'd be happy to just sit down with these two, a loaf of bread, and a glass of wine.

But Micaela's set to lead me in another direction. She's a young, energetic *signorina* in her early thirties who teaches out of her sweet little apartment kitchen at the edge of Parma's historic center.

We'll make tortellini stuffed with that parmigiano, along with ricotta and chard. The prosciutto will get wrapped up in beef and cooked up in wine with a little rosemary to become Rosa di Parma.

These are recipes Micaela learned from her *nonna* Elena. Elena is now up there on my list of heroines. Not only for the cooking she taught Micaela that she passed on to me, but for the stories Micaela tells me about this amazing woman as we mix eggs together with flour to make pasta dough.

Elena was a partisan—one of the brave, underground group who formed an Italian resistance movement during World

War II. They carried out brilliant covert moves from their mountain hideouts, fighting the fascists and the Nazis.

Elena took on the dangerous job of delivering messages to her compatriots in the mountains. Once, riding her bike through a tunnel, she was stopped by German soldiers. Hidden in her long, black, curly hair were rolled up notes. She was a cute young girl, kept her head steady, flirted a bit. Got away with it.

I'm stretching and kneading pasta dough on a big pine board as Micaela tells me this story, awed and thinking of Elena. Micaela shows me just what part of my palm to use, the right pressure, when to turn it. She's encouraging, like a soft-spoken coach. And there's more to the story...

Up in the hills outside La Spezia, Elena met the man who became Micaela's grandfather. They were in the back of a truck, lying flat, hiding in an empty water tank. German soldiers stopped the driver and opened fire, riddling the tank. *If they'd been standing...* From that day on they vowed to always be together. He died when Elena was thirty-seven. She had his wedding ring forged to hers and never re-married.

Now I have shivers, the good kind you get from a good story. And the dough, miraculously, has actually turned out.

We spend relaxed hours here in the tiny kitchen, stuffing the tortellini, making tiramisu, picking rosemary from Micaela's little terrace herb garden to add to the roast. It's cozy.

Micaela has me laughing when I asked her how she learned to speak English so well. She was a high school exchange student and lived with a family in Wisconsin. She almost didn't make it all the way through, because the first thing she saw when she arrived was a just-killed deer hanging in the garage. "When I told my mother she wanted to get on a plane and bring me back home." But Micaela called it an adventure. An adventure where she ate "Deer and deer and deer." She even went out with bow and arrows to hunt. And every night the Wisconsin *mamma* would slice that deer, put it in a microwave, pour a can of cream of mushroom soup or ketchup over it. That was dinner.

I am so glad I'm having dinner here and not in Wisconsin. Micaela sets a round table in the living room with an elegant white cloth and china. She pours Lambrusco, the wine of the Emilia-Romagna region, thankfully not a real fizzy one. Then she brings over a framed photo: It's Nonna Elena as a young woman, looking strong, with the exact same curly, dark hair that Micaela has. "That's where she hid the notes," Micaela reminds me.

We keep the picture on the table as we dig in.

TOURS

The International Kitchen (www.internationalkitchen.com) offers cooking classes in Parma and throughout Italy.

RECOMMENDED READING

The Splendid Table: Recipes from Emilia-Romagna by Lynne Rosetto Kasper

Mamma Agata Cooking School–Ravello

IN ITALY I OFTEN FIND MYSELF GUSHING, "Life is beautiful!" But in Ravello, high above the Amalfi Coast, the gushing gets elevated to "Life is more beautiful!" The sky is bluer. The sea more sparkly. The horizon more hypnotic. The tomatoes more delicious.

It's fitting that in such a divine spot there lives a Goddess of Amalfi Coast Cooking: Mamma Agata. She's an irresistibly adorable woman—pleasingly plump, with twinkling, almond-shaped eyes. Her smile warms my heart. She's been cooking for most of her seventy-four years, and to watch her move around a stove is simply marvelous.

This one-day Mamma Agata Cooking Class takes place at her home: an eighteenth-century villa, surrounded by terraced gardens, perched on a cliff with a to-die-for view of the sea. Chiara Lima, Mamma's daughter, is the gracious mastermind behind the whole operation.

www.amalfi.it/scapariello

Chiara even turned my traveling pal Carol and me on to fantastic digs nearby at the **Villa Scarpariello**. It's an amazing mix of old buildings, and a tower from the twelfth century, hidden in a seaside nitch. It feels like a well-kept secret, but here I go blabbing about it, because that's the way I am. Each balconied suite of rooms is unique, and most have kitchens, so it's a temptation to check in for a week and just bliss out—especially because the prices are so reasonable. One of the many zigzags of stone steps on the property took me right down to the water for a refreshing before-school swim.

Class at Mamma Agata's begins with lemon cake and coffee. "It was Humphrey Bogart's favorite," Chiara tells us. When Agata was thirteen, she began her pro-career working in the Ravello villa of a wealthy American woman who entertained star visitors. "Baby Agata" was what Bogey called her, and he wasn't the only one among the glitterati who was wowed by her cooking. Agata has great stories about making *pasta e fagioli* for Anita Ekberg, *spaghetti alla puttanesca* for Fred Astaire, and *insalata Caprese* for Jacqueline Kennedy. "Jackie was Mamma's favorite," Chiara says. "She always talks about how she was a real lady, so kind she'd even insist on washing her own coffee cup." The lemon cake is phenomenal. And eating it out on the terrace surrounded by the very trees where the lemons came from makes it all the more delicious.

The class is mostly demonstration. Twelve of us students are gathered in the tiny kitchen, with Agata at the stove and Chiara narrating. Practically everything she makes uses what's grown right here in her gardens. There's rolled eggplant appetizers, eggplant parmigiana, pappardelle with sausage and peppers, and lemon chicken. We get tastes of fresh tomato sauce, sniffs of just-picked basil, as Chiara tells us Mamma's "secret techniques." This is simple cooking—it's the details that make it divine. "Listen to the sound of that sizzle, that's when you know the garlic is ready, now's when you put in the tomatoes for the sauce" says Chiara. She's printed out all the recipes for us in a glossy handout and CD, so we don't even have to take notes. We can just sip wine and watch the master at work.

It's delicious fun. We take breaks to walk around the gardens with all of us *oohing* and *aahing* over the paradise we are in.

After three hours, we take our places at a long, wooden table on the terrace. Lovely *signorine* magically appear with platters and pans of everything we've watched Mamma have her hands in. The sun streams through the pergola. More than one of us says, "This is the best lunch I've ever had."

For the grand finale, Agata comes out with her exquisite homemade limoncello. The day has gone along like a song.

I can't resist giving Agata a hug goodbye. My arms don't reach all the way around. She tilts her cheek to me for a kiss. "*Grazie, grazie, grazie,*" is all I can whisper to her smiling face, again and again and again. I don't hold back. I am in Ravello, after all, where everything is elevated.

TOURS

Mamma Agata Cooking School (www.mammaagata.com) offers cooking classes, and can arrange private dinners or even a wedding party.

RECOMMENDED READING

Simple and Genuine: Recipes of Mamma Agata by Chiara Lima

79

Cook at Seliano—
Paestum, Campania

I'M A GUEST OF THE BARONESSA. I like saying that. Not that
Baronessa Cecilia Bellelli is one of those bejeweled, barking,
"Where's my fish fork" type baronessas. She does have a grand-
ness about her. But it's in a southern Italian generous woman-
of-the-world kind of way. She tells me to call her Cecilia.

I am in the kitchen of the Baronessa's *agriturismo* called
Masseria Eliseo. Loosely translated that means Elysian Farm.
Not quite Elysian Fields, where kings and gods went to enjoy
eternal bliss, but for me the large white-tiled kitchen is pretty
heavenly. I'm stirring tomato sauce that's been simmering with
beef and sausage for two hours—just like I did when I was a kid at
my nana's house in Newark, New Jersey. Except out the window
there are water buffalo grazing on flat green fields.

This is Paestum, south of Naples, in the region of Campania
where the foods we think of when we first think "Italian" originated: tomato sauce and pizza. It's where *mozzarella di bufala*—which
Italians say is the only real mozzarella—comes from. To have a
bite of that cheese here, in its primal state, with the buffalo that
were milked just hours before right outside the door, is such a
fresh, creamy, burst-in-the-mouth revelation it'll spoil you for
the rest of your mozzarella-eating life.

My husband and I, along with four other couples, are here
for Arthur Schwartz's Cook at Seliano program. Four times a

year, the Brooklyn-based award-winning cookbook author leads
week-long tours that include cooking classes, visits to Naples,
Salerno, wineries, and olive farms. For me, the grandchild of
southern Italian immigrants, it was a chance to get to the roots
of the kitchen of my past.

It was Arthur's *Naples at Table* that was my siren's call to sign up.
Reading it gave me an eerie feeling—as if he'd followed my nana
around, writing down all the recipes she'd never bothered to.
In addition, he delves into the history of Campania, with spicy
details. For example, he writes that Nana's *ragu napoletano* was also
called *il sugo della guardaporta* (sauce of the door-keeper) because it
needed frequent stirring, which was the traditional job of the
woman who guarded the courtyard door. Then he adds: "In a
typical Neapolitan way, a joke proposes that by the same theory,
ragu could as well be the sauce of whores." Nana would have wal-
loped him with her wooden spoon for that comment. I thought
it was hilarious, and when I finally got to meet Arthur in person,
found him to have that perfect combo of humor and smarts
which makes for a great teacher.

Arthur's co-host for the program is the Baronessa, whom he
met while he was researching the book, and they've been friends
ever since. As a pair, they could pass for brother and sister.
Both are in their early sixties, with broad expressive faces, and a
boundless enthusiasm for Campania's cuisine.

The Baronessa has two *agriturismi*, and we stay at one near the
cooking class, **Tenuta Seliano**. It's three eighteenth-century
converted farm buildings surrounded by olive groves, orchards,
and fields of escarole, artichokes, and fennel. To add a rich-
ness to the rural scene, right down the road are the **Temples
of Paestum**, three of the best preserved Greek temples in the
world.

Arthur leads the cooking class, with all ten of us tying on aprons and following along with his recipes. The best is the afternoon of New Year's Eve, when we make *timballo*, a pastry drum filled with macaroni, meats, and cheeses. I've wanted to make this ever since I saw the movie *Big Night*, where the two chefs obsessed over it for days, and cutting it open was the climax of the film. Arthur's rendition is a little simpler, but still a twenty-step process that has us making the *ragu*, then the pastry crust, and grating, chopping, and sautéing the filling ingredients. We're very high-spirited, with all the fantastic smells in the kitchen and the wine flowing.

That night we gather in the Tenuta Seliano dining room with over a hundred party guests—Cecilia's family and friends. There's a blazing fireplace, long wooden tables. Our *timballi* are served along with others made by Cecilia's pro-chefs. We've marked ours with an "X" in the crust, and I'm cringing thinking they're going to stand out as "the student's attempts." Breathless, I watch Cecilia's family take their first bites of one of ours. It's the *Big Night* moment. Unanimously, they look up and smile in approval.

That triumphant note takes the class into the New Year. We toast with prosecco as kids run out the door to set off Roman candles. I look around and see faces that could pass for doubles of relatives I've celebrated holidays with long ago. I feel a rush of them smiling down at me. We all get up to dance.

Cook at Seliano: Programs take place four times per year (www. foodmaven.com).

RECOMMENDED READING

Naples at Table by Arthur Schwartz

80 Cooking in Tropea–Calabria

WITH HER MOM JEANS AND GOLD MADONNA on a chain swinging between her breasts, Marianna Giuditta reminds me of mothers I grew up around in my New Jersey neighborhood. It makes sense, since so many of them were descendants of folks from Calabria, this region in the toe of Italy's boot. Marianna even moves around the kitchen like they did—a tigress going in for the kill.

"The pig is the meat of Calabria," she tells me, hacking away at a chunk of pork and tossing big fatty pieces of it into a pot to start off her *sugo Calabrese.*

Cooking by Marianna's side is taking the straight shot into the rustic, generous spirit of the region.

Her classroom is a hilltop cottage, what around here is called a *casetta.* It's surrounded by lemon and fig trees, a chicken coop, tiny gardens where Tropea's famous red onions, herbs, chard, fava beans, peppers, tomatoes, zucchini, and melons grow. There's an outdoor woodburning stove. It's a typical Calabrese set-up: a slapped-together country getaway townies build to have a place to grow their own food and cook great fresh meals.

Marianna's evening class is a whirlwind of picking vegetables from the garden and then working on a huge outside table, doing everything from chopping onions to making meatballs that go into *pasta al forno*. Her husband Franco pours prosecco and adds fresh-picked strawberries to our glasses. We nibble on pecorino paired with the garden's fava beans—a divine combo.

While the tomato sauce bubbles along, Marianna teaches me how to make *fileja*, Calabria's signature pasta. It looks a little like what back in Jersey was called *cavatelli*, pronounced *gava-deels* by those moms of my past.

The sunset turns the sky pink and orange. It's dark out by the time class is finished. Loads of stars. We dine outside by candle-light, and when Marianna breaks out the limoncello, we realize it's two in the morning.

The Cooking in Tropea school is the creation of Tania Pascuzzi, an Australian-Italian whose parents were born in Calabria and then emigrated to Melbourne. Tania, who grew up around delicious Calabrian food, came to live in Tropea after fourteen years of high-pressure work as a New York stylist. She's a sophisticated woman in her forties, the type who looks chic even when she's wearing faded jeans.

Tropea is a beautiful school base. It juts out above the sea, a jumble of crumbling sandstone baroque buildings, tiny piazzas that look like opera sets. I'm staying in a seventeenth-century renovated palazzo, right off the main square. Inside is a mod-ern surprise: a spacious suite, sleekly designed, with filmy taupe curtains, balconies, a laptop with internet access.

The cooking program includes a food tour of Tropea, where with Tania by my side, everyone treats me like I'm part of *la famiglia*. This is hot red pepper territory. They're dried and tied up in garlands all over the place. They're minced up and made into *n'duja*, a spread that sizzles on the tongue or has me choking and gasping, depending on intensity.

Another day of class brings me to neighboring **Capo Vaticano**, a village set on cliffs with ocean views of the Aeolian Islands.

There I get to meet another local cook: Rosanna, a hip mother of two in her thirties, who looks like a grown-up Meadow Soprano, and has a totally different style from Marianna's. Rosanna's an Encyclopedia Brown of Calabria's culinary traditions, and her recipes add subtle, elegant notes to the region's classics. There's a heavenly dish of peppers, pecorino, and breadcrumbs. She sauces her *filea* with tomato and tuna that was caught that morning, and we have fresh grilled swordfish spiced with herbs.

Her menu is loaded with vegetables grown on a huge organic farm she runs with her husband, Roberto. We ride around it in a golf cart, past patches of flowering chamomile, stalks of wild fennel surrounding vineyards, orchards, and fields of greens. There are Arabian horses, cows, llamas, pigs, chickens, gaggles of geese.

Most entertaining are the couple of ostriches we catch during mating season. The male squats, spreads his feathers, and sways his neck in figure eights—a move Roberto calls "*a danza d'amore.*" The gal ostrich pays no attention, maybe because we're watching. It's the only display of cool behavior I've seen during my time in Calabria, where hugs and kisses come at me at every turn.

We eat lunch on the terrace of Rosanna and Roberto's **Capo Vaticano** resort, a sprawling modern beachside complex with guest apartments and a swimming pool. Rosanna brings out homemade ricotta covered with fresh strawberries. The sun sparkles off the sea. Like so many moments in Calabria, this is one I want to take home in a bottle.

TOUR

In Italy Tours (www.initalytours.com) offers cooking classes in
Tropea, throughout Calabria, and even on a private yacht while
circling the Aeolian Islands.

RECOMMENDED READING

Sapori di Calabria by Emilia Fusco

X Learn Italian Crafts and Culture

Becoming a student instead of a tourist in Italy pulls you in closer to her. It gives you the chance to immerse yourself deeper into the culture and pursue a particular passion while you're at it.

While for decades there have been lots of language schools to choose from all over the country, these days more and more art workshops are being created. They are headed up by pros who teach using the age-old master-apprentice model. Here's where you can roll up your sleeves and take time to learn one of Italy's traditional handicrafts, such as mosaics or ceramics. Classes are open to beginners, who simply want to explore their creative side, or advanced artists, who want to get to the source—the place where the art form that's captured their passion all began.

You may be amazed at how relaxing these experiences are. Italy can be overwhelming, so when you focus on one of its aspects, it's less so. Instead of flitting from place to place with your guidebook and map, you are rooted in a dreamy environment, where your creative side can flow.

An additional wonderful thing about the workshops is that you'll be spending time in Italy with others who share your passion. The built-in creative community is perfect for a solo traveler and often leads to lifelong friendships.

Once you open the door to the idea, possibilities flow...

81

Maskmaking at Tragicomica–Venice

AFTER DAYS OF MUSEUM–MUSEUM–MUSEUM, Sandy Osceola and her two daughters needed to step off the tourist treadmill. So they stepped into the Tragicomica workshop, spending a morning decorating masks. It turned out to be a highlight of their vacation. Not only was it great fun to be together painting and gluing on feathers and sequins, but they also got an entertaining art history lesson while they were at it.

Tragicomica is one of the finest spots in Venice to pick up traditional masks, and rent hats, sumptuous ball gowns and capes for Carnevale. The store is packed with these fantasy-inspiring goodies, and a wonderful place to browse even if you're not heading to the back for the workshop.

Gualtiero Dall'Osto is Tragicomica's master maskmaker, following in the footsteps of artists who began dressing up Venetian partiers in the thirteenth century. His creations have been exhibited internationally, and he's designed costumes and set pieces for theaters all over Italy, including La Scala in Milan.

In the 1970s Dall'Osto was one of a group who fought successfully to bring back the Venice Carnevale which Mussolini had put an end to in the 1930s. The traditional pre-Lent party began in Venice in the twelfth century. It was named Carnevale from the Latin for "Farewell meat!" because the forty days before Easter were days of abstinence.

Though masks were first worn only during Carnevale, in wild eighteenth-century days with guys like Casanova running around, being in disguise became useful to fun-loving Venetians. Fellas who were in debt could wear a mask to gambling rooms and play undiscovered by creditors. Married gals could slip away for romantic trysts without damaging their reputations. Ultimately the government stepped in and banned mask-wearing except for Carnevale, as they felt things with the citizenry were getting way out of control.

The Osceola's three-hour workshop kicked off with an entertaining demonstration by Dall'Osto's assistant, Alessandra. Putting on maks, she showed how each one has a story behind it, corresponding to a Commedia dell'Arte character or a bit of Venetian history. Next came a demonstration of how papier–mâché is molded on to forms for the first stage of the mask-making process.

Sandy and her daughters picked out blank masks to decorate and got to work in the backroom, right where expert artisans turn out the pretty things that fill the shop. Sandy chose a Medico della Peste, the Plague Doctor mold. That's the one you've seen in so many photos, with the long-beak-shaped nose and tiny eyeholes. It originated in the sixteenth century when doctors would stuff the nose with a sponge soaked in vinegar, so they could move plague victims around and be protected from the disease. Sandy's daughters, Jessica (21) and Marissa (12), went for styles that they decorated with paints and sequins to look as though they could be eighteenth-century ladies on their way to a Carnevale ball.

By lunchtime they had three one-of-a-kind souvenirs. Now back at home, the masks bring back great memories of the trip the Osceolas took to celebrate Jessica's graduation from college. Moreover they'll always remind them of the entertaining spirit of the unique city of Venice.

Tragicomica: Calle dei Nomboli, off Campo San Toma in San Polo, 041 721102 (www.tragicomica.it).

TOUR

European Connection (www.europeanconnection.com) arranges mask-making classes and is an excellent company that custom-designs itineraries for trips throughout Italy.

82 International School of Ceramic Art— Deruta, Umbria

"EVEN SOMEONE WHO'S NEVER PICKED UP a paintbrush can spend a little time here and come away with something beautiful," Florence Welborn told me. She's a retired schoolteacher from Tacoma and self-described "arts and crafts person." Florence and her husband fell in love with Italy, bought a place in Umbria, and every time they have visitors, this Deruta school is on the itinerary. What great hosts.

The class set-up here is freeform and casual. Which is surprising, because the school building is also a major ceramics institution (opened in 2001), with lecture halls, galleries, a retail shop, and professional workshop. But as far as ceramic painting classes, anyone can just call or e-mail a day in advance, make a reservation for a few hours (at least four is good for a beginner), and get one-on-one tutoring to learn traditional techniques that have been going on here since the Renaissance.

If you're a beginner, you choose what design you'd like to paint from a selection of tiles, and then you're set up at a work-table with all the supplies you need, including a blank tile that's stamped with the design. It's like paint-by-number.

Well, not that easy. Which is where the one-on-one tutoring comes in and you're taught how to mix the paints, and hold the brush, which is different for ceramics than it is for painting on canvas.

Here's the important thing: make sure Nicola Boccini is there, unless you speak Italian, because Nicola is the only instructor at the school who speaks English. He's a thirty-something-year-old master, not only an expert with traditional designs, but he also paints ceramics in a modern style that's critically acclaimed. Best of all, he's a fantastic teacher, expert at guiding you according to your level. From time to time he's called away for lectures and workshops all over the world, so once again, check in to make sure he's there before you make plans.

The school was founded by Romano Ranieri, a world-renowned ceramic painter and teacher, whose masterpieces sell for high prices and are in museums around the world. Despite his mega success, he's a humble sort who's been teaching and painting for fifty years. You'll definitely see him here—he's that artsy looking gentleman with the shoulder-length salt-and-pepper hair, passionately working on some incredible project. Inevitably, hawk-eyed teacher that he is, he'll break away from his painting to stand over your shoulder and give you advice if he sees you straying in the least.

You can also take classes in pottery making, like Ekta Nadeau did after she saw a You Tube of Nicola working at a wheel and decided to fly to Deruta from Vancouver to learn his technique. She set her trip up so she spent a few days throwing pottery Italian style, then left to tour around for a week, so by the time she came back her pots and jars had been fired. Then, with the help of Maestro Ranieri, she chose a pattern that was just right for their shape and stayed a few days to learn ceramic painting.

The big perk of being in Deruta is that right out the door are hundreds of artisan shops and a ceramics museum, so you get an education just walking around.

The school will give you lots of recommendations for accommodations nearby, from apartments to B&Bs. Gina Garner, who's been here twice for classes, usually stays at the **Hotel Melody**, a simple three-star, which she says is "Great, as long as you don't eat there!"

Deruta's a very relaxing place to stroll about, especially when you're feeling so artsy. The natives, accustomed to visitors, are warm and welcoming. The same goes for the staff at the school. Don't be surprised if Floriana Spaccini, the *scuola* president, stops by with a tray of *caffè* and *biscotti*. Yes, they're for you. Put down your paintbrush and take a little *pausa*.

International School of Ceramic Art "Romano Ranieri": Via Tiberina Sud 330, Deruta, 075 972 383 (www.schoolofceramics.org).

83 Leathercraft at Scuola del Cuoio— Florence

I NOW KNOW WHAT "TOUGH AS LEATHER" really means. Believe me, a lousy steak is a cinch to cut through compared to a piece of leather. I've come to the Scuola del Cuoio to get a taste of what this handcrafted leather tradition is all about—in Florence where it all began. The Scuola is in a building that was a monastery in Renaissance days, tucked behind the Santa Croce church.

I'm thinking about the Santa Croce, where I saw Michelangelo's tomb yesterday. I'm thinking about all the shops around there that say "Handmade Leather." How do they cut this stuff?

This is a professional workshop, and there are two American gals sitting at another table who are part of its longer programs— three months to a year. They're working on adorable purses. I've signed up for a three-hour class to make a journal cover, which I thought would be easy-peasey. Now I'm imagining the sun setting, everybody leaving, and here I still struggle just to cut a square, the worst student who ever crossed the Scuola threshold.

My teacher Carlo, a man who's spent most of his seventy-something years working here, is Father Patience standing over my shoulder, non-plussed. "The first time..." he says, gently shifting the angle of my hand. And then, "*Piano, piano...*" Slower? Could I possibly go any slower? Something clicks when I take his direction. I break through the leather. A triumph.

This is about working the old-fashioned way, with precise attention, and *pazienza, pazienza, pazienza.* Cutting's the hardest for me, but every step that follows that would seem so easy, I have Carlo over me with exacting instructions for folding, pressing, hammering holes along the border.

I give into the rhythm of "leather-crafting" time. I've spent the last few days running around looking at stupendous masterpieces. Now my vision is totally focused on pulling one thin strip of leather through tiny holes along the edge of this piece to make a braided edge. The room has an overwhelming scale of aromas—from the deep smell of leather to top notes of nose-tingling glue. Church bells ring. It's simply divine to be here.

The Scuola del Cuoio was founded in 1950 as a leather-making school for boys who'd been orphaned after World War II. The goal was to teach them a trade so they could earn a practical living. It was initiated by the Gori family, who'd been leather artisans in Florence since the thirties. They teamed up with the Franciscan friars to create this place, turning the monk's dormitories into a workshop. And not just any old dormitory—it was built by the Medici in the fifteenth century. The section that's open to visitors is a gorgeous fresco-lined hall, where senior artisans at old-fashioned wooden workstations turn out some of the best handcrafted leather you can buy in Florence.

The three Gori daughters now run the place. They are the epitome of fashionable Florentine women—the crisp haircuts, the wool suits.

My journal cover is finished. "Congratulations," Carlo says, as he fills it with a book of fine blank Florentine paper. We walk across a garden and upstairs to the professional workshop, stopping at a workbench where he hands it over to a venerable, bald-headed artisan named Bosco. Bosco works some magic over it, with eggwhite, a flame, and twenty-two carat gold. When he hands it back to me, my initials are embossed on the cover.

My initials in gold bring back the feeling of getting a star stamped on my paper in third grade. I hold on to it and shake Carlo's hand. "*Pazienza, pazienza*," he laughs.

Scuola del Cuoio: Piazza Santa Croce 16, 055 244 533. Half-day, full-day, short-term to year-long courses. This is also a great place to stop by to see artisans at work and buy beautiful handcrafted leather.

84

Jewelry Making Classes—Cortona and Florence

MY FRIENDS SHERYL AND ERIN SHOCKED their Mommy and Me group when they announced they were taking off for a week to go to this Cortona workshop. They're both mothers of two children. "Go ahead, you could use the break," said their respective wonderful husbands.

So off they flew to an **Arcangelo Art and Life Workshop**, created by Stacey Matthews and Rob Friedman. Stacey and Rob live part time in the Tuscan hilltop town of Cortona, and call in guest artists to head up workshops that mix a creative experience with the delicious flavors, friendly natives, and surroundings of this beautiful place. Along with four full-day studio classes, the weeklong itinerary includes wine tastings, cooking classes, and visits to nearby hill towns. You're set up in a B&B in Cortona's historic center, and there's free time to simply bliss out wandering around town and enjoying the food in its homey restaurants.

Sheryl and Erin signed up because Sally Jean Alexander, a beloved reliquary jewelry artist, was teaching. That's not "reliquary in the finger of John the Baptist under glass" sense. Reliquary jewelry is wearable collage art—charms bordered in silver, encased in glass, that hold tiny mementos, bits of photos, or antique fragments. The style became popular in Victorian times, when Italian women would have jewelry made that contained locks of hair or tiny photos from loved ones. Alexander's contemporary take on reliquary is whimsical and eclectic, as she says, "like wearing your sentiments around your neck."

Cortona is the perfect base to scavenge for pretty little things to incorporate in the jewelry. The workshop began with a trip to the Arezzo Antique Market, where the ten students gathered old buttons, lace, or crystal pieces from broken chandeliers. Back in the studio (a converted convent), Alexander taught them how to design their necklaces and solder silver. It turned into a creative weeklong party.

Sheryl is one of those gals who loves to do arts and crafts projects, but has to sneak it in back home, in between taking care of her family. In Cortona, she said being immersed in such an inspiring environment with unlimited studio time "was like a dream where time totally stopped."

She and Erin went back to their families rejuvenated from the artsy Italian break, wearing their pretty necklaces.

Jewel on the Arno—Florence

Ken Scott, originally from New Zealand, is an artisan who has worked for major jewelry companies in Florence for fourteen years. He has created an exquisite line of his own designs, and also teaches jewelry making at Florence's prestigious professional institutions. Passionate about sharing what he knows with travelers, he offers a program where you spend four mornings a week learning about the history of Florentine jewelry and get workbench sessions to create something to bring home.

Here's a man with a great wry sense of humor, whose walking-tour history lesson is wonderfully entertaining. He brings you to the Ponte Vecchio, the Oltrarno Goldsmith workshops, Pitti Palace, and for lunch at "The Jeweler's Trattoria." For the rest of the time he's by your side helping you design and make something that will become a treasured souvenir.

TIP: *If you're having thoughts about going in for serious jewelry study in Florence (for at least a month or maybe even a longer certificate program), my friend Alexa Taylor recommends you check out:* **Art Fuji Studio** *(www.artfuji.com, classes in English) or* **Perseo** *(www.perseo.com, classes in Italian only).*

Arcangelo Art and Life Workshops: One week sessions take place in the spring and fall. www.arcangeloproductions.com

Jewel on the Arno: Sessions run Monday through Thursday for three hours each morning. www.kenscottdesign.com

85

Landscape Painting— Buonconvento, Tuscany

IMAGINE STANDING ON A TUSCAN HILLSIDE, looking out over a vineyard, with that gorgeous golden light all around. Instead of gasping at the view for a few moments, you're at an easel for a couple of quiet hours, capturing it with your brush and paints. The light changes. A gentle breeze blows through carrying the smell of earth, lavender, grass. Birds twitter. There may be butterflies.

Landscape painters Maddine Insalaco and Joe Vinson run workshops where this is how it goes for a whole week. O.K., the reality is maybe it'll rain and they'll set up a tarp overhead to cover you. There will also be lunch breaks in the shade, where Maddine, who's an expert cook as well as painter, mixes up what she's got fresh from the local market into a delicious meal. You'll have a glass of wine and take a break with your fellow painters, then it's back to the easel, so you're painting as the sun sets.

The goal of these workshops is to give beginners to advanced painters a rigorous, focused experience of the open-air style of painting, called *plein air*. The tradition of artists coming to Italy to paint outdoors goes back to the eighteenth century, when painters from France and England traveled to Rome to see Renaissance masterpieces. They were amazed by the countryside surrounding the Eternal City—the light, rolling hills, and architectural ruins. They lugged their easels out there, developing new techniques to capture these scenes, working quickly and spontaneously. It was a liberating experience, in contrast to working in a studio. Camille Corot's landscape paintings from this time paved the way to Impressionism.

Maddine and Joe follow in the footsteps of this tradition and are passionate about the form. They've been landscape painters for twenty years and their work is shown in American and Italian galleries. They're also passionate about Italy, and divide their time between an apartment in New York and a place in Buonconvento (southern Tuscany), where they base their workshop. Here students get Maddine and Joe's enthusiastic, expert instruction as they paint, along with the joy of being integrated into the local scene through the couple.

www.landscape-painting.com

"What was so wonderful is that everything was taken care of—the only decision I had to make all week was what to paint and what colors to use," said Voni Schaff, a student from Minnesota. Voni had studied art in college, then put it aside for thirty years while she brought up four children. The week in Tuscany was a kick start for her to pick up where she left off. It turned out to be amazingly productive—she went home with a suitcase full of paintings and liked it so much she returned for a second time.

"Spending a week there is equivalent to a semester in a college art course," said Rachel Newman, who went to her first workshop with no experience, hoping it would help heal a heartbreak. She's since returned for three more sessions. The heartbreak is long behind her, she's had gallery shows of her paintings, and ended up buying a place in Buonconvento because she loved the area so much.

The program is an art-high week, where you'll be painting for a total of around fifty hours. Maddine and Joe intensely focus on giving detailed, basic instruction and encouragement for everyone to paint according to their own style. "They're not making clones of themselves," said Elizabeth Garat, an artist from Tennessee, who has worked as a studio painter for many years and loved learning new outdoor painting techniques.

The pace of the work, completing a painting in two hours, is a thrilling challenge. It's all about being connected to nature and responding to it with your brush and colors. At the end of each day, the student's paintings are hung up in a display they call the "Tower of Power" and a critiquing session follows. "It's not just patting on the back," said Elizabeth, "It's honest, specific, constructive, and encouraging."

An art teacher once told Maddine that landscape painters were the happiest people he knew. Maddine and her students understand why. There's something quite wonderful spending the day outside, especially in Tuscany. Add to that the great satisfaction of quick creation, learning something new, and the camaraderie that naturally evolves in the group.

In the evenings, you'll find yourself sitting in a cozy restaurant, still in your painting clothes, drinking wine and talking late into the night about art, naturally.

Landscape Painting: Workshops are held in the spring through fall. The program includes most materials, accommodations at a converted twelfth-century abbey, meals, slide-show lectures, a visit to a Siena museum, and canvases small enough to fit in your suitcase. Enrollment is limited to twelve students.

RECOMMENDED READING

Seasons in Basilicata: A Year in a Southern Italian Hill Village (written and illustrated) by David Yeadon

86 Giuditta Brozzetti Weaving and Embroidery Workshop Perugia, Umbria

I LOVE THE SOUNDS IN THIS CHURCH CLASSROOM. I'm not talking bells or heavenly choirs. It's the clickety-clack of wooden looms. It's a calm, rhythmic beat that echoes softly through the vast gothic **San Francesco delle Donne**, The Women's Church of Saint Francis. The building was turned from a holy place into a weaving workshop in the nineteenth century when 300 women had jobs here.

Now that craft tradition is beautifully preserved. Pale light filters through big curved gracious windows onto nine looms. In the space that was once an altar, round tables are draped with enticing creations for sale—royal blue, gold, and red patterned cloths. Their designs are callbacks to medieval times—grape leaves and that mythological griffon (half-bird, half-lion) that's the symbol of Perugia. On another table delicately embroidered pieces add a light, elegant touch.

This is an extraordinary place to stop by and browse around even if you aren't taking a class. You could even spend some time at a simple loom to get a feel for how to work the threads as you pedal, like I did. *It's not easy!* Nearby is the **Perugia Duomo**, where the BVM's wedding ring is enshrined and from there you have the whole charming mix of Perugia's cobblestoned streets lined with designer and artisan's shops.

If you have a day or a week to sign up for a workshop, a step-back-in-time experience awaits. You'll be learning to weave on simple shaft looms and then Jacquard looms, all built over a hundred years ago, that are scrupulously maintained here.

"I was in awe to be experiencing this small part of Italy's history—to be a part of that continuity," said June Rogovin, a student from California who's been hand weaving for twenty years. "The teachers were so welcoming and patient, it was absolutely humbling at times."

The Brozzetti workshop began in 1921 when Giuditta Brozzetti, who was the headmaster of Perugia's elementary schools, was riding around in her horse and carriage and heard that clickety-clack sound coming from the looms of surrounding farmhouses. Weaving had begun in Perugia in the twelfth century, when the town became a textile-making center, turning out table coverings that were renowned all over Europe. Giuditta decided to open a workshop not only to preserve the handicraft that was dwindling away because of the Industrial Revolution, but also to give women jobs so they could become financially independent.

Now Giuditta's molto-chic great-granddaughter Marta teaches the weaving classes. Marta (also an interior designer) is the only one around who knows how to repair those antique looms. In addition, she's an extraordinary weaver, who recreates designs from medieval paintings that feature those famous Perugia tablecloths. Marta's mother, Clara, leads the afternoon history lessons, which is where her passion lies. She's intensely studied the traditions of weaving and written books about it.

www.brozzetti.com

One of the history classes is a trip to Citta di Castello, to visit the Tela Umbra studio, and see a different style of weaving. The studio was created from the same inspiration as Brozzetti, to preserve the tradition and give women jobs. And since those women had children, Maria Montessori was brought in to open up a classroom that became her first training ground for teachers.

If you'd like to learn embroidery, Lina Montagnoli, who has been at it for fifty years, is the maternal and meticulous teacher. She'll go simple for beginners or teach intricate medieval designs to the more advanced. When local women show up to her classes, she says, "They see it as group anti-stress therapy."

Giuditta Brozzetti: Via Tiberio Berardi 5/6, 075 40236. Classes are June through September, one day or one to three weeks.

TOURS

Bella Vista Tours (www.bellavistatours.com) arranges group artisan workshops here and throughout Italy.

87 Italian Language Classes

"GET AN ITALIAN BOYFRIEND," is what girlfriends tell me is the best way to learn the language. Learning to speak Italian while falling in love is a lot like how a baby makes its first attempts. First it's all about *amore*, then it moves on to basic necessities where you're like a demanding two-year-old, and if things go farther you'll inevitably be expressing feelings, which could lead to anything from a tearful breakup or, in the case of my friend Lisa, a happy marriage and two adorable bi-lingual children.

Going another route, you could follow my friend Louise's lead. She's a card-carrying Italophile and has taken lots of language classes in Italy. For her it's been a good way to take a trip that feels "rooted" and gets her more deeply immersed into the culture. And since she's past the backpacking days of meeting fellow travelers in youth hostels, the classes have the perk of a built-in social scene for those times when she's traveling solo.

If you do an internet search, you'll find schools all over Italy—from Elba to every major city. Most are reasonably priced and have sliding scales of accommodations, so you can stay in a low-priced dorm or private apartment. Italians have become professional in setting these schools up all over, as so many people from all over the world want to learn Italian. As far as accreditation, you may want to check with your local Italian teachers to see if they have any recommendations.

So the question is: *Where to study*? Since it's Italy, every place where there's a school has its charms.

You could break the question down to, "Do I want a village or city school experience?" If you choose a city, as Louise says, "It's like going to a commuter college in America. There's the advantage of having so much interesting culture around you in a place like Rome, but it's going to be a bit more expensive than a village school. And most likely the other students will be running off after class to do their own thing."

If you choose a village, it's like going to college in a small town. There's camaraderie with the other students, and since you'll be in a place where most of the natives don't speak English, it's a good "sink or swim" situation when you're not in class. A middle ground choice would be a town like Siena or Perugia, where you have a lot of cultural activities, but it's a more closely knit community than a major city.

www.ciao-italia.it
laboratoriolinguistico.it

Taking Louise's advice, years ago I went to **Ciao Italia**, a small school in Rome, near the Colosseum. They fixed me up with budget accommodations (my own bedroom and bath) in a huge Trastevere apartment, where I was hosted by Antoinella, a half-deaf, 70-something-year-old widow. She insisted on feeding me and I got a kick out of hanging out and watching blaring TV with her just like I'd done back in Jersey with my nana.

My classmates were a writer from Edinburgh who was working on translating Belli (his favorite Roman poet), a thirty-something-year-old Venezuelan gal who'd married an Italian and was on a job hunt, and a Japanese chef who worked in an Italian restaurant in Tokyo. This mix of nationalities is typical. "Most of the time I'm the only American at the school," Louise says.

At Ciao Italia the instructors were enthusiastic types, who rode Vespas to work and looked like fashionistas even when they were just wearing jeans and zip-up jackets. The classes were excellent and structured as most schools are: three-hour morning sessions, broken up into grammar and conversation classes, and optional afternoon activities that ranged from cooking classes to a walking tour of the Jewish Ghetto, or watching *Cinema Paradiso* without subtitles.

I loved the two weeks. It was rigorous classwork, but fun. At the same time, there were distractions, like my American-Roman friends who I'd have dinner with and break my "only speak Italian rule." And then the endless sights I'd want to get to or re-visit from past trips, which cut into what I could've gotten from the afternoon programs.

One of Louise's favorite language school experiences was in the small port town of Milazzo, Sicily, where she signed up for a few weeks at **Laboratorio Linguistico**. The classes were small, the school had sailboat excursions to the nearby Aeolian Islands, there was a beach to hang out on, and a historic town center that wasn't touristy. Louise now speaks excellent Italian, and she says taking this class really helped to improve it.

Wherever you choose to go, you should have basic Italian 101 under your belt, as most schools teach using the "direct method," with classes totally in Italian. And though there is fun to be had, keep in mind there will be homework.

What's best about taking classes in Italy rather than back home is that the learning curve is speedy. All of a sudden you'll be out in the street, overhearing conversations you can actually understand or having interactions with Italians, using what you've just learned. Ah—those "Eureka!" moments.

88 Mosaics at Orsoni Studio–Venice

CONNIE GIOCOBBE, A FIFTY-THREE-YEAR-OLD mother of two grown-up kids, had been a hairdresser in Kansas City for years, painted as a hobby, and had just begun mosaic work when she thought, "If I really want to learn this, I should get to a place that has one of the longest traditions of mosaic-making: Venice." And lo, up on her computer screen popped a mosaics workshop at the **Orsoni Studio**.

Orsoni is hidden behind high walls in the Cannaregio district, off a *fondamenta* that wasn't even on my *Streetwise Venice* map. Since 1888, when the foundry was taken over by Angelo Orsoni, the *smalti* (colored opaque glass) and gold-leaf mosaics that it produces have been used to restore churches, such as the Basilica di San Marco, and shipped off to provide materials for some of the world's most beautiful buildings—from Gaudi's Sagrada Familia church in Barcelona, to the Golden Room in Stockholm where Nobel Prizes are awarded, to buddhas in Bangkok.

Even though what's made here is such a major deal, the place has a low-key, family business vibe. Everybody from the workers to the staff and students seems especially upbeat, I'm guessing because they're surrounded by all this pretty sparkly stuff all day.

Like Orsoni students on their first day of class, I got in to see the production facility, where men gathered around a blazing furnace and moved with a riveting choreography, scooping out glowing liquid glass to a rotating metal belt where it solidified in seconds and then was slid away to cool, like iridescent pancakes. Next door women cut the *smalti* into *tesserae* (small pieces used in mosaic art), that formed what looked like piles of glittering hard candy. Finally, there's the color library: a huge warehouse of rickety wooden shelves stacked floor to ceiling with over two thousand hues of *smalti* to choose from.

"The library is one of the things that makes it a dream to take class here, to have access to all that," Connie told me.

The Orsoni Workshop was opened in 2003 by Maestro Lucio Orsoni, the great-grandson of the company's founder and a world-famous mosaic artist. Classes here are kept small (six students max), so there's lots of individual attention given by instructor/artist Antonella Gallenda, who's been working by Lucio's side for thirty years. The school attracts a range of international students, from beginners to those with years of experience. Some simply sign up for three days to add a little cultural zing to their Venetian vacation and make a small mosaic. Others opt for the one- or two-week sessions to learn basics, micromosaics, or portraiture.

When I stopped by the workshop, catching a two-week class at its midpoint, it looked like they were all pros. Then the gal from Chicago whose portrait of her adorable five-year-old son I admired said she'd never done it before. Instructor Antonella strolled about offering encouragement and suggestions—stopping by Connie's project to help her out with the tricky problem of getting her portrait's mouth just right. There was a fun, focused, creative spirit in the air as the students hammered and glued away.

"I came here as a beginner three years ago, and now I'm back for my third time," Connie said. Her technique has advanced so much she's gotten commercial commissions for her creations.

A fab feature of the program is that in the same renovated Orsoni villa as the workshop is **Domus Orsoni**, a bed and breakfast designed by mosaic artisans, where students can stay during their course. It's the only *artiturismo* I've ever seen, and when it's not filled with workshop participants it's available to visitors looking for bargain digs in an under-touristed Venice neighborhood.

"I love staying here and waking up to the foundry workers singing," Connie said. "Everyone around here has become like family to me."

The classes have also given Connie the opportunity to make friends with mosaic artists from all over the world. "A lot of nights after dinner, we'll go back into the workshop with a bottle of wine and cheese, put in a Pavarotti CD, and get to work. Sometimes we're up until three in the morning. It's completely relaxing."

Orsoni Studio and Domus Orsoni: For workshop information, to make an appointment to tour the foundry and gallery, or to book a stay at Domus Orsoni, go to www.orsoni.com.

XI

Be Entertained

While you're often surrounded by tourists in museums and restaurants, if you venture out to a jazz club, puppet show, or soccer game, you'll be blending in with Italian life. How fantastic to be in the midst of cheering soccer fans, elegantly dressed patrons of the opera, or adorable children cheering at a puppet show. Where's Fellini's camera?

You may want to plan your entertainment in advance (recommended for opera), or there's sure to be something wonderful going on you could just happen upon during your travels.

Italy is also world renowned for its **summer festivals**, which attract international artists and audiences. Here's a chance to stay in one place and enjoy a variety of entertainments: theatre, symphony orchestras, ballet, and film. Two of my favorite festivals:

* **The Ravello Festival, Amalfi Coast**
  Late June to September, www.ravellofestival.com
  An outdoor stage is set up on a cliff overlooking the sea at the Villa Rufolo, where Richard Wagner came in 1880 and was inspired to write *Parsifal*. To be there on a moonlit night to hear an orchestra under the stars is an experience of a lifetime. The festival also includes dance, film, and art exhibitions.

* **Festival of Two Worlds (Festival dei Due Mondi), Spoleto, Late June to Mid-July, www.festivaldispoleto.com**
A showcase for new and insightful theater and music, here you'll find exciting events such as a play directed by Robert Wilson or opera directed by Woody Allen.

FOR WHAT-WHERE-WHEN IN ENGLISH

Rome: www.inromenow.com
Florence: www.theflorentine.net
Venice: www.aguestinvenice.com

Opera

"WHICH EXPERIENCE DO YOU WANT: the prima donna or the diva?"

That was Fred Plotkin's response when I asked him for advice about where to see the best opera in Italy. Fred is a modern-day Renaissance man—an expert on Italian food and wine, classical music, and opera. Then there's me—definitely a neophyte, in need of help, because all the opera I've seen in Italy has been shockingly disappointing. Not that I didn't enjoy the pleasant experience of taking a nap on the red velvet cushions in a box at Teatro San Carlo in Naples, but I do expect more from opera in Italy.

"Every Italian knows the difference," he said. "A *prima donna* is a demanding, difficult woman. A *diva*, from the Latin *divus* (god), is a woman who has powers beyond those of the average person, someone who can transport you to emotional heights. Diana Ross is a prima donna. Aretha Franklin is a diva."

Don't we all want the diva? Isn't getting spectacularly transported what opera is all about?

That was the original intention. Opera began when a group of radical academics and musicians (the *Camerata Fiorentina*) got together in Renaissance Florence with a vision to create a new kind of performance, unlike the stiff style of the day. Inspired by the spectacles of ancient Greece, they invented an art form where the human voice expressing emotion was the focus, with music composed to support a dramatic text.

At first opera was "only for royalty" entertainment, but by early eighteenth-century Venice, regular folks had become avid fans. The shows were as popular as the Broadway musicals of our day. Seventeen Venice opera houses would be filled to the rafters with courtesans, merchants, and noblemen. Though women's roles were first performed by *castrati*, soon composers realized they needed real female voices, so out onto the stage stepped Italy's first divas.

Which gets us back to the question: Where do we go today for the diva experience?

According to Fred, the cities that first come to mind when we think Italian opera—Milan, Venice, and Naples—are all prima donnas. Yes, their opera houses are astounding to be in, and it's wonderful to take a tour of them. Historically, they're important because they're where the world's beloved Italian composers—like Verdi and Puccini—had their premieres. But as far as the quality of performances: all prima donna. These places are resting on their laurels from days gone by. So for the "diva experience," go to:

Teatro Regio, Turin

Not only does this northern Italian town have fabulous food, wine, and chocolate, but its cultural scene is outstanding. The principal conductor of Teatro Regio is Gianandrea Noseda, a brilliant young musician of world-class stature, who's also Chief Conductor of the BBC Philharmonic. The Torino opera house was built in 1740 and its shell still exists, but the building's been stricken with fires and renovated, so inside you'll find a contemporary design. The Regio is surrounded by great restaurants and caffès for a fun before-and-after social opera scene during its September through June season.

Opera in The Marches

The seaside and mountain towns in this central coast region are home to over seventy *teatri storici* (historic theaters)—from jewel boxes to arenas—built between the seventeenth and nineteenth centuries. Here in this under-touristed part of Italy, you can experience great opera in beautiful settings, such as:

● **Pesaro**, the birthplace of Rossini, of *The Barber of Seville* fame. This is a lovely beach town that's home to an annual August **Rossini Opera Festival**. Three theaters are involved, one from 1637 and two other modern spaces. Rossini's home is also fun to tour, and Pesaro has a fascinating old Jewish quarter, a family-oriented beach scene, loads of bookstores, and a university.

● **Macerata** is a quintessential Italian hill town, loaded with Romanesque, Renaissance, and Baroque architecture. In July and August, operas are staged outdoors at its **Arena Sferisterio**, a huge neoclassical structure that was built in 1820 for handball games. According to Fred, coming here for the *al fresco* opera experience far outshines the Verona Arena scene. In Verona, you are typically packed in with crowds of drunken tourists, while in Macerata you're surrounded by Italians who truly love and appreciate great opera.

www.teatroregio.torino.it
www.rossinioperafestival.it
www.le-marche.com
www.teatropergolesi.org

❀ **Jesi**, an elegant, fortified medieval hill town hosts an opera
festival every fall. Here you'll have an outstanding intimate
experience, in its small (680 seat) **Teatro G.P. Pergolesi**,
named in honor of the composer who was born there.

So go and cheer *Brava!* to the Divas. Join in with the natives
and call out, "*Bis! Bis!*" for an encore. Hopefully you won't hear
whistles, which in Italian is the sound that means "Boo!"

RECOMMENDED READING

Opera 101: A Complete Guide to Learning and Loving Opera by Fred Plotkin

Classical Music

YOU MAY BE WALKING ALONG AND HEAR VIOLINS. The music is coming out of a church. Take a peek inside: a chamber ensemble is at the altar, surrounded by luscious baroque architecture. Heavenly.

You're in Italy where this kind of thing isn't rare, especially in the major cities. Yes, there are impressive symphony halls, opera houses, and outdoor summer festivals where you can go to hear excellent classical music. But there's something about the intimacy of the church setting, where the music is often not miked, the surroundings pull you back to the gentler times when the pieces were composed, and there you are up close to a handsome fella soulfully playing a cello...

Many chamber ensemble concerts are free, none are very expensive. This is an experience you could plan ahead for, but you're bound to just be walking along and see a banner announcing the event and decide to go that evening. There's no set seating, so get there early if you'd like to be up front. If you or your beloved traveling partner grumbles "Classical music, not me," try an "It'll only be an hour or two tops" nudge. This will probably become one of the most memorable experiences of your trip, and theirs.

Venice—Home of Vivaldi

Venice reveres Vivaldi, that romantic baroque musician of *Four Seasons* (*Quattro Stagioni*) fame, who was born here in 1678. He was a revolutionary composer, boldly bringing emotion to the violin and its sister string instruments—from heights of joy to depths of melancholy. His ornate music matches the Venetian spirit.

All over Venice you'll see posters for chamber ensemble performances where Vivaldi is the headliner. And there will often be other greats such as Corelli, Rossini, and Mozart on the bill. You'll also be approached by beaming costumed folks who are putting on Vivaldi shows. To put it as nicely as possible, the costumed folks are not who I mean when I'm talking great Vivaldi in Venice, so don't confuse them with the authentic chamber ensembles.

www.interpretiveneziani.com
www.ensembleantoniovivaldi.com
www.collegiumducale.com

Tickets are easy to get online, at tourist kiosks, or through your hotel; I've also done fine off-season just showing up right before the concert. Performance nights vary and most starting times are 8:30ish.

❀ Interpreti Veneziani—Chiesa San Vidal (San Marco)

The very best! A young, exuberant ensemble that's received critical raves since they came onto the scene in 1987. The seventeenth-century church setting is enriched with paintings from Carpaccio and other Venetian masters.

❀ **Ensemble Antonio Vivaldi–Chiesa di San Giacometto (Rialto)**
The cherry red interior of one of Venice's oldest churches makes for an especially romantic experience. This is also an exceptionally well-heated venue, perfect for a chilly night.

❀ **Collegium Ducale–Chiesa di Santa Maria Formosa (Rialto) or Palazzo delle Prigioni (San Marco)**
This seven-piece ensemble has a repertory spanning from baroque to jazz, with jazz only on the bill when they play at the Palazzo. Why is the Chiesa di Santa Maria so curvy, you might ask? It was built when a bishop had a vision of the BVM who came to him looking quite voluptuous, so he passed on that inspiration to the architect.

Rome

❀ **Concerts in the Sacristy of Borromini–Piazza Navona**
Right off Piazza Navona, in the back of the Church of Saint Agnes in Agony, is this recently restored jewel box, designed by the baroque master Borromini. Here guest artists—from award-winning young players to musicians of international fame—bring in a varied repertoire. Your program may include either Schubert, Paganini, Debussy, Mozart, Brahms, or Chopin. Admission includes a free post-concert drink at the nearby **Cul de Sac** (one of Rome's best wine bars), where you can meet the musicians. Evening performances usually start around 5 or 6 P.M.

www.santagneseinagone.org
www.orcafi.it

Florence

❖ **Orchestra da Camera Fiorentina–Chiesa di Orsanmichele**
Critically acclaimed as the best chamber orchestra in Europe, this forty-piece ensemble performs chamber music and symphonic concerts, from such composers as Pergolesi, Schubert, Beethoven, and Haydn. Star guest musicians often add flash to the bill. It's on a grander scale than most "music in churches" experiences, but fitting for the vast Orsanmichele, a granary turned Gothic sanctuary. Performances take place March through October.

91 *Jazz*

ITALY GAVE AMERICA PIZZA. America gave Italy jazz.

Just like there's pizza in even the smallest American burb, the same goes for jazz in Italy. Italians went gaga over the style in 1904, when a Creole group, hailed as "the creators of the cat-walk," performed in Milan. With great enthusiasm, orchestras were formed. Over the decades star players emerged, bringing Italian twists to this American form.

From the start, American jazz musicians who came to Italy were welcomed and revered. Louis Armstrong toured through in the thirties, Chet Baker lived in Turin for a while, Ella Fitzgerald celebrated her fortieth birthday (really her forty-first, she was tricky about it) with a concert in Rome that's one of her best recordings.

These days in Italy you'll find top American players on the bills, along with legendary natives such as Enrico Rava and Gianni Basso. As far as Italian jazz gals to look out for, there are vocalists Tiziana Ghiglioni (called Italy's "Lady of Jazz"), and Maria Pia de Vito, a Naples native whose take on Joni Mitchell tunes is wonderful.

Or you may find yourself in Italy enjoying Patti Wicks, an extraordinary American jazz pianist and singer, who performs in Italy often. Her trio, which includes two native Italians on bass and drums, won Best Jazz Album of the Year at the 2008 Italian Jazz Awards.

Patti's take on the Italian jazz scene is, "It's all set up with such elan. The audiences are so effusive, there's absolutely no chatting when there's music, and they're always calling for encores."

As a backdrop to the cool players, the varied performance venues are exquisite. You may find yourself at one of Italy's many jazz festivals, mostly held in summer, when an entire small town is filled with music and you can see shows in baroque theaters, chic clubs where the food is fantastic, or in amazing outdoor settings, where often the performances are free.

Like pizza in America, jazz in Italy varies greatly in quality. As in, you wouldn't want to spend a euro to hear the sour saxophonist who played "Strangers in the Night" outside my Rome apartment again and again.

Here are some great spots—my recommendations mixed in with Patti's.

Clubs, reservations necessary:

* **Alexanderplatz**—Via Ostia 9, Rome, 063 974 2171, closed Sunday
  A super-sophisticated spot on the Vatican City side of Rome, where you feel part of the in-crowd as you take a winding staircase down to a room where legends like Wynton Marsalis got their start.

* **Ferrara Jazz Club**—Torrione San Giovanni, Via Rampari di Belfiore, 167, 339 788 6261
  Chic, intimate spot to see headliners, with fantastic food of the Emilia-Romagna region.

- **Osteria del Caffè Casolani**–Via Casolani 41, Casole d'Elsa, 057 794 8733, closed Thursday
  In a perfectly preserved teensy medieval town near Siena, is this quaint restaurant where Tuscan specialties are served family-style. Jazz ensembles perform in the attached garden during warmer months and inside otherwise. Patti says she's met people from all over the world here—Norway, Britain, and America, along with Italian jazz fans.

Festivals

- **Umbria Jazz Festival**
  The largest jazz festival in Italy, which takes over the town of Perugia for ten days in July. Two hundred thousand fans flock in to see what's been called the best in the world. The more low-key **Umbria Jazz Winter** takes place in December in Orvieto, in venues such as Teatro Mancinelli (built in 1886) and the Palazzo del Popolo, from the eleventh century.

  www.umbriajazz.com
  www.anconajazz.com
  www.argojazz.com

- **Ancona Jazz Festival**–The Marches
  The seaside town on the northern Adriatic is filled with jazz all year long and every July with this festival, featuring performances at the historic Teatro Della Muse and beautiful gardens in the neighboring medieval town of Offagnia.

- **Argo Jazz**–Basilicata
  A 2003 newcomer, centered around a beach resort, that also features poetry, film, theater, and photography exhibits. The main stage, set seaside, is awesome.

* **Lucca Jazz Donna–Tuscany**

For one week in February, top female players and vocalists reign here. The event includes gallery shows and films, and often performances that pay homage to a particular legend, such as Billie Holiday or Ella Fitzgerald.

WWW. www.luccajazzdonna.it www.thebrassgroup.it

Also:

* **The Brass Group**–Palermo

All year long, this non-profit jazz foundation hosts performances at various Palermo venues. The most beautiful is **Santa Maria dello Spasimo**, a roofless former Gothic church.

TIP: *For complete listings of jazz performances all over Italy by dates and regions: www.jazzitalia.net or www.jazz-clubs-worldwide.com*

Puppet Shows

WHEN I WAS A KID, PUPPET SHOWS creeped me out. I'd make a run from the birthday party as soon as a scary grownup got up to hide behind a dark curtain. So I never sought out Italian puppet shows. But there I was in Naples, in a great mood because I'd just eaten a *sfogliatelle*, the seashell-shaped pastry the city is deservedly famous for.

Timing is everything. A dinky portable puppet stage appeared right on the Via Toledo route that led to the apartment I'd rented. Mammas and *bambini* crowded around it, clapping and laughing. I stopped and saw Pulcinella, the rascal clown who's the mascot of Naples, get whacked in the head by a *signorina* puppet. I laughed. I was cured. And hooked.

Italian puppet shows are hysterical spectacles that have a Warner Brother's cartoon-like style. They're great fun even if you aren't a kid and don't know a word of Italian. They'll pop up spontaneously in parks or can be found elaborately produced in theaters, with locals of all ages making up a rapt audience.

The puppet tradition in Italy goes back thousands of years, and though the shows are full of laughs, creating them is taken very seriously, with artists crafting characters, sets, costumes and music to make enchantment.

The characters and stories you'll see will depend on the region you visit. In Naples, you'll always find Pulcinella, whose name translates to "little chicken." He's the hook-nosed guy in the baggy white costume who's always causing trouble. Sometimes he's making a play for the perky servant gal, *Columbina*, who's traditionally dressed showing lots of cleavage and typically turns the story around by saving the day with some tricky smart move. Tambourines rattle, there is much whacking with sticks—its rhythm blends with the mercurial Neapolitan spirit.

In Palermo, right across from the Cattedrale, you can see grand puppet opera created by the Argento family that's been in the biz since 1893. Their shows tell stories of the Knights of Charlemagne battling the Saracens, with marionettes dressed in fancy armor saving damsels in distress. I'll never forget watching one of their action packed finales: Knights charged a king, split his head open with their swords, each head-half plonked to the stage, and then in rushed a clown marionette to cheer the happy ending.

Free outdoor puppet shows:

* **Rome**: I Burattini di Carlo Piantadosi, Janiculum Hill (behind Garibaldi's statue, 06 582 7767). Show times may vary: Monday-Friday at 4 & 7, Saturday & Sunday at 10:30, 12:30, and 4:30.

* **Florence**: Il Cappello di Merlino, Piazza Pitti 3r (055 230 2594). Every Saturday at 5.

Theater shows:

* **Rome**: Teatro Verde (www.teatroverde.it)

* **Florence**: Teatrino del Gallo (www.teatrinodelgallo.it)

- **Palermo**: Near the Cattedrale, at Opera dei Pupi di Vincenzo Argento e figli, via Pietro Novelli 1, 091 611 3680.
- **Milan**: Teatro Colla (www.teatrocolla.org)

Soccer

ARE YOU UP FOR EXPERIENCING the most intense display of passion in this most passionate of countries? The soccer stadium is where it's ratcheted to awesome heights.

You'll get some idea of why the sport is regarded as the country's religion if you're there on a Sunday. You're bound to hear a huge explosion of yelling-screaming or moaning bursting out of bars, restaurants, and kitchens. Take a seat at one of those places if you can't make it to a game.

But you won't really get it till you're in the stadium. The most enthusiastic American sports fans look like they're on lithium compared to *calcio* fans. Italian enthusiasts form clubs that can be as big as 10,000 screamers, who sit in special reserved sections in the stadium. They arrive three hours before the games with banners and flags to rehearse chants, songs, and choreography for the big event.

And what an event! The game takes place in two thrilling halves: ninety riveting minutes of those *bellissimi* players. There are no Jumbotron dot-racing breaks, no flashes of "Candy Will You Marry Me?" It's all about what's happening on the field, moment by thrilling moment.

"It's a way of life, it's all heart," says Bruno Dascanio, a dedicated fan of Inter-Milan. "You have bragging rights when your team wins, you take it personally when they lose, get sick over it, have fights with girlfriends over it."

Bruno, in collaboration with **Europe at Cost** tour operators, takes travelers on soccer weekends to Milan, that include dinners, hotel, and an escort to the game. If the timing is right, you may even meet some players. This is a perfect set-up for those of you who've been warned that going to a stadium is dangerous. It's true that in some stadiums there have been horrendous outbreaks of fan violence in recent years. But the police have cracked down on the hotheads and these days things are under better control. The much larger majority of fans go to the stadium to have a great time.

The Italian Soccer League has four divisions, with twenty teams making up the top tier, called Serie A. These are the most exciting games, and best to see at stadiums in Milan, Rome, Florence, or Torino. You can get less expensive tickets seeing Serie B-D, and some of these teams play on Saturdays, if that's more convenient for you.

When you go, sit on the home team's side. The away team section has different exits and entrances and you won't get the booming local experience over there. Pick up your sausage or *porchetta* panino at a stall before the game. And leave behind your prudish self, because inside you're bound to get a thorough education in swearing Italian style. Get into the spirit. It may give you goosebumps.

Tickets can be obtained from www.1st4footballtickets.com or www.lega-calcio.it (official Italian soccer site).

TOUR

Europe at Cost (www.europeatcost.com) will custom design tours to Italy, including soccer weekends.

XII

Advice from Writers

I love to read books that take place in Italy. They fling me around through its history; give me a chance to see the country through a different lens. They take me beyond guidebooks, bringing another layer to my experience of a destination.

Sometimes I'll get caught up with historical fiction—learning about the Jewish ghetto in Venice through Erica Jong's heroine in *Shylock's Daughter*. Or on my last trip to Rome, I reread Tennessee Williams' *The Roman Spring of Mrs. Stone*, a hoot of a melodrama, which brings *La Dolce Vita* days back to life. What was there to do after I finished it, but get myself to the Rosati in Piazza del Popolo and order a Negroni.

When I'm not in Italy, reading one of the many memoirs that's come out over the past decades has been an excellent way to hold me over until my next trip. I've gone along, vicariously restoring several farmhouses and getting over various heartbreaks. Wondrously, there's that "reading as communion" thing that happens when these writers pour their passion for Italy on the page. That's me on the couch, sighing along as I read.

While writing this book, I've been thinking about some of my favorite female writers who've taken me around "their" Italy. So I checked in with them to talk about Italian travel. Each generously shared with me some of their favorite places, so now I share them with you...

Frances Mayes

> "I came to Italy expecting adventure. What I never anticipated is
> the absolute sweet joy of everyday life—la dolce vita."
> -FRANCES MAYES, *Bella Tuscany*

WITH VIVID WRITING THAT CAPTURES sensual moment by moment details, Frances Mayes has turned readers all over the world on to the joys of life in Italy. For any of you who missed it, she's the author of *Under the Tuscan Sun*, *Bella Tuscany*, and *A Year In the World*.

Her books have taken me along with her—hacking away at weeds in her Cortona garden, discovering Saturnia's thermal springs, and temples in Sicily. It's engrossing writing that gets me daydreaming about my next trip. Plus her recipes are wonderful.

Always, she connects the experience of her outer journey to the fascinating, ever-changing inward journey. "In Italy you can find the place that corresponds to your soul more easily than any other place in the world," she says.

Frances first traveled to Italy after studying its art and architecture in college. She remembers landing in Bologna one autumn morning:

"It was staggering. I was sitting under one of those big arcades...all around there were people drinking coffee and smoking, and I remember thinking...*Ah! this is really fun.* That's when I started getting intrigued by the vivacity of the Italians. I have that great attraction us pale-faced people have to it, like a moth to a light bulb."

That great attraction led Frances to find her "soul" place: rural Tuscany. As much as I love reading about her life there in Cortona, I also get thrilled by her writing when she takes off to explore other parts of Italy. She brings such a great spirit of whimsy, curiosity, and passion to her traveling. When I spoke to her, she naturally had lots of recommendations:

"For women traveling solo, I would love to be in Venice. You can just revel in being there, riding around on the boats and walking. And Capri, off season, is paradise. It's one of the best places for walks—glamorous and quiet. It would be a marvelous place to work."

As far as traveling with a sweetheart or friends, Frances raved about **Friuli-Venezia Giulia**. This region in Italy's northeastern corner is world-renowned for its wines. And it's (so far) unspoiled by tourism. As Frances said, "You get a sense of discovery there, like it's yours. But of course, you're not the first one to discover it!"

On a recent trip, she and her husband explored the area in and around **Cormons**. "We're wine fanatics," she said, "and the experience visiting wineries there is completely different from northern California, where places are set up for commercial tourism, with stores selling t-shirts. When we were driving around Cormons, we'd just pull up to a vineyard, and there was the owner who came out and showed us around. Then we sat with him under a pergola and tasted his wines."

What's also attractive about the small, fun-to-walk-around town of Cormons is the chance to blend in with the community at the local bar where everyone gathers for wine tastings. And, as

Frances says, "The food was wonderful, with Austrian influences and lots of fish from nearby Trieste."

Frances was in her North Carolina home, cooking broccoli soup with her six-year-old grandson, when I spoke to her from my apartment in Los Angeles. But just as she'd brought me to Tuscany through her books, when she spoke (with her lilting southern accent) about Cormons, I was there: "The countryside is quite mellow, with vineyards full of that...that *golden* light...."

Tuscan Sun Festival: Mayes describes this annual Cortona event as "A camp for grown ups who love music." It takes place for ten days every August and was started by two of her friends. "I'm the godmother of it," Mayes said. Events include concerts, art exhibits, lectures by writers and poets, cooking demos, wine tastings, and wellness sessions. (www.festivadelsole.com)

RECOMMENDED READING

All of Frances Mayes' books, including:

Bella Tuscany
Under the Tuscan Sun
A Year in the World

95 Erica Jong

> "Venice is ever the fragile labyrinth at the edge of the sea
> and it reminds us how brief and perilous the journeys of
> our lives are, perhaps that is why we love it so."
> —ERICA JONG, *Shylock's Daughter*

I DISCOVERED ERICA JONG THROUGH HER POETRY, which I read ferociously in high school, turning down Joni Mitchell albums to share it with my girlfriends on my front porch on the Jersey shore. Her first novel, *Fear of Flying*, became the woman's bible of the '70s sexual revolution, and she's followed that up with many bestselling books, each cutting to the core complexities of the feminine experience, in a luscious, richly entertaining style.

And Erica's connection to Venice is strong.

She'd visited Venice on a college trip, but didn't really get to know it until years later when, in her words, she was drawn there by "an impossible love." Throughout the '80s and '90s she rented apartments in Venice, delving into the history, mysteries, and literature of the island. She saw it as similar to her Manhattan hometown—an island that became a cultural center in part because of immigration, a place that welcomed enterprising Jews who helped to make the city great.

Erica calls Venice a magic place where the imagination is unbound. It was in Venice that she was inspired to write *Shylock's Daughter*—originally titled *Serenissima,* the nickname for Venice, which means "The Most Serene"—a riveting novel about a beautiful, troubled actress who magically time travels back to the town's sixteenth-century Jewish Ghetto, where she meets young Will Shakespeare. As the actress becomes the heroine in his play, passion and adventure ensue.

Her writing captures the spirit of La Serenissima, with such passages as:

"Each time one comes to Venice, it reflects back another self, another dream, as if it were partly your own mirror. The air is full of the spirits of all those who have lived here, worked here, loved here. The stones themselves are thick with history. They whisper to you as you walk the streets at night."

When asked what advice she'd give to women about Venice, Erica said, "It's such a romantic place. But if you stay in a hotel you just get the money-grubbing Venice, the Venice where everybody wants something from you. To get the real Venice, rent an apartment in a neighborhood like the Dorsoduro and stay for a period of time. You'll realize it's very much an island. And a very tight little island where everybody knows everybody. And everybody *watches* everybody because they get so bored on the island!"

"The best way to see Venice is by getting someone to take you around on a private boat," she said, and went on to rhapsodize about the Romanesque mosaics in the church on the island of Torcello. "And Chioggia," she said, "Chioggia is amazing—a tiny fishing village with cobbled streets..."

For info about Erica and her books: www.ericajong.com

RECOMMENDED READING

Shylock's Daughter by Erica Jong (and all her books, found at www.
  ericajong.com)

Erica recommends:

Watermark by Joseph Brodsky

Venice Is a Fish: A Cultural Guide by Tiziano Scarpa

Marcella Hazan

*"Eating in Italy is one more manifestation of the Italian's
age-old gift of making art out of life."*
—MARCELLA HAZAN, *The Classic Italian Cook Book*

MARCELLA HAZAN, THE QUEEN OF ITALIAN CUISINE, whose award-winning cookbooks have inspired me for many years, was perfect to ask for advice about eating in Venice. She and her husband Victor lived and taught there in the '80s and '90s. Now that Marcella's eighty-four and all the steps and walking there became too much, the couple lives on another island, in Longboat Key, Florida, but they still visit Venice often.

She was eager and generous about sharing her tips for eating and shopping in her favorite city.

"Order *canocchie*," she told me, "It's a type of spider shrimp that you can only find in Venice and Japan. It's very soft, very sweet, very delicate." She also recommended *moleche* (soft shell crab) when it's in season, which is usually April and November. Then there is sole: "For Americans, Maine has the lobster, but Venice has the sole," she said. It's much smaller than American sole and served as *sole in soar*, where the fried fish is put in a sauce with vinegar, pine nuts, and raisins.

As far as shopping for food at the **Rialto Market**, she sighed, "I'd like to shop there every day of my life." And, "You should notice how each item is marked to tell where it came from. What's local is more expensive than what's imported, like asparagus from Sant'Erasmo or fish marked *nostrane*. It's the freshness that costs much more," she explained. "Salmon is cheaper, it's not Italian."

When it came to restaurant recommendations, **Fiaschetteria Toscana** was her immediate response. "It doesn't have anything to do with Tuscany, that was its name from the beginning and now Mariuccia who cooks there is very good, it's very Venetian, and she makes wonderful desserts." When I stopped in there for lunch recently, sure enough Mariuccia showed up carrying a freshly baked apple tart and then made her way around the restaurant to chat with the locals who were obviously long-time regulars of this spot near the Rialto bridge. "Marcella sends her regards," I told her. Mariuccia held her hands over her heart and said, "She is like my aunt!"

If you mention "Victor and Marcella Hazan sent me" to the owners of any of the restaurants listed below, they will give you a warm welcome.

The woman whose voice that comes across so strict and uncompromising through the pages of her cookbooks, got soft and nostalgic talking about Venice: "Every corner you turn is unbelievable. Have you ever seen it in the snow? It looks like embroidery on the Ca' d'Oro, like it came from Burano. And the light...the fog...when you can see Venice coming out little by little and you wait and it is coming to life...Venice..."

Places to say "Marcella sent me..."

* **Fiaschetteria Toscana,** ask for Mariuccia. Salizada S. Giovanni Grisostomo, Cannaregio 041 528 5281, closed Tuesday and Wednesday lunch.

- **Da Ivo**, ask for Giovanni. Ramo dei Fuseri, San Marco, 041 528 5004, closed Monday and January.
- **Da Fiore**, ask for Maurizio. Calle del Scaleter, San Polo, 041 721 308, closed Sunday and Monday.

RECOMMENDED READING

All Marcella Hazan's cookbooks and *Amarcord: Marcella Remembers*

Mary Taylor Simeti

"*Sicily is a fun-house mirror in which Italy can behold her national traits and faults distorted and exaggerated.*"
—MARY TAYLOR SIMETI, *On Persephone's Island: A Sicilian Journal*

AT JUST THE MENTION OF FEMALES in Sicily, Mary Taylor Simeti comes out with: "There's that pre-Greek ancient sculpture in the archaeological museum in Syracuse. A large seated woman, with two infants, each suckling a breast. And her head's been lopped off. Such an image of the Great Mother! And of motherhood in general!" That's typical of Mary's wry, personal take on the island's legends.

Mary's writing—whether it's memoir, travel story, or cookbook—weaves together her expatriate-in-Sicily experience with her extensive knowledge of mythology, history, and culinary traditions. It's a rich mix that really prepared me for my first trip to the island—giving an honest picture of Sicily's light and dark sides.

Mary arrived in Sicily in 1962, a New Yorker who'd just graduated with a degree in Medieval History from Radcliffe. Her plan was to spend a year volunteering at a community development center in Partinico, west of Palermo. In the prologue of *On Persephone's Island*, Mary's self-deprecating look back at her naïve but determined younger self hooked me. I won't spoil it. Pick up the book.

Mary's year in Sicily turned out to be much longer. While working at the center, she met an agronomist, Tonino Simeti. They married, had two children, lived in Palermo and then rebuilt Tonino's family farm. Now, almost fifty years after she first set foot in Sicily, Mary lives on that farm, called Bosco Falconeria.

"It was all accidental," she laughs. These days, part of Bosco is being converted into a B&B. So if you drive to Alcamo, forty miles west of Palermo, you could stop by and get a taste of those white mulberries Mary writes about, or whatever delicious thing happens to be growing in their organic fields and orchards.

When we spoke more about women and Sicily, Mary focused on **Erice,** about an hour's drive west of her farm: "A fascinating place, laden with Venus myths."

Erice is dramatically set overlooking the coast, on a mountain so high that there's often a haze shrouding the view. It's a tiny town of narrow cobblestoned lanes, hidden courtyards, medieval architecture, with sprinklings of baroque.

Venus worship here goes back to the Carthaginians, who worshipped her as Astarte, Goddess of fertility. Every spring, priestesses would release a flock of white birds from the Erice promontory to fly off to Astarte's temple in Carthage. The birds would return nine days later with a red dove leading them, symbolizing nature's renewal.

Greeks, who came later, claimed that the goddess (as Aphrodite) rose from the sea below Erice in a cockleshell chariot, making the mountain her sacred spot. It was where Aphrodite's ancestor—the primordial God of the Sky Uranus, and his Titan son Cronus-clashed. Cronus sliced off Uranus's balls with a sickle, then threw that sickle (where the name Sicily comes from) into the sea, along with his father's balls. Up splashed Aphrodite! Once on her mountain, she bedded the Argonaut Butes, and gave birth to a son, who she named Eryx.

During Roman times, a huge Venus Erycina cult swept the Mediterranean. She was worshipped not only as Goddess of Beauty, but also of Sacred Prostitution. Romans would come to Erice to lay (in the Biblical sense) with Venus Erycina's priestesses.

"Venus worship continued in Erice well into Christian times, all the way into the Middle Ages," Mary said. "So the main church **(The Matrice)**, was purposely built right at the city gate. The idea was the Madonna would catch the women before they could get to Venus, on the opposite side of town. It was a ploy by the Roman Catholics to put an end to pagan practices."

Now the **Castello di Venere,** built by the Normans in the thirteenth century, stands where Venus's temple once was. It's a grand spot for amazing views. Also, as Mary writes, take a good look at the succulents growing out of the castle walls. The ones with smooth circular leaves, dented in the middle, are called Venus's navelwort—or *ombelico di Venere* in Italian.

"And definitely stop by Maria's for the pastries," Mary said. That would be **Pasticceria Maria Grammatico**, a shop run by a woman who grew up in a convent orphanage, where she learned to make these traditional sweets. Maria is a sort of Erice celebrity, thanks to the book, *Bitter Almonds*, which tells her life story. It was co-written by her friend, Mary Taylor Simeti.

In Alcamo: Taylor Simeti's Agriturismo: Bosco Falconeria (www.boscofalconeria.it).

In Erice: Pasticceria Maria Grammatico, Via Vittorio Emmanuele 14.

RECOMMENDED READING

On Persephone's Island by Mary Taylor Simeti
Travels with a Medieval Queen by Mary Taylor Simeti
Pomp and Sustenance by Mary Taylor Simeti
Bitter Almonds by Mary Taylor Simeti and Maria Grammatico

XIII

La Famiglia
Experiences

These are the places you go where everlasting memories are made; trips that will live on for generations. And as welcoming as Italy is to any traveler, when you arrive with children, or for a wedding, or to visit your Italian relatives, the heart of Italy expands even more for you.

These trips may begin as daydreams. Find a way to make them come true. Especially when it comes to taking children or visiting family over there, don't delay. There will always be reasons to stay home and put off going until next year or the next. But keep in mind the obvious: children grow up fast, grandparents don't live forever. *Carpe diem.*

And don't forget your camera.

98 Places for Children

MANY CALL ITALY THE MOST WELCOMING country in the world to children. Italians adore their own children and will roll out the red carpet for yours on sight.

If you take a baby through a city market, I'm warning you, you're going to have a slow go of it. Inevitably, *signoras* will be leaning down to pinch their cheeks. You may even have the shock of seeing Roman waiters, notorious for their rudeness, drop their "I'm-a-very-important-person—too-busy-to-deal-with-you-attitude" and bend over backwards to bring treats.

Along with its welcoming spirit, Italy has an infinite number of places children will love. Little ones are awestruck by its fountains and castles. School-age kids get to see their history books come alive and will get giggles and thrills from all the nude statues. There are parks or beaches to frolic off the energy. Then there's pizza and gelato. Winning combinations all around.

If you'd rather leave the planning to others, group adventure trips (with companies such as **Backroads** or **Country Walkers**) are there to take the pressure off, and they offer family trips so the kids can make new friends during the week. Also, if you're thinking of bringing the kids to one of the major archaeological sites like the Roman Forum or Pompeii, save yourself and get a children's guide.

For expert help setting things up, check out **Ciao Bambino.**
The company was created by Amie O'Shaughnessy, a
mom herself, who's traveled to Italy often, and along
with her staff, checks out properties and chooses the
best of the child-friendly. You can go to the website
and find them rated according to what age ranges
they're best for, from "Baby-Ready" to "Cool for
Teens." The company can also help you find kid-
friendly restaurants and sites, guides, playgrounds,
and English speaking babysitters in any region.

www.ciaobambino.com
www.italiakids.com
WWW.

Amy's advice for one of the best places to land if
you're traveling with young children is a rural resort in
Tuscany. These are converted villa or farmhouse estates,
which are well set up with cribs, laundry, and a pool for
older kids to mingle with travelers their own age. They're well
located for day trips to charming towns nearby, but you may
just find yourself staying put for at least one idyllic restful day
at what will feel like your Italian home.

Some fun places for kids:

Rome

* **Borghese Gardens**
  Sixty-five acres of manicured green, shadowed by umbrella
  pines. In the Porta Pinciana area, you can rent surrey-style
  pedal carts, roller skates, plain ol' bikes, or even give your
  child a pony ride treat. There are paddleboats available at
  the park pond, you can see puppet shows on weekends, and
  there's a tiny tram that takes you to the Bioparco, a huge
  zoo. That about covers it. (For puppet show schedule: www.
  sancarlino.it)

Florence

❁ **Museo dei Ragazzi–Palazzo Vecchio**
Costumed characters lead kids through this palace where
the Medici lived, for entertaining adventures that may
include shadow shows or dressing up in sixteenth-
century costumes. There are a few programs to
choose from, for children ages four and up.
Reservations necessary.

Venice

❁ **Sant'Erasmo (The Secret Garden of Venice)**
Children easily slip into the fairytale aspect of Venice
(Walt Disney's favorite city), and all the boating makes for
easy entertainment.

But if you're in Venice for more than a few days, and with
kids who like biking, vaporetto to Sant'Erasmo, an island that
lies between Burano and Murano. It's covered with vegetable
gardens and orchards that have supplied Venice markets for
centuries. If you get there in June, lucky you: there will be
fields of purple artichokes in bloom. The bike loop around
the island is 3.5 miles/5.5 km, and you may want to join
Venetian families at the tiny beach for a swim—this is where
the natives come to escape the Lido crowds.

❧

Golden Day: Take Vaporetto 13 to the Capannone stop at
Sant'Erasmo—it's about a forty-minute ride. For bike rentals,
walk up Via Forti to Lato Azzurro (Via Forti 13, (041 523 0642,
www.latoazzurro.it). Eat at **Ca'Vignotto Ristorante** (Via Forti

www.museoragazzi.it

71, 041 244 4000. Lunch daily, dinner Saturday only, reservations essential). It's the only restaurant on the island, beloved by locals, that serves course after course of just-picked deliciousness grown on the island.

RECOMMENDED READING

The Italy Discovery Journal, an interactive guidebook (www.kidseurope. com)

99 An Italian Wedding

IF YOU GET AN INVITATION to an Italian wedding, don't waffle about how you're going to pay for airfare or take time off work. Go for a once-in-a-lifetime unforgettable event. Prepare yourself for an extravaganza of delicious food and dancing until the wee hours.

It'll be a rare invitation. These days Italians say it's not practical to get married, so most are shacking up together for years, and the statistics for Italian marriages are at a historic low. Along with that, there's the trend of "*mammoni*" or mamma's boys, that is, men living at home and having their mothers cook for them and do their laundry until they're well into their thirties. It's inspired the government to step in to get things moving, and beginning in 2008 tax breaks will be offered to those earning low incomes who leave home to live on their own.

Still, if you're in Italy, especially in June (thanks to Juno, Goddess of Marriage), you'll run into Italian weddings in churches. I spent a week in Palermo one June where almost every church I peeked into had a marriage ceremony going on, with wonderful music and stunning get-ups from the bride on down. You'll never see a real Italian wedding on a Tuesday or Friday, as that's considered not a good day to begin any venture.

Which is why when I was last visiting Ravello's Villa Cimbrone on a Friday, the wedding party posing for pictures were Americans from Massachusetts.

Speaking of which, you may be considering getting married in Italy. It's naturally a great place for a wedding, completely romantic, with locations from castles to vineyards to cliffs overlooking the sea that can satisfy every fairytale fantasy.

A major advantage to getting married in Italy is that you can cut your guest list down to a core group of dearest family and friends, who'll be thrilled to be in on the adventure. Plus, what better place is there for a jumping off point for a honeymoon?

As far as the nitty-gritty, it's better to have a symbolic wedding in Italy rather than an official one, as the paperwork to make things official is complex and time consuming. To help get things set up, here are some companies that specialize in Italian weddings:

* **Doorways, Ltd.** (www.villavacations.com)
  One of this company's top "I Do" spots is a sixteenth-century villa on the outskirts of Lucca, which sits on 300 acres of vineyards, olive groves, and woodlands. A special perk is a pre-wedding cocktail party exclusively for the bridal couple and all the service people involved in the festivities. Here, according to Doorway's President Kit Burns, "Everyone becomes a family and the bride's pre-wedding anxiety vanishes when she's met everybody who'll be doing the work."

  There's a fantastic frescoed bridal suite at the villa, an arts and crafts workshop area for younger guests, and it's perfectly located for day trips before the big event, such as a boat ride to the Cinque Terre.

* **Italy 4 Real** (www.italy4real.com)
Intimate country weddings in Tuscan and Umbrian agritur-
ismos, are Italy 4 Real's specialty. The company's philosophy
is for clients to fully experience the environment they're
in, so they bring in local expert chefs and musicians and
it's all very traditional. Marriage ceremonies feature stunning backdrops of vineyards and olive groves. Brides and
grooms are whisked off to nearby picturesque hill towns such
as San Gimignano or Assisi for photo shoots. The company
is owned by Rem Malloy and his Roman-American mother,
Deborah de Maio, who Rem made a point of telling me he
does not live with.

* **The Italy Specialists** (www.italyspecialists.com)
Silvia Giardin, company founder and Veneto native, has been
planning Italian weddings for thirty-three years. "Nothing is
impossible" is her motto.
    I would love to have been invited to just one of the
weddings she told me her company put together: a sunrise
ceremony on a Venetian dock where the bridal couple wore
pajamas and the party continued with a palazzo brunch...
an extravagant affair at the Lake Como estate now owned by
George Clooney...a wedding in Taoromina, Sicily where the
ceremony took place at the Greek amphitheater and was followed by a reception at The Grand Hotel Timeo.

RECOMMENDED READING

Italy, a Love Story edited by Camille Cusumano
In Love in Italy by Monica Larner

100 Go Find Your Mammas

LIKE MANY ITALIAN AMERICANS, as soon as I land in Italy, a deep, powerful connection to the *mammas* of my past takes hold of me. It's more than just seeing those look-a-like faces from my maternal line. It's a sensational hit to the core, a feeling of belonging, joining into the continuity of *la famiglia*. Even when I'm not with my relatives face-to-face, when I'm in Italy, I feel those roots. For many that feeling will be enough, but to travel to your ancestor's hometown and maybe even connect with long lost Italian relatives can be life changing.

Meeting my Italian cousins and eating together (which takes up most of our time) is one of the gifts I'm most grateful for in my life. If your family is still in touch with your relatives over there, you're lucky. The door is open. Plan your trip so you'll have time for a visit, even if they live off your tourist track, which is most likely the case.

It took me a few visits to Italy before I got my sister to come along with me to Vinchiaturo, a postage-stamp-sized town in the region of Molise, where my nana grew up. How can I begin to tell you about our times together in their twenty-room villa (which they only live in part of), left to them by my great-great-uncle, the wealthy Monsignor? Let's leave it at absolutely extraordinary, full of affection, and a salt-encrusted baked fish.

There are many of you whose families have lost touch with their roots. Over 4 million Italians `immigrated to the United States between 1820 and 1920, most from the impoverished south, never to return to their homeland. They became Americans, worked hard, and didn't pass on much family history. Often "somewhere near Naples" or "a town in Calabria" are the only answers families have to "Where was nana from?"

There are lots of ways to get the facts to help you reconnect and the research can be fun. Google "Italian Genealogy" and a whole bunch will come up, including **Italian Geneology** (www. italiangenealogy.com), which has a helpful forum. There is also the **Family History Center** (the Mormon-hosted site, www. familysearch.org), which has an extensive database of records. While others I have known had luck with those two, as a test, I put my grandparents' names in there and struck out.

But I did find them on the **Statue of Liberty-Ellis Island Foundation**'s site (www.ellisislandrecords.org). Two million Italians immigrated to the United States between 1900 and 1914, and many came through there. A search got me to a ship manifesto with nana's name along with her siblings, mother, and father—who was bringing in $120.00. It listed that they were from Vinchiaturo and headed to a church address in Newark— coincidentally the one that rich great-great Monsignor Uncle had built—good move! It's a cool site that even has photos of the ship your ancestors came in on, along with lots of info about genealogy research.

To travel to the place where your ancestors came from, meet relatives, or look up their names in record books is something that takes planning and a helpful pro if you don't know Italian. There are those fairytale stories of someone showing up in a little town, flashing a passport with their Italian surname on it, and the next thing they know there's a spontaneous welcome banquet. But in reality, when we're talking small Italian towns, that's rare. *La famiglia* is a sacred and private thing, and just like here, Italians aren't going to open their doors to a stranger. That said, once the preliminaries are done, and that door is open, you are in for smotherin-lovin.

One great resource to help you out is Carol Dimopoulos, who runs the Italian division of **Celtic Tours**. Since Carol has gone through finding roots in Italy for herself, she's dedicated to giving clients the same experience.

"My mother died when I was twenty, and it was important for me to have my kids see where they came from," she said, telling me about her visit to meet long-lost family members in the town of Gaeta. "I was treated like a celebrity, it was overwhelming for my children—so much affection!" Carol provides everything from assistance with genealogy research, to trip planning that includes chauffeur services, and a local who acts as translator.

I do hope someday you find yourself smack in your ancestral town. You may find yourself saying: "There's no place like home."

&

Golden Day: Sit down at the table with your Italian relatives. That'll take up the whole day.

www.celtictours.com

Appendix 1
Tips for Italian Travel

1. **Lie about when you're leaving and returning.** Tell yourself and those in your world you'll be away the day before and the day after whatever it says on your airplane ticket. It's not really lying. Mentally you're in Italy those pre- and post-travel days. This helps me to not leave packing until the last minute, and spares those around me from being with getting-on-the-plane-to-Italy-obsessed Suz. The day after you return, you'll be on an Italy high, unpacking, and will get no sympathy with your "I'm jet-lagged, just got back from Italy" spiel. Consider these border days gifts to yourself, to ease in and out of the journey. If you do tell anyone your *real* return date, have it be a masseuse.

2. **Get psyched.** Your destination has probably been featured in movies or *You Tube* videos to watch and books to read to enhance your experience. Before you get on the plane, use them to familiarize yourself with your chosen region's history, art, and cuisine. And though the natives you'll encounter in the major cities will most likely speak English, learn at least some words of the beautiful language—*buon giorno, buona sera, grazie*. You'll be thrilled with the Italians' cheerful reaction to your efforts to speak even a little bit of their language.

3. **Spread the Word.** Tell your friends and family where you'll be traveling, and inevitably they'll have a friend, someone they met when they were going to school in Florence, or a kind cousin once removed who lives in your destination. Make contact in advance and enjoy time with a local. It'll be a treasured part of your trip.

4. **Go Solo.** Italy is a fantastic place to wander solo, following your very own desires. As Italians are such wonderfully social people, you'll rarely find yourself feeling lonely. Even when I'm traveling with my husband or girlfriends, I love having time on my own during the day to explore at my own pace—it makes dinner times more fun, when we join together to share our separate adventures. If you are on your own and would like to break up your solo time, log on to Lonely Planet's Thorntree (www.lonelyplanet.com), CouchSurfing (www.couchsurfing.com) or Connecting Solo Travelers Network (www.cstn.org) to find out who else is around that you could meet up with. You could also check out **Florence for Fun (www.florenceforfun.org)**, an organization that arranges events for English speakers in the city and beyond. Or you could join a group tour that's focused on an active adventure, sightseeing, or a workshop that focuses on your interests. In other words, "I have no one to go with," doesn't have to be an obstacle to your Italian travel dreams.

5. **Flirting.** There's a shrink in New York who prescribes a trip to Italy for women who need a boost to their self-esteem. Italian men have mastered the art of flirting—it's one of the country's masterpieces. Females of all ages are adored here. Enjoy, without taking it too seriously. It's all

in the spirit of: *You are women, we are men. We are alive! And what a fun game we play!* If you get harassment rather than flirting, a loud *"Vai Via"* ("Go Away") is the age-old stopper, and it usually works.

6. **Take a Guided Tour.** I resisted this for many trips, with visions of traipsing behind a screaming person hoisting an umbrella. At the same time I had the frustrating experiences of waiting in line for the Sistine Chapel while tour groups were ushered through in front of me, being baffled in the Forum where nothing is marked, and so on. It's great to join a *small* tour group—my favorite is Context Travel (www.contexttravel.com), a company that runs tours in Italy's major cities, and limits them to six participants. Their guides are scholars and authors (not at all pretentious), so you get the experience of seeing a part of Italy with someone who's like an in-the-know friend. Also, in Rome, if you can get any time with the exquisite guide, Iris Carulli (www.imcarulli.com), you'll have a golden time.

7. **Stay Healthy.** You'll inevitably be in crowds of coughers, so starting with the airplane, take Airborne or loads of Vitamin C and bring along anti-bacterial hand wash. And (God forbid), know the number to dial for an ambulance is 118.

8. **Bidets** are found in almost every hotel room. Even in a simple convent where I stayed, there was a spigot gizmo attached to the toilet to do the job. Answers to most frequently asked questions: (1) you can sit either facing the faucet or not, (2) Use after your normal toilet routine. To avoid surprises, test it out to see if it's the basin type or has squirting jets.

9. **Keep an Eye on Your Stuff.** Please don't become a paranoid traveler, but the truth is there are expert purse-snatchers out there, who target tourists in places of major distraction: public transportation, outdoor markets, and crowded sights. Get your offensive style down, so it becomes second nature, and then you can roam around comfortably. While some prefer a secret money belt, neck pouch, or bra stuffing, I copy the native's style. Stand back and observe for a moment, and you'll catch on. I carry a shoulder bag tucked under my arm, always closed, on my inside-of-the-street arm, to avoid whizzing *motorini* thieves. At sidewalk restaurants, keep it hooked to you or your seat. You'll get extra warnings regarding the fantastic city of Naples—warnings that made me feel like I'd be robbed the minute I stepped off the train. Instead I met the kindest people I've ever met on earth in Naples and fell in love with the city. So don't miss Naples, but like anywhere you travel, use common sense, don't flaunt expensive jewelry or large bills, and leave what you don't need back at the hotel.

10. **Experience *Il Dolce Far Niente*—The Sweetness of Doing Nothing.** Though you'll have "must sees" on your itinerary, take time to escape from an agenda and simply be in the moment in Italy. It may be sleeping late with the sound of church bells in the distance, lingering at a caffè while beautiful-people-watching, or meandering around a vineyard—such bliss! Ideally, plan a "vacation from your vacation"—at least a day or two outside a city where *Il Dolce Far Niente* peacefully awaits.

Appendix 2
Packing

What am I going to wear? This will undoubtedly be at the top of your thoughts once you book your trip.

Think simple: Italian women dress stylishly without a lot of fuss. Color coordinate, be neat, and all shall be well. Over-packing (don't bring that coffin-sized suitcase again, Kristin!) will end up being a drag on your trip. You can always hand wash, or get to a laundry or dry cleaner while you're there. Plus, what's the hardship in *having* to buy extra clothes or shoes in Italy?

Don't pack:

* **Your hairdryer:** Even budget hotels have them.
* **Spike heels:** They get stuck in the cobblestones.
* **Shorts:** You'll feel odd unless you're biking or on a beach.
* **Sneakers:** Meaning your gym shoes or white sneakers. That said, comfortable shoes are important as you'll be doing lots of walking. Check out Ecco or Arches for good styles. Rubber soles are best for hill towns, where leather slips on the slopes.

Do pack:

* **Umbrella:** To always carry with you on "iffy" weather days. You'll regret having to buy one from eager street vendors who jack up the price the moment the sky opens.

- **Tissues:** To double as toilet paper. There will inevitably be places that are lacking.

- **Band Aids and moleskin:** In case of foot blisters.

- **Travel-sized toiletries:** This is the stuff that can really add weight, so bring only what you need. Hotels generally supply shampoo, conditioner, and body lotion.

- **Lightweight duffel bag:** To fill with souvenirs for your return trip.

- **Copy of your passport, credit card numbers, and toll-free numbers to call in case of credit card loss.** Give another copy and your itinerary to someone who can easily be reached, so they can be sent to you if necessary. Before you go, call your bank and credit card companies to give them a heads up, as in these days of high security, they may block your card if they aren't forewarned about your foreign spending.

- **Pages of guidebooks:** Rip out those that apply to your destination. Don't take the whole heavy book.

- **Streetwise Maps** for the cities you'll be visiting. These laminated, purse-friendly, well-indexed maps are far superior to the ones hotels and tourist kiosks hand out. You can buy them in U.S. bookstores or online: www.streetwisemaps.com.

- *Italy: Instructions for Use* (www.italyinstructions.com):* A unique, practical, lightweight guide and phrasebook containing all the nitty-gritty details you'll need as you travel—trains, driving, eating, making phone calls, public transportation, etc.

Packing à la Susan:

- **Use Wire Hangers:** I know Joan Crawford would be horrified, but putting all your clothes on wire hangers, which you then roll up in plastic to prevent wrinkling and then whoosh into your hotel closet when you arrive, cuts down on unpacking time, which gives you more time for Italy.

❋ **Have a Dress Rehearsal**: Here I go confessing my corny secret packing ritual: I take my inspiration from Cher in *Moonstruck*—the scene where she gets ready for her date with Nicholas Cage. To get psyched for my date with Italy, I put my mirror center stage, have a glass of white wine nearby, Andrea Bocelli blaring in the background, and all the wardrobe possibilities on the bed, including jewelry and scarves. Then I dress for the plane, for that day I know I'll be touring a museum, for that special dinner, etc. Inevitably, this is where I'll figure out what to mix and match, what shoes won't work, and cut out half of what's on that bed. And so the light, lovely adventure begins...

Calendar of Madonna Holidays and Female Saints' Feast Days

No matter when you visit Italy, you're bound to come upon a celebration of the Madonna or a Saint. Which means colorful processions and great food.

The saints are traditionally honored on their feast days with big time celebrations in their home towns, as well as in less elaborate (but still impressive) *festas* in other parts of Italy. For example, in Catania, The Feast of Saint Agatha is a two-day extravaganza (one of the largest processions in the world), and also on February 5 in Massa Lubrense, a coastal town in Campania, a smaller *Festa* is held in her honor.

JANUARY 21	Saint Agnes of Rome
FEBRUARY 5	Saint Agatha of Catania, Sicily
FEBRUARY 22	Saint Margaret of Cortona, Tuscany
MARCH 8	*Festa della Donna,* International Women's Day *Italian women are given yellow mimosas by their admirers*
MARCH 25	The Annunciation *Big celebrations in Florence and Venice to celebrate The Angel Gabriel's announcement to the BVM*
APRIL 27	Saint Zita of Lucca, Tuscany
APRIL 30	Saint Catherine of Siena, Tuscany

MAY	The Month of Mary *Celebrations honoring the Madonna all over Italy*
MAY 4	Saint Monica (entombed in Rome)
MAY 22	Saint Rita of Cascia, Umbria
JULY I5	Santa Rosalia of Palermo, Sicily
JULY 26	Saint Ann, Mother of Mary
	Celebrations in many Italian towns
AUGUST I2	Saint Claire of Assisi, Umbria
AUGUST I5	Feast of the Assumption—*Ferragosto* *Biggest holiday in Italy after Christmas and Easter,* *celebrating the BVM's rise into heaven.*
NOVEMBER 22	Saint Cecilia of Rome
DECEMBER 8	Feast of the Immaculate Conception *The celebration of the BVM's purity is the start of* *Christmas festivities.*
DECEMBER I3	Saint Lucy of Syracuse, Sicily

Resources

(Van Allen's Favorites)

WEBSITES

* Italian Government Tourist Board: www.italiantourism.com
  For info on events and festivals, and helpful details for every region

* Life In Italy: www.lifeinitaly.com
  For insights into Italian culture

* Slow Travel: www.slowtravel.com
  A community of discerning travelers with a great forum

* Dream of Italy: www.dreamofitaly.com
  An online newsletter for up-to-date advice for travelers

TOUR OPERATORS

* Italian Travel Promotional Council: www.goitpc.com
  An organization of tour operators who are seasoned experts when it comes to Italian travel. Check out the site for everything from custom-designed tours for individuals or groups, escorted group tours, car rentals, active adventures, villa rentals, weddings in Italy, or cooking classes.

* La Dolce Via Travel: www.ladolceviatravel.com
  High quality custom travel planning

* One Step Closer: www.onestepcloser.net
  Run by discerning Florentines who custom design exclusive itineraries

❀ The Women's Travel Club: www.womenstravelclub.com
Women-only escorted tours to Italy.

BARGAIN PACKAGE TOURS

❀ Club ABC Tours: www.clubabc.com
Quality independent or escorted tour packages for great bargain prices

ACCOMMODATIONS

❀ World By: www.worldby.com
For good prices on B&Bs, Hotels, Apartments, and Villas all over Italy

Budget

❀ Convent Stays: www.santasusanna.org
Lodging In Italy's Monasteries: www.monasteriesofitaly.com

Unique and Charming Accommodations (Moderate to Expensive)

❀ JDB Fine Hotels and Resorts: www.jdbassc.com

❀ Karen Brown's World of Travel: www.karenbrown.com

Apartments

❀ Roma Rentals SPQR: www.romarentals.net

❀ Florence: www.bepiolga.it

❀ Venice: www.venicetostay.com

❀ Also Craig's List: Your Destination

TRANSPORTATION

❀ Train: www.trenitalia.it

Ferry Services

Be sure to consider traveling by boat (for example from Naples to Sicily—a dreamy way to go)

* A great service to get to the Amalfi Coast from Naples is Metro del Mare Ferry: www.metrodelmare.it

Car Rental

* Auto Europe: www.autoeurope.com

Private Drivers

* Rome: Valentino Moscatelli, www.romewithvalentino.com, 06 7707 2393 or 340 585 8933

* Florence: Gianni Marranini, 338 106 8454

* Venice Gondolier: Roberto Righetti, 339 438 4154, recommended by Marcella and Victor Hazan

* Amalfi Coast: Claudio Lucibello, www.amalficoastcarservice.it, 089 873 063 or 339 702 8395

RESTAURANTS

* Chowhound: www.chowhound.chow.com

* *Italy For the Gourmet Traveler* by Fred Plotkin

* *Flavors of Rome* by Carol Coviello-Malzone www.flavorsofrome.com

* *Divina Cucina* by Judy Witts-Francini www.divinacucina.com,

* *Chow Venice: Savoring the Food and Wine of La Serenissima* by Ruth Edenbaum and Shannon Essa

Index

Acknowledgments

Why do authors so often leave husbands till the end of these sections? In my book, he's first:

With thanks to my dearest one, Jonathon Leifer, for EVERYTHING—that includes Latin translations and chocolate deliveries during this process.

Every writer should be so lucky to have such an angel-of-a-sister as Patti Sullivan, my first draft reader whose smart editing and encouragement were invaluable. Thanks to all my family, whose loving support I feel across the miles and from those in *Paradiso*. Particularly for help in the research process, I thank my father, Robert Van Benthuysen, who showed me by example what that's all about.

At the Italian Government Tourist Board in Los Angeles, Emanuela Boni has been a blessing and a joy to work with. For her assistance, along with that of the wonderful people in the L.A. office and the Italian Government Tourist Board in New York (the kind-hearted Marzia Bortolin and Riccardo Strano), I give my heartfelt thanks.

To each of you who's traveled with me somewhere along this journey to write this book, I raise a glass, with everlasting gratitude for what you've done to help make it happen: Gioia Acon, Maxine Albert, Sheila Balter, Irma Becerra, Risa Bell, Alessandra Bolzagni, Baronessa Cecilia Bellelli, Joann

Biondi, Lauren Birmingham, Liz Brewster, Tita Cahn, Sheryl Cancelleri, Elena Cappalini, Iris Carulli, Sara Chamberlin, Erin Champion, Maria Laura Chiacchio, Jill Clark, Paul and Suzanne Codiga, Rosanne Cofoid, Carol Coviello-Malzone, Sandy Cutrone, Cornelia Danielson, the D'Aquilas, Bruno Dascanio, Betsy deFries, Susan Engbrecht, Robin Epstein, Eurofly, Maureen B. Fant, Babs Fasano, Cydney Fowler, Elizabeth Garat, Gina Garner, Deb Gaughan, Julie Genovesi, Dorris Goodrich, Marlene Grimaldi, Valentina Grossi Orzalesi, Inge Hansen, Heather Hanson, Anne Heck, Karen Herbst, Julia Bolton Holloway, Marina Innocenzi, Barbara Kossy, Hope Levy, Maddine Insalaco, Chiara Lima, Maria Lisella, Jo Ann Locktov, Lauren Maher, Joe Maniscalco, Lori Mayfield, Megan McDonnell, Nan McElroy, Petulia Melideo, Joanne Morgante, Mario and Lexi Marmorstein, Kathy McCabe, Mona Lou McConnaughey, Yan Moati, Vittorio Muolo, Ekta Nadeau, Rachel Newman, Rachel Norman, Wendy O'Dea, Sandy and Jessica Osceola, Kristin Overn, Tom Paris, Tania Pascuzzi, Lisa Pieracini, Veronica Puleo, June Rogovin, Meredith Rolley, Phil and Monica Rosenthal, Sirpa Salenius, Voni Schaff, Jessie Sholl, Erin Shachory, Arthur Schwartz, Bryna Skuro, Jean Sondhi, Fiorella Squillante, Kristin Stasiowski, Jessica Stewart, Adrienne Storey, Bill and Patty Sutherland, Alexa Taylor, Anna Lisa Tempestini, Elfride and Bob Vaughan, Monica Vidoni, Tina Villano Chase, Joe Vinson, Margaret Vos, Wendy Walsh, Florence Welborn, and Louise Wright.

I'm thankful for the women who paved the way: Patricia Schultz with *1000 Places to See Before You Die*, and Stephanie Elizondo Griest, with *100 Places Every Woman Should Go*. And for all the writers out there who've guided me in my travels and writing about Italy.

I am especially grateful for James O'Reilly and Larry Habegger of Travelers' Tales, not only for this book, but for being editors who keep us travelers inspired with their essay series. Heartfelt thanks also to Christy Quinto and Susan Brady, the magicians of production over there.

Thanks to Saint Anthony, who has helped me find words.

Always, I thank the people of Italy who have welcomed me with their open hearts.

About the Author

Susan Van Allen has written about Italian travel for National Public Radio, *Town and Country*, *Tastes of Italia*, and many other publications. She has also written for TV, on the staff of the Emmy Award winning sitcom, *Everybody Loves Raymond*. When she's not traveling off to Italy, she lives in Los Angeles with her husband.